Guns and Hunting

Guns and Hunting

Two Decades of Thoughts on Guns and Calibers

by

Finn Aagaard

Safari Press

This book is dedicated to all Finn's fans—
past, present, and future.

The trademark Safari Press ® is registered with the U.S. Patent and Trademark Office and with government trademark and patent offices in other countries.

Aagaard, Finn

Second edition

Safari Press

2012, Long Beach, California

ISBN 978-1-57157-367-4

Library of Congress Catalog Card Number: 2010939009

10 9 8 7 6 5 4 3 2 1

Printed in China

Readers wishing to receive the Safari Press catalog, featuring many fine books on big-game hunting, wingshooting, and sporting firearms, should write to Safari Press, P.O. Box 3095, Long Beach, CA 90803, USA. Tel: (714) 894-9080 or visit our Web site at www.safaripress.com.

Table of Contents

Foreword

The job of "gunwriter" is a rather odd one. For one thing, very few people aspire to the profession when young. I know two men who claim to have majored in journalism in college specifically so they could become gunwriters, and while each succeeded, it took them just about as long to become a full-time gunwriter as for most others in the profession. The problem with gunwriting is that it takes much more than college to even begin to be competent. While this is also true of many other professions, gunwriting requires more experience than most, the reason that many gunwriters essentially fall into the job somewhere in middle age.

Many (if not most) gunwriters in America are really gun-and-hunting writers. While it's possible to learn to teach algebra in four years, or even to become a Wall Street wizard (legal or illegal), becoming a gun-and-hunting writer requires long post-graduate experience with many different firearms. As a gun magazine editor noted a few years ago, "Somebody who's only hunted with a .308 Winchester can't write a really good article about the .308 Winchester because he has little perspective."

Finn Aagaard may have been born to be a gun-and-hunting writer, even though there's no indication he aspired to the profession when younger. He was born in Kenya in 1932 to parents who emigrated from Norway and settled on a farm. Finn attended an agricultural college, but always had more interest in rifles and hunting than in farming. He gained some hunting experience on the farm itself, since farming in Kenya in those days meant hunting both for meat and to protect crops and livestock. His father had to be a farmer-hunter, and evidently was a good shot, though he apparently didn't have the same passion for hunting as his son.

Finn eventually became a professional hunter rather than a farmer, guiding clients after the spectrum of Kenyan big game, so he was able to observe other people using a wide variety of rifles. In many ways this is more educational and useful to a gunwriter than personally owning and shooting a lot of rifles. Just as someone who only hunts with a .308 Winchester doesn't have much perspective about where the .308 fits into the hunting-rifle world, a hunter whose only experience is his own is often blind to the individual problems of other shooters.

This isn't an uncommon failing among gunwriters. How often have we read that the .308 Winchester is a mild-kicking cartridge? Perhaps it is to most he-men gunwriters, but not to some other people. I personally developed a bad flinch from starting my big-game hunting in junior high school with a .308 Winchester that hurt my skinny little shoulder. During Finn's guiding career, he encountered many people who flinched when shooting big-game rifles, including a lot of he-men who refused to acknowledge the fact.

Of course, it's still possible to observe a lot of hunting and still not gain any perspective. I can immediately think of two American gunwriters of the past who spent some time guiding, yet often made flat statements about what rifles are "perfect" for different kinds of hunting because that is what they found perfect for themselves. That the same rifles might kick too hard for other shooters, or be too heavy or too long, apparently never occurred to them. Of course, we are all products of our individual experience, but their problem was ego: If their rifles worked perfectly for them, well then they should work perfectly for everybody.

Finn apparently didn't have this problem. This isn't to say that he wasn't a man of firm opinions, but they were fairly earned opinions, gained by not just his own experience but that of other people. Consequently, one of his favorite questions was, "And how do you know that to be true?"

Aside from observing a lot of hunters in the field, another advantage of his African experience was a freedom from some of the commercialism of American gunwriting. Now, there is nothing wrong with commercialism; in fact it's the basis for being a professional gun-and-hunting writer. However, America is not just the land of hope but of hype.

American gun magazines have always contained a large dose of "New and Better!" This is all well and good because, apparently, one of the basic human needs is some hope of better things coming, whether an afterlife or a new hunting rifle. But we also need things that are tried and true, and in his forty-five years in Africa, Finn learned to depend on the tried and true. Anything new and improved first had to prove itself to him, and not once but repeatedly.

In the meantime, he tended to ask his question, and from the evidence he often asked it of himself. He learned to believe in proven cartridges like the 7x57 Mauser, .30-06, .375 H&H, and .458 Winchester Magnum, in proven bullets like the Nosler Partition, and in proven rifles like the 98 Mauser and Model 70 Winchester.

One theoretical disadvantage he may have had in Kenya was that handloading was outlawed. However, many of his clients handloaded, especially Americans, and Finn read a lot about handloading. Since he was definitely what I call a "rifle loony," this was only natural. He also remained distant from some of the hype about handloading that infects many American shooters, especially the striving for every last foot-second of velocity, or tiny groups shot off a benchrest.

Part of the reason for his lack of intense interest in another 100 feet-per-second or half-inch groups was that since Kenya was a British colony until 1963, Finn also grew up with the British perspective on big-game hunting, especially with its strict codes of sportsmanship. Ideally, a hunter never pulled the trigger unless he could place the bullet properly for a quick, clean kill. Consequently, among Finn's convictions was that a hunter should get as close as possible to the game before shooting.

While this was partly due to the code of British-based sportsmanship, it also came from his own love of the hunt. He got no satisfaction from "hunting" from a vehicle, sitting in a blind, or shooting at long range. He preferred to use his own still-hunting skills to approach game on its own grounds, close enough for that ideal one-shot kill.

I don't know whether Finn read Jose Ortega y Gasset's little book *Meditations on Hunting,* but I suspect he did. One chapter is devoted to technology and the hunt, and its main point is that when humans started hunting for anything beyond the simple need to survive, we ran head-on into the fact that our brains and technology are an enormous advantage over the game we pursue. In order to hunt, we therefore must limit our use of technology in order to engage the natural defenses of wild animals; otherwise, we aren't hunting but merely killing.

Finn definitely knew and believed this, even if he never articulated it in his writings quite so specifically. In one story he described being at a hunting lodge, where in the evening the other guests bragged about how far away they'd shot their deer. Finn thought this was completely backward, that instead we should take pride in how close we could get before shooting.

That was reflected in his hunting rifles, even after his family relocated to Texas after hunting was abruptly and arbitrarily banned in Kenya in 1977. In Africa his collection of rifles was limited, but when he moved to Texas, he reveled in the freedom of arms that was part of America's Constitution. Even his new rifles, however, remained fairly simple, with fixed-power scopes and little ornamentation, though he did have some nice custom-built walnut stocks. He also started handloading, and apparently had read and talked about it enough in Africa that some people thought he'd been doing it all his life.

Writing came harder for him, even though he'd been doing it without pay for many years. He'd long kept extensive hunting journals, which became great references for his articles, but he took a long time to write a story for publication, laboring over every sentence until he felt it was just right. His formal education in English was British colonial, so his writing had much of the dry, wry understatement common to many British writers. Like his rifles, it was also unembellished and direct, so sometimes his writing didn't appeal to those readers who prefer their hunting stories (especially about Africa) full of exaggerated adjectives and desperate encounters with angry beasts. But it did appeal to readers who prefer practical truth.

Among them was me. I read Finn's articles for a number of years before finally meeting him at the SHOT Show in 1987, a decade after he moved to Texas. I saw him walking on the other side of a big display and almost ran him down, sticking out my hand and saying, "Finn, I'm a big fan of yours." He smiled and said he was also a fan of mine, having read my articles in *Field & Stream* for some time.

We saw each other at SHOT almost every year after that, and corresponded occasionally in between, both by letter and telephone. Finn invited me to visit him in Texas, but my career was becoming busier and somehow the visit always got pushed back, and then he was gone. I never met Berit until a few years later, but we quickly became friends as well, and for many of the same reasons. One of my most prized possessions is a copy of the original edition of *Aagaard's Africa, A Hunter Remembers,* inscribed in 1993 by Finn: "To John Barsness, Who would have fitted in—Good Hunting, Bwana." Below that, written in 2007, is a note from Berit, thanking me for my friendship. She and I have gotten together in Texas a couple of times, but it needs to happen more often.

Among Finn's (and Berit's) other convictions was that most wild animals are for eating. By the time he came to America he wasn't much on hunting predators, though I suspect he would have learned to like hunting black bears if he'd eaten one taken at the right time of year. He also wasn't a super-dedicated trophy hunter himself anymore, having seen perhaps too much of that while guiding, though he was apparently a very good trophy guide. One of the things that always appealed to me about Finn's writing was his frequent mention of how the meat of a certain animal tasted, even if it had large horns or antlers, for that is still the original essence of the hunt.

Time is the true arbiter of the worth of any writing. There have been a number of gun-and-hunting writers who were very popular in their day, but most have been essentially forgotten. A few, however, remain timeless, even though the rifles they wrote about are now considered passé. Their writing transcends time because instead of being about trends of style and technology, it is about the eternal hunt. I suspect Finn Aagaard will be read and remembered for a very long time, because he was that fine combination of hunter, painstaking writer, and seeker of truth.

John Barsness
April 2010

A Guy You Should Meet

J ohn Wootters said to me, "There's a guy by the name of Finn Aagaard that you should meet."

"Why?" said I.

"Because he is Kenyan, a former PH and partner in a safari outfit, and knows guns pat. He has a zillion stories to tell, writes and properly spells the King's English, wants to be a gunwriter, and has offered to guide us on an axis deer hunt in the Texas hill country."

"Oh . . . welllll . . . OK."

We did, he did, and two weeks later Finn signed a contract to write exclusively as field editor for *American Rifleman* and *American Hunter.* For the following sixteen years Finn's love and knowledge of the sports of hunting and shooting and the rectitude he brought to them contributed mightily to the success of both titles.

Now a friend is gone, and though our days in the field together were not as many as I wish, I value each the more.

George W. Martin
Former Executive Director, NRA Publications

A Son's Worthy Praise

Finn Aagaard, whom I'm lucky to have had as my father, was a good man, an avid gunwriter, an ethical hunter, and a patriotic citizen. He slipped away quietly 3 April 2000, after a long battle with cancer. He made this world a better place in which to live and he will be sorely missed by all.

He had a strong sense of ethics and always did the right thing. He took the moral high ground. He accepted responsibility for his actions. He spoke nothing but the truth and was good for his word wherever he went. In a time of slogans, sound bites, and spin doctors, his reputation was beyond reproach and his actions spoke louder than words. He built his house on the solid rock, while many others waffled in the shifting sand. He was a good friend to many and set a fine example for them to follow.

Through his writing, Finn was in a unique position to influence more than just his friends. He started writing seriously in 1983 and gained quite a following ever since. I don't know how many articles he wrote during that time, but a compilation of his works would probably fill several volumes. He really loved his job. He got to hunt and shoot and reload ammo every day. Finn joked that all he had to do was write about it and get paid.

Writing, however, never came easily for him. He wrote and rewrote and wrestled with every sentence to get it just right. He spent hours and hours doing meticulous research and testing. He kept detailed diaries of all his hunts and painstaking notes of all his tests. Finn wrote what he believed, not what he thought others wanted to hear. He was honest in his reviews of hunting outfits, rifles, cartridges, and equipment. He used his vast experience and interesting stories to support his straightforward writing style. This agreed well with his readers. Modest as he was, fame left him unchanged.

He felt very strongly about gun safety. Through the years, he saw or heard of many negligent firearm discharges and shooting deaths. This prompted him to write one of his favorite articles on the subject, "The Four Commandments." They can be summed up as follows:

1) Treat every gun as if it is loaded.

2) Don't point it at anything you do not want to shoot.

3) Keep your finger off the trigger until you are ready to shoot.

4) Be sure of your target and what lies beyond.

Finn was also a big proponent of hunting ethics. In a time of deer blinds, feeders, and guaranteed kills on any tiny parcel of land, he believed in fair-chase hunts. The animals he hunted had an even chance of getting away. They roamed free while he stalked them on foot in their natural environment, pitting his hunting skills against their wits. Far more than collecting trophies, he enjoyed pursuing game for the sake of hunting. He loved the time spent outdoors searching for game, and he enjoyed the excitement of a long stalk on his hands and knees. (My last and most memorable hunt with my dad yielded nothing but a good time together.) He respected the animals and would not fire unless he had a clear shot and was assured a clean kill. In his mind, bullet placement was far more important than gun caliber. If an animal was ever wounded, he went to great lengths to track it down so it would not have to suffer.

Finally, my father was a patriotic citizen. He loved this country and all that it stood for. We flew the flag at half-mast for him at his memorial. Finn was a big defender of the Constitution and the Bill of Rights—especially the Second Amendment. Guns were his livelihood. He couldn't imagine giving them up. He felt it was his duty to be armed in order to protect his family and fellow citizens.

I have been very fortunate to have Finn Aagaard as my father. He taught me about gun safety, hunting ethics, and Second Amendment rights. He passed on to me his .375 magnum and to my brother his .458 Winchester Magnum. He left us with a legacy to pass on to our children. My hope is that through his writing he has also passed on to others his morals and values. I know that he made this world a better place in which to live.

Harald Aagaard, Lt. Col., USMC

Finn Aagaard

1932–2000

Finn Aagaard, former field editor of *American Hunter* and *American Rifleman*, died 3 April 2000, after a long battle with cancer. He is survived by his wife, Berit, sons Harald and Erik, and daughter Marit.

Over the past two decades Aagaard was one of the world's most popular and highly respected writers on shooting and hunting. His background as a big-game guide in both Africa and Texas, along with a lifelong fascination with firearms, provided an admirably versatile and prolific bibliography ranging from adventure tales and hunting tactics to ballistic performance and shooting techniques with all types of guns.

If ever a man was born to educate and entertain hunters, it was Finn Aagaard. A native of Kenya, where his father was a coffee and sisal planter, he was trained to shoot at an early age, hunting for the family table and protecting crops. After education in Britain and Nairobi, Aagaard went on to serve in the Kenya Regiment and saw action in the Mau Mau uprising of the 1950s. In 1967 he helped launch Bateleur Safaris, and over the next decade earned a reputation as one of East Africa's top professional hunters. After Kenya banned big-game hunting in 1977, Aagaard moved his family to the U.S. and soon was guiding hunters for white-tailed deer and free-ranging exotics on ranches in the Texas Hill Country.

An extremely literate man with a wealth of know-how and insight to share, Aagaard began to submit articles to the firearms press and by the early 1980s was rapidly building an audience. In 1983 he signed on as field editor with NRA Publications and was a regular fixture through 1994. In addition to scores of his articles, NRA published two books, *Hunting Rifles and Cartridges* (1990), and *Aagaard's Africa* (1993). The role he played in helping build this magazine to national prominence was tremendous. Says former *American Hunter* editor Tom Fulgham:

When Finn Aagaard joined the *American Hunter* staff, we encouraged him to write about the challenge, adventure, and techniques of big-game hunting in Africa and North America. Always he wrote on these subjects with authority, and always he wrote with honesty. But what I respected most about Finn's writing was its pervasive insistence on fairness and integrity in hunting. I'll remember Finn as an expert hunter, a talented writer, and, above all else, an honorable man."

Perhaps even more than his field experience and technical expertise, Aagaard's unflagging truthfulness and decency made him a great writer. He never allowed trophy hype to cloud his vision of the hunt, he never minced words when critiquing guns and ammo, and he never compromised the ideal of firearms freedom. For all of us who valued his work, there remains a place for Finn Aagaard at our campfires.

John Zent, Editor
American Hunter magazine, an NRA publication

Acknowledgments

During this entire endeavor I have been stunned and humbled by the enthusiasm and support from everyone I contacted. When I approached Jim Land, secretary, of the National Rifle Association, and requested permission to republish some of my late husband's stories that appeared in *The American Rifleman* and *The American Hunter,* he contacted Michael Blaz, NRA assistant general counsel. Together they graciously provided me with the necessary permit that enabled me to make a dream come true.

John Barsness, a fellow writer and old friend of Finn's, replied that he would be honored when I asked him to do the foreword. I felt John would be the right person for the task; his values and ideas correspond closely to what Finn stood for: honesty, common sense, no frills.

I also need to thank Don Polacek of Wolfe Publishing for allowing the reprint of my story "The Tracker," which was published in *Successful Hunter* magazine, July–August 2005 issue. Kinuno, my late husband's tracker, featured in so many of Finn's hunting stories and he was such an important part of Finn's hunting career I felt he belonged in this volume.

Bill Pace, my second love and a former NRA board member, introduced me to Jim Land and thereby facilitated this enterprise. He has patiently coached and guided me through this whole endeavor and been my constant support in the world of business and publishing.

Finally, a thank you to Ludo Wurfbain of Safari Press who recognized the value of the treasures contained in these stories, and for providing the willingness and means to produce a quality book to preserve them in.

My heartfelt thank you to each and everyone.

Berit Aagaard
Houston, Texas
April 2010

Introduction

Not until after Finn was gone and the family was flooded with letters of condolence did I begin to grasp the far-reaching impact of his writing. Readers, not only in the States, but from all over the world took time to express their sense of loss. One sentence still grabs me: "I will miss his unwritten stories."

I went through mounds of old magazines searching for Finn's articles in order to make a complete collection for each of our three children. What I found was an astounding volume of technical, well-researched information. There was so much always relevant wisdom, common-sense advice, and entertaining hunting stories, all coupled with Finn's sturdy integrity. Finn had a way to make it all interesting, even to the nongun enthusiast.

More than ten years after his death, people still remember him with admiration. Often I am told: "I grew up reading Finn" or "I always read his stories first when a new magazine arrived." It is heartwarming to know how much he is still appreciated. His writing contained all his practical experience, disciplined research, endless test shooting as well as his honesty, dry sense of humor, and excellent grasp of the English language.

His writing style flows effortless. What most of his readers never knew was how he struggled with each sentence and paragraph. He strived to communicate so others could understand in an intelligent and informative way, seldom writing about things he had not personally experienced or tested. Finn would not praise a product if he did not approve of it. While writing, he was thoroughly absorbed in his work, often forgetting time and place. His office was a jumble of reference materials, books, and his meticulously kept African diaries, notes on bullet performance, rifles, and ammo. I never dared to move anything while he was in the middle of a story; the room looked like a disaster to me, but there was always a method in the mess.

I really want to talk about the photo sessions we had together. The two of us would use the granite hills on the ranch where we lived as dramatic backdrops to take pictures of the rifles, of Finn holding firearms, of Finn in different shooting positions. It always amused me when the magazine wrote: "Photos by author" when he was clearly in the picture himself and I had taken the pictures!

Going through all the articles, it struck me that here was so much timeless wisdom and information that the newer generation could also benefit from and enjoy. The idea grew in my mind to gather some of the stories in book form. In the end we talked to Jim Land, secretary of the NRA who contacted the NRA Intellectual Property Committee. They kindly gave me the necessary permission to publish a compilation of some of the articles Finn wrote for the NRA. We can thank Safari Press for making it happen.

We will all "miss his unwritten stories," but now at least some of the best ones will be preserved in a more permanent form than in mounds of old magazines gathering dust in the garage.

Berit Aagaard
Houston, Texas
April 2010

A Tale of
Two Sevens

 **Chapter 1**

A pair of venerable 7x57 rifles span a half-century of hunting. (American Hunter *magazine, December 1989)*

Why is it that the 7x57mm Mauser, one of the very first smokeless-powder cartridges, is still going quite strongly after ninety-six years while many of its contemporaries, such as the .30-40 Krag, have virtually been dead and buried for decades? The answer probably lies in its fortuitous blending of good killing power with relatively mild recoil. Almost anyone can become accustomed to the kick of even a light and portable 7x57mm and learn to shoot it well, while the reliability of the round on everything but the largest dangerous game has been so thoroughly proven in the field all over the world as to be beyond much dispute.

When my father arrived in Kenya from Norway as a young man in 1927 he brought with him a Husqvarna double-barrel 12-gauge hammer gun and a Browning .32 auto pistol, but no rifle. One of his first acquisitions therefore was a 7x57 Mauser-Werke M98 sporter with a 28-inch barrel (or 27.56 inches, to be exact). It remained his only rifle throughout most of his active hunting career. How much game he killed with it I do not know, but it certainly tallied 1,000 heads and likely more, given that he was expected to provide meat to help feed the large labor force on the coffee and sisal plantation he managed.

The local white settlers had built a clubhouse where they would often gather in the evenings to play tennis, hold dances, talk, and in general get together and socialize. My father was probably still embarrassed by his schoolboy English, and in any case he had no money for that sort of thing. Instead he spent many evenings hunting in the sisal. *Agave sisalana,* a relative of the century plant, was grown for its fiber. It was planted in tight double rows about ten feet apart and provided perfect havens for reedbuck and duikers.

My Old Man would kick the reedbucks out of their beds and more or less wingshoot them as they jumped the rows. At first he used the shotgun and buckshot, but found that too easy and so graduated to the rifle. If there is a better way to learn fast and accurate close-range rifle shooting, I do not know what it might be, and he soon became quite deadly at it. He tried to get them at the top of their leap, and told me that although he might very occasionally miss with the first shot, he would always bag his game if given two shots.

On weekends he and Harry Heppes, the senior manager, would go farther afield. They were up in the Ithanga hills once while my father was still very new in the country. He came across a large, horse-size antelope with curving horns, of a species he did not recognize, and shot it. Harry was utterly horrified when he saw it. It was a roan antelope, which even then was strictly protected in Kenya. They cut it up on the spot and buried the hide and the hoofs. But my father took the chance of keeping the horns, which hung on our veranda over the living room door for many years.

They hunted a lot on the open plains as well, taking elands, zebras, wildebeests, *kongoni*s (one of the hartebeests), and gazelles at ranges that were perforce sometimes quite long, especially for open sights. Harry Heppes was a South African who had been raised in the old Boer tradition in which a boy was sent out with a rifle and two rounds of ammunition. He was expected to bring back meat or both cartridges, else he risked a licking. A harsh schooling, certainly, but it did teach a fellow to make sure of his shot, and to conserve his ammunition.

Harry was an extremely fine shot who later represented Kenya at Bisley. One of his favorite tricks was to wait on an anthill until he had two gazelles lined up so that he could drop both with one round. My father swore he had seen Harry lie down, raise the 600-yard leaf, and nail a little Thomson gazelle that was walking directly away with its nervous tail going like a windshield wiper.

He never got that good himself, but by becoming thoroughly familiar with his rifle and its trajectory, he was able to do creditable work with it at quite long range despite its roundnose 175-grain bullet and modest 2,300-FPS muzzle velocity. The bullet had a lot of lead showing at the nose. It expanded well but retained enough weight in its shank to penetrate deeply, and was a reliable killer on anything up to and including eland. I cannot remember the Old Man—or anyone else for that matter—complaining of a failure that could honestly be attributed to that load in the 7x57mm.

He did not hunt elephant or buffalo, but did bag a couple of lions with the Mauser. He killed a zebra for bait and tied it to a tree. In those days lions were still considered vermin, and it was a common practice to build an impenetrable thorn *boma* (enclosure) in which to sit up for the lions and shoot them at night. My Old Man did not do that. He came back at dawn, crawled up over a little rise fifty yards from the bait, found a lion and a lioness on it, and took them both with one shot apiece.

Later he started to use the Kynoch load with a 140-grain bullet at a listed 2,900 FPS (which it might nearly have attained in his long barrel). He said that it dropped the small and medium antelopes a little quicker than the 175-grain bullet, and was easier to hit with at long range. But he also thought it caused more wear, and blamed it for the fact that by the beginning of World War II the Mauser's barrel was shot out, though I suspect corrosive priming may have played some part in that.

For a long while there were no 7mms in the family, until my brother-in-law, Peter Davey, bought a used Brno 7x57 in 1958. According to Ludwig Olsen's *Mauser Bolt Rifles,* it is a Model 21, a slightly modified small-ring M98 Mauser with integral scope-mounting bases, shotgun-style trigger guard, "butter-knife" bolt handle, 23.6-inch barrel, double set triggers, and a slender stock with a neat and unobtrusive Schnabel fore-end tip.

Pete took it along on a rhino hunt that year, near Makueni. This was the district where John Hunter recently had to shoot 1,000 rhinos so that Kamba tribesmen could settle there. The government thought there were still too many rhinos and issued a limited number of rhino licenses to hunters at reduced cost. However, they were still expensive enough that we would have to sell the rhino horns to cover costs, so Pete and I agreed to pool our resources, buy two licenses, hunt together, and split whatever profit or loss there might be in the venture evenly between us.

When we eventually found a suitable rhino, Pete had his .458 and I a .375 H&H, but Joe Cheffings, who did not have a license, was carrying the 7x57 Brno in case we chanced on an impala or such for camp meat. Pete belted the rhino in the shoulder area. It went into a spin, as they often do. It received a .375 bullet in the center of the chest as it turned toward us, then a .458 in the other shoulder, but still remained on its feet as it swung completely away from us. Joe stuck a 175-grain softnose into its rear end and it promptly fell down. He claimed that it was perfectly obvious it was he who had killed that rhino, with the 7x57mm!

(This was 30 years ago, when the situation was quite different from today and rhinos were numerous. Nevertheless, I concluded that there was little sport in shooting a poor bloody *kifaru* and have never had the slightest desire to do so since.)

A couple of years thereafter a leopard started preying on Pete's cattle, killing two calves. He recovered one of the carcasses and hung it up in a big fig tree. Ten days later the cat started feeding on it. Pete drove by in the evening and found two leopards at the bait, a big male up in the tree and a smaller one, probably a female, on the ground. There was no cover between Pete and the tree, just a tangle of brush around the base of it, so he shot from where he was. The leopard tumbled out of the tree into the brush. Pete approached and circled the thicket but could see nothing of the leopard, and because it was getting dark he wisely decided to leave it for the night.

Next morning he eased into the brush with a shotgun and soon found the leopard dead. But the ground and vegetation were torn up all around it, so it may not have been entirely defunct the previous evening. Pete got quite a shock when he paced out the range and found it to be 150 yards—an awful long way to be shooting at a leopard with iron sights. He had hit it a little too far back, through the stomach and the very rear of the lungs. The 175-grain softnose of the 7x57mm did about as well as almost any other cartridge could have been expected to do under the circumstances. The leopard was a very big tom that registered 240 pounds on the scales, with its stomach full of calf meat.

In 1972 Pete brain-shot a large, 13½-foot crocodile in the Tana River. We had to use the winch on his Toyota to haul it up the bank. Apart from that, Pete used the Brno mostly as a meat gun, bagging various small and medium-size antelopes and gazelles for the larder. Not too long after the leopard incident, he had a Weaver 2½X scope mounted on it, using a set of Kesselring low, quick-detachable rings that are still on the gun, and which are the only ones that I have found will fit the

Brno bases. At some point we replaced the double-set triggers with an excellent Timney adjustable trigger.

Over the years, Pete, always an ardent wingshot, drifted away from big-game hunting. Then in 1977 Kenya banned all hunting and announced that (with a few exceptions) licenses for sporting firearms would not be renewed. Pete gave me the 7x57 Brno, and I immediately shipped it off with my other guns to the United States, where I was eventually able to take possession of it in 1978, almost exactly twenty years after I had first seen it.

I had always wanted a 7x57mm. But when I went into Shaw & Hunter, the Nairobi gun store, looking for one to replace my worn old 8x60mm Mauser, I found they had none in stock, and the closest we could come was a 7x64mm on a Mauser action. The 7x64mm, ballistically a twin to the .280 Remington, served me superbly for fifteen years, but it was not a 7x57! So I was delighted to receive the little Brno. The only thing wrong with it was that its comb was too low for me when using a scope sight, which was easily fixed by having it built up into a moderate Monte Carlo.

I went to work for an outfitter in Texas who guided for white-tailed deer as well as exotic game. Almost immediately I lent the 7x57 to a party of Mexican clients who wanted to avoid the hassle involved in crossing the border with their own guns. They took four deer and an exotic sheep with six shots, using a handload with 140-grain Nosler Partition bullets, so the Czech Brno got off to a good start in its new homeland. Since then I have loaned it to quite a few other hunters, who have used it on deer, mouflon sheep, hogs, axis deer, and aoudad (Barbary sheep). It has also become my personal favorite whitetail gun.

Some years later I needed a .280 Remington in a hurry for an article I was working on. I ordered a .280 finishing reamer, and a buddy and I rechambered the Brno by hand. We were lucky and it turned out well, except that fired cases came out of that chamber with a stepped neck. Then we looked at chamber drawings and found that the 7x57 chamber has a greater neck diameter than does the .280 Remington. The .280 reamer does not clean up all the 7x57 neck, hence the two-diameter neck on fired cases. It did no harm, and the cases survived many firings with no problems. Regardless, when rechambering a 7x57 to .280 Remington, it is proper to set the barrel back enough so that the reamer will clean up the neck completely.

Although I killed a six-point bull elk with one shot with the Brno in its .280 guise (using a 160-grain Nosler Partition bullet), and a lot of other game as well, I came to regret the conversion.

I still wanted a 7x57mm. So finally I ordered a 22-inch Light Sporter 7x57 barrel from E. R. Shaw and had gunsmith Joe Sherrod fit it to the Brno. The Shaw "light" barrel is actually quite substantial and gives the rifle a slightly muzzle-heavy hang. It has a barrel-band sling swivel and a bead-blasted, satin bluing, and with its 4X Leupold compact scope it weighs right at eight pounds unloaded. I could have saved some weight by having Sherrod turn the barrel down, but I like its balance, and have learned my lesson. I am going to quit messing it about. The gun is as close to perfection for my purposes as I am likely to get, so I am just going to use it the way it is, and enjoy it.

And I do thoroughly enjoy hunting with it. In various hands it has now accounted for precisely fifty game heads in North America, of which twenty-seven were white-tailed deer. Only one of the deer required more than one shot, which is a very satisfying record, especially as I do not shoot deer from blinds as is common here in Texas, but still-hunt them on foot.

Because it is not used on anything bigger than 250-pound aoudad, or at ranges of much over 200 yards, I generally use fairly mild handloads with 140- to 154-grain bullets at around 2,600 FPS. They do all that is required under these conditions, as does any of the factory-loaded ammo I have tried. Winchester and Federal loads with 175-grain bullets in my rifle generally give about 2,350 FPS, while the Remington ammo with 140-grain bullets averaged 2,638 FPS for 25 shots the last time I chronographed it.

Two new factory loads have recently been announced for the ancient cartridge. Winchester has a 145-grain PowerPoint bullet at a listed 2,690 FPS, while Federal is offering a Premium load with the 140-grain Nosler Partition bullet at 2,660 FPS, both velocities being from 24-inch barrels. I have not been able to try either one as yet, but both ought to be excellent choices for game up to the size of caribou, at least.

Because many old, weak, or worn-out rifles chambered to the 7x57 may still be in use, American ammo manufacturers conscientiously tend to hold pressures down to not much over 45,000 CUP. However, the reloading manuals suggest that in strong, modern rifles in good condition that will safely tolerate chamber pressures of up to 50,000 CUP, such as the Ruger M77, velocities of over 2,800 FPS can be achieved with 140-grain bullets in a 22-inch barrel, and up to nearly 2,700 FPS with 160-grain bullets.

If I were going to hunt moose or elk with the 7x57, which I would not hesitate to do, I would most likely use the 160-grain Nosler Partition bullet at as close to 2,700 FPS as I could comfortably get. Otherwise I really do not see much sense in pushing the 7mm Mauser to the limit, and think that when high velocities are needed it is better to step up to the 7mm magnum, or at least to the .280 Remington. But because I believe in stalking to within as dead-certain a range as possible, and have consequently not fired a shot at game at over 250 yards in years (and darned seldom even back when), I find the 7x57 amply sufficient for almost all my hunting. Of course, I like and use many other cartridges as well, but the fact remains that the little seven will do a thorough job on about any of our non-dangerous game in the hands of a responsible hunter.

Many European makers still regularly chamber to the 7x57mm Mauser. Rifles in that caliber can be had from our custom gunmakers, and from some semi-custom makers like Ultra Light Arms. But among our large-scale manufacturers, only Ruger presently lists rifles in 7x57mm. It offers the chambering both in its M77 bolt gun and in the No. 1 single-shot rifle. While I am very happy about that, it does not concern me personally. I already have my 7mm.

Rifles for Dangerous Game

 **Chapter 2**

Whether you're off to Alaska for grizzly or Africa for buffalo, the author offers advice on firepower and rifle designs. (American Hunter *magazine, October 1988*)

T he hunting of dangerous game holds a fascination for many of us above and beyond that engendered by more innocuous beasts, no matter how elusive and challenging they may be. A large part of it probably derives from a natural urge to prove to oneself that he can handle danger, that he can perform when his life may be at stake if he screws up. Whatever the psychology, most hunters dream of one day going to hunt brown or grizzly bears in Canada or Alaska, or buffaloes, lions, and elephants in Africa. A surprising number of them make it, even those of quite modest means if they are determined enough to save up for it, so a discussion of the proper arms for the purpose may not be entirely irrelevant.

There is no one cut-and-dried answer to the question of what is the best rifle for dangerous game. It all depends on what one will be hunting; on where, how, and under what conditions; and on his own abilities and limitations. The ideal tool for warding off a brown bear at two paces in a dripping-wet Alaskan alder tangle might not be the prime choice for precisely dropping a dimly seen leopard stone-dead out of the tree at fifty yards in the dusk, for instance. A few chaps could apparently handle a double-barrel .577 Nitro Express as easily and as casually as a 20-gauge shotgun, while others have trouble with anything that kicks more than a .30-06. And so on.

I am a firm believer in employing "enough gun." But I am even more firmly convinced of the necessity for putting the bullet into the right spot no matter how mighty a cannon one is using. The most powerful sporting rifles presently available cannot be counted on to make up for poor bullet placement to any significant degree. Even on an elephant, a 6.5mm solid in the heart or lungs is vastly preferable to a gut shot with a .600 Nitro Express. On the other hand, with equally well-placed body shots that do not affect the central nervous system, the big gun is indeed likely to stop the animal a little quicker on average than the small one.

A chap once wrote to me asking advice. He was going to Africa to hunt a lion, but had found that he could not tolerate the recoil of a .375 H&H. Should he take his familiar .30-06 loaded with 200-grain Nosler Partition bullets, which he shot very competently, or the bigger gun that was too much for him? Of course I replied that a 200-grain Nosler in the right place would kill any lion in Africa quite promptly, and that he would be far less likely to land himself and his professional hunter in a lot of grief with an '06 he could handle than with a .375 that caused him to flinch. A better answer, though, would have been to suggest that he learn to handle the .375.

We make too much of the recoil bugaboo. None of my hunting companions and acquaintances in Kenya had much trouble accustoming themselves to the recoil of the .375, and we were by no means a bunch of supermen. We were just motivated: If we wanted to hunt buffalo and other dangerous game, we had by law to use at least a .375. Likewise, I notice that a good proportion of resident Alaskan big-game hunters tend to use the .300 magnums, the .338 Winchester Magnum, and even the .375 H&H.

I believe that any adult who does not suffer from some physical disability, such as bursitis in the shoulder or a whiplash neck injury, can learn to handle a .375 H&H and, in most cases, a .458 quite adequately for shooting at game. One mistake most hunters make when graduating to rifles of heavy recoil is to fail to hold them firmly. The butt should be pulled back firmly into the shoulder, and the fore-end gripped tightly enough to absorb some of the recoil and to control and moderate muzzle rise. One has to overcome the natural inclination to hold a rifle of which he is frightened away from himself else it gets a running start, and that really hurts. The butt pad should be held against the muscles of the shoulder joint with the toe over the armpit, not farther in toward the chest where it can hurt the collarbone, and not out on the upper arm.

Given a reasonably well-fitting stock and an effective recoil pad like the Pachmayr Decelerator, a properly held big-bore rifle may startle and shock a neophyte, but it cannot physically hurt him unless he is shooting from an awkward position, from the bench, or with his back against something solid so that his body cannot roll with the punch. A muzzle brake or Mag-Na-Porting may help, though the latter serves mostly to suppress muzzle rise, in my experience.

The ideal way to accustom oneself to a heavy rifle might be to start out with very mild reloads and then to gradually increase the charge over a number of shooting sessions until he can eventually handle full-power ammo. Until he has become quite comfortable with its recoil, the rifle should be fired only from the standing position, not from the bench. When one does have to sight-in a big gun from the bench, a "sissy-bag" of sand or small shot placed between the butt and his shoulder is a useful aid.

Weight in a rifle reduces felt recoil, but it also reduces portability, and if taken too far it can hinder quick handling. A client of mine in Kenya brought a Remington M700 .375 with a heavy 26-inch barrel that weighed over 12 pounds with scope and ammo. It was a dream to shoot, but it about wore him out when we spent a morning tracking up buffalo on foot. At the other extreme, there has been a minor fad recently for ultralight big-bore rifles that has resulted in .375 magnums weighing a scant six pounds and the like. Those who like them may keep them; personally I want a .375 to weigh around 9½ pounds field-ready, and think that 8½ to 8¾ pounds is about right for a .338. Conversely, my .458 "stopping" rifle weighs 9¼ pounds with a full magazine, and I would not have it any heavier for the work I put it to.

A "stopping" rifle is the rather specialized tool that a professional hunter (guide) uses to get his clients out of trouble, and to clean up messes. It is designed for quick handling and fast shooting at close range, while delivering as big a bullet and as heavy a blow as is practical. But it is not always the best choice for the hunter on a guided hunt.

The way to stay out of trouble with an animal that can fight back is to hit it so well with the first shot that no charges can develop. To this end I always told clients who were coming to hunt dangerous game in Kenya that I preferred them to bring a scope-sighted .375 H&H rather than an iron-sighted .458 because they would be more likely to place their shots vitally with it.

African stopping rifles are usually fitted with the traditional Express-type shallow "V" open rear sights. They are a third-rate choice, with low-power scopes and "ghost-ring" aperture sights being preferable on all counts. But stopping rifles are normally used at such close range that it does not matter. Jack O'Connor described how on one of his African safaris he and his companion (probably Herb Klein) tested their professional hunter's heavy double rifle and found that it was shooting half a foot off at 100 yards. He remarked that because the professional never used it at ranges over 25 yards, that was good enough. Actually, most of the time he probably did not use the sights at all, but just pointed the piece like a shotgun.

A more precise sighting arrangement is definitely to be preferred, as even professional guides may have occasion to try to stop a wounded beast at quite long range. Many years ago Soren Lindstrom (who did not yet have a professional's license) and I took his father out for buffalo. Finally we got him a shot at a very good bull that was standing broadside at well over 100 yards. It was farther than we liked, but we were running out of time—the buffalo were alerted and about to go, and besides, Erik Lindstrom was a capable shot. He hit it a touch far back in the lungs with my .375, and it ran into an isolated motte of thornbrush. Now we had trouble.

Then I noticed that the buffalo was peering out at us through a gap in the thorn. Only its head was visible. The range looked to be 200 yards or a little more, but we had nothing to lose. I sat down with the .375, held the cross hair in the Weaver K2.5 scope on top of the boss of the bull's horns, and gently pressed the trigger. The buffalo disappeared, and when Soren and I worked our way into the thicket we found it dead with my bullet through its brain. There was a good portion of luck in that shot; nevertheless, I could never have pulled it off with the iron-sighted .458.

On the other hand, I have used the same .375 to follow up and finish off a couple of wounded buffalo in thick cover when my .458 was out of action, and found the scope no hindrance. On another occasion, when we had a wounded bull standing in dense shade in heavy brush, I could not make it out through the iron sights of the .458, so I took the scope-sighted .375 from the tracker and solved that problem. Clients have used the rifle with its 2½X scope to flatten a buffalo at 10 feet, to stop a charging elephant at 14 paces, and to kill a lot of the big stuff quite neatly both near and far. I am absolutely convinced that a low-power scope sight of from 1½X to 3X, or a variable-power scope with a 4X maximum, is by far the best sight for a guided hunter's dangerous-game rifle.

The only exceptions I can think of might be leopard hunting, when a little more magnification could be an advantage, or when one has to hunt in extremely wet and thick cover. From what little I have seen of Alaska, scopes would seem to be entirely appropriate for much of the bear hunting there also. All the clients we had in one Alaska camp used scopes successfully and with no problems. Phil Shoemaker, the registered guide, had a little Leupold 2½X scope on his .458 stopping rifle and liked it very well. It had survived some pretty rough treatment and was still moisture-proof. Good lens covers were an essential, though. Wide bands cut from automobile inner tubes are as good as anything—if you can find an inner tube! I do think it is good insurance to have standby iron sights on the rifle and to use a mounting system that allows the scope to be readily removed in the field if necessary.

Phil had a fiberglass stock on his rifle, which I think is wise in that wet climate. He had also painted most of the external metal with a black, matte, rust-proofing paint, and had reinforced the stock with a bolt through the recoil shoulder. Fiberglass stocks are said to be stronger than wood. That may be so, but only if they are properly designed and well made. Heavy recoil has been known to tear the recoil shoulders out of some synthetic stocks. In the drier climate of East Africa, wood stocks served me perfectly well, though I insisted on a crossbolt behind the recoil lug on rifles of .375 power and up, and bedded the actions in fiberglass. A second recoil lug under the barrel is usually fitted to .458 rifles, and sometimes even to a .375.

The old double rifle versus bolt-gun controversy is pretty much passé—not that many doubles are around anymore, and few of us can afford them. Obtaining ammo may be difficult as well, though B.E.L.L. of Bensenville, Illinois, can supply cases for many of the obsolete British double-rifle cartridges, and loaded ammo for some of the calibers, as can A-Square Company of Madison, Indiana, and perhaps others. Doubles are available chambered to cartridges like the .458 and .375 belted magnums, but extraction can be unreliable with rimless cases. Personally, I would want a flanged (rimmed) cartridge like the .470 Nitro Express if I were to hunt dangerous game with a double rifle.

A good double rifle does handle rather like a double-barrel shotgun, and I believe that provided it fits the shooter, it probably is faster than a bolt-action (or autoloader) for two shots at close range. But when more shots are needed in a hurry, or the range extends to any distance, then the advantage tends to be with the magazine rifle. I doubt there is anything to the contention that doubles are more reliable than bolt guns—many of their parts are quite delicate.

A rifle for dangerous game must function with absolute reliability. Provided the shooter has remembered to load it, it must go bang every time the action is cycled and the trigger is pressed, without fail. Because of their superior extraction system and their "controlled feed," whereby the extractor engages the case before it enters the chamber, I prefer the old Mauser M98 and the pre-'64 Winchester M70 actions to the more modern ones. But my present .458 is a post-'64 M70, and I would not hesitate to depend on a Remington M700 or a Ruger M77 either. Three of the four bear hunters in Shoemaker's camp were using Browning A-Bolt rifles and liked them well.

A smooth-working action that allows the rifle to be reloaded easily with the butt in the shoulder is another requisite. To get it, I would be prepared to pay a good gunsmith to work on the gun. I would also consider it money well spent to have him alter the stock (if necessary) so that the rifle came up to my shoulder with the sights quite closely aligned to the target. A decent trigger facilitates getting the bullet into that vital spot, but because one is often tense when dealing with dangerous game, it ought perhaps to have a slightly heavier pull than normal.

The optimum barrel length is another consideration. In heavy cover, short is better—at some cost in power and in range limitations. Actually, I used that old M70 .375 quite happily in plenty of thick African brush and forest and never found its 25-inch barrel to be any real handicap. I learned something, though, when I followed Shoemaker into Alaskan alder patches. The leaves were mostly gone and visibility was not too bad. But the closely packed, upright stems really could catch the rifle barrel if one had to swing it urgently to deal with an upset bruin coming in from the side. For that particular application, an 18-inch barrel would be dandy, but otherwise I think 22- to 24-inch barrels are generally the best choice.

There exists some disagreement, to put it mildly, as to what cartridges are suitable for dangerous game. The first, most essential attribute is penetration. The bullet must have sufficient penetration to reach the vital areas of any animal on which it will be used, at any angle and distance from which the shot may have to be attempted. Without that ability, none of its other qualities is of any avail. Too much penetration is infinitely preferable to too little, which is why solid full-metal-jacket (FMJ) nonexpanding bullets are appropriate for elephants and, in my opinion, for buffalo as well. For bears and the big cats, premium "controlled expansion" bullets such as the Nosler Partition or the bonded-core bullets offered by some of the small, specialized bullet makers are good choices.

Every species of terrestrial dangerous game has been bagged quite handily with such mild cartridges as the 6.5mm Mannlicher and the 7mm Mauser. If I had nothing else, I would be willing to tackle any of it with which I have had any experience with suitable loads in a .30-06. But given the choice, I would nearly always opt for more power.

For elephants, for backing up clients, or for following any wounded dangerous animal into the "puckerbrush," I want my .458. For hunting unwounded lions or buffaloes, I like a scope-sighted .375 H&H, but I acknowledge that a .416, which combines the virtues of both the .458 and the .375, might be better yet. I think the .338 Winchester Magnum with 250-grain Nosler Partition bullets is excellent bear medicine, as is the .340 Weatherby Magnum and even a .300 Winchester Magnum with the right loads. But I expect they are less effective than the .375 when it comes to using solid bullets on the larger African beasts.

The essentials, then, are that the rifle must be absolutely faultless and smooth-functioning; have rapid availability of follow-up shots and the ruggedness to withstand rough conditions; deliver loads with sufficient penetration to reach the vital areas under almost any circumstances; have good fit and balance to promote fast handling and quick pointing; weigh enough to moderate recoil and to aid steady holding without impairing portability; have a sighting system that permits both very fast shooting at close range and precise aiming at longer distances; and deliver as much power as the shooter can comfortably handle while remaining confident of placing his shots where they need to go. Above all, shot placement remains the key.

Kudu Days

 **Chapter 3**

Fond reminiscences of stalking greater kudu in Kenya. (American Hunter *magazine, May 1988)*

Outh-West Africa, otherwise known as Namibia, is the place for greater kudus. There they are among the commonest of the large antelopes, and are as much a nuisance and a danger to motorists as white-tailed deer are here in central Texas, or so they say. In fact, though, kudus inhabit a far-flung range that extends from a little below the Congo River in Angola through Namibia, South Africa, Botswana, Mozambique, Zimbabwe, on up the eastern half of the continent through Zambia, Tanzania, Kenya, Somalia, and Ethiopia to the fringes of the Red Sea hills, whence it hooks back through southern Sudan to parts of Chad and the Central African Republic—a grand, sweeping arc that traverses some seven thousand to eight thousand miles of Africa.

Although their numbers are sadly reduced in much of this range, and the guerrilla wars that ravage back and forth across Angola, Mozambique, Chad, and Ethiopia have no doubt taken their toll, greater kudus have been brought back in South Africa and are still plentiful in Zimbabwe, Botswana, Zambia, and relatively so in Tanzania.

They may be common in some areas, but no one has ever accused the kudu of being commonplace. A mature greater kudu bull weighs six hundred to seven hundred pounds and stands a good five feet at the shoulder, which is to say that it is not significantly smaller than your average Rocky Mountain bull elk. Kudu bulls are a blue-gray color with a white chevron between the eyes and six to ten vertical white stripes on their flanks. Their ears are large, while their hoofs are surprisingly small for the size of the beast, a not uncommon family characteristic among the tragelaphine or spiral-horned antelopes. (One notable exception is the swamp-dwelling, almost amphibious sitatunga with its greatly elongated hoofs.)

Kudus appear almost slender compared to the burly roan and sable antelopes, a fact that, combined with their aristocratic bearing and the incredible magnificence of their horns, puts them among the most handsome and elegant animals on earth.

The heavy, ridged horns typically make 2 to 2½ complete spirals and may tower 4 feet above the head. According to Rowland Ward, they are properly measured along the outside surface, not around the spiral.

The longest set on record, to my knowledge, is listed in the 1922 edition of Rowland Ward's *Records of Big Game* as measuring 71½ inches on the outside curve and 51¾ inches in a straight line from tip to base. A photo of this head, which was taken by J. Cole Rous (or Rouse) in the Lyndenburg district of the Transvaal, is included in that edition. It looks quite stupendous!

The East African greater kudus have smaller heads, on average, than the southern race and are listed separately in the record book. The minimum length for inclusion in "the book" used to be 49 inches for East African kudus when it was about 56 inches for southern kudus.

Kudus are animals of the dry brush country and in general seem to prefer hilly terrain. They are principally browsers. The big bulls run in little bachelor bands or are very often solitary, while the cows and younger animals are normally found in groups of around four to six, though famed African hunter Frederick Courteney Selous reported once seeing a herd of almost thirty kudus.

In addition to their large ears and love of cover, kudus share other traits with our white-tailed deer. They are skulkers and hiders that depend more on concealment than on fleetness of foot, and the way a kudu can remain invisible in a patch of skimpy, leafless bush is uncanny.

They seem to have extraordinarily keen hearing, a good sense of smell, and excellent eyesight. Like whitetails, they have quick and nervously alert dispositions, and at the first hint of trouble an old bull is likely to lay his horns down along his back and sneak away into a thicket before the hunter has any inkling of his presence.

Greater kudus were quite rare in Kenya, found only in scattered pockets. For many years there was no open season on them, but eventually it was realized that the population was stable and could tolerate a carefully limited harvest.

Mostly we hunted them on steep, hot, rocky hills in the arid Northern Frontier District of Kenya. We climbed and glassed for them in country that looked like parts of Arizona, and in many ways the hunting resembled accounts of hunting the desert bighorn sheep.

A lot of African trophies, particularly many of the antelopes, are collected by chance; one happens on them while hunting something else. This was not the case with the kudu in Kenya; they entailed a serious quest that concentrated on them exclusively, and even seeing one was an event. Therefore I liked to hunt kudu.

I first hunted them on Pyramid Ranch (named for a hill) in the Loldiagas to the northwest of Mount Kenya, when Ray Mayers ran that spread. Born in Australia, Ray was one of those glorious characters who made Kenya such a marvelous place to live. He had served as a district commissioner in the military administration of Somalia during World War II. There he kept the peace with the aid of the Somalia Gendarmerie, a unit whose British officers were, by all accounts, as rare a mob of far-gone eccentrics as one could wish to meet. Ray had an inexhaustible store of humorous tales, and had seen far too much of life to be able to take any of it very seriously. He and his wife, Helen, were probably the most hospitable couple I have ever known. A ranch house they built later, near Voi, had no doors whatsoever. Anyone could walk in and be welcome.

There was a drought that year in the Loldiagas—in fact, not a drop of rain had fallen in eleven months and the country was burned up. I climbed the hills behind Ray's house in the black predawn every day for a week and glassed and searched both high and low till near dark. I saw several cows and a young bull with but one curl, but never a sign of the half-dozen mature bulls that normally ranged the property. It turned out that there had been an isolated, heavy thunderstorm up to the north near Dol Dol ten days previously, and it is likely that the big boys had migrated over there for the new browse.

Some years later I did hunt kudu near Dol Dol, with Laird Mooney, while Ken Clark guided his uncle, Chip Loomis. After three days of hard hunting, during which we got only a fleeting glimpse of one small party of cows, we spotted a solitary bull high up on a hill. We went around behind the hill, dodging a bunch of agitated elephants on the way, climbed it, and crawled expectantly over the crest. The kudu was gone.

A brushy draw ran partway down the otherwise open slope. I left Laird where he had a commanding view, and walked noisily down one side of the draw, allowing my scent to drift into it. It was a good guess. Presently the kudu burst out of the brush into the open, and Laird nailed it at 200 yards with the third shot from his .375 H&H.

There was a total eclipse of the sun that afternoon, but it seemed a minor event to us. Laird and I will always remember that day as "The Day We Shot the Kudu."

It proved to be a candidate for the record book, with horns measuring 51 inches along the outside curves. The next day Chip and Ken collected another beauty with 47-inch horns but a much wider spread. Getting two kudus in two days in Kenya is fantastic, and if memory serves, we bagged a record-book Grant gazelle and gerenuk here also.

The other main kudu ground in Kenya lay just to the south of Lake Turkana (formerly Lake Rudolph) in hunting Block 52, which included Ol Donyo Nyiro (roughly, "The Dark Mountain") and some isolated, rough-hewn hills with names like Kowop, Koitokoi, and Sartin.

It was home to the "Butterfly People," the Samburu, who are close kin to the Masai and to the wild Turkana. There we found the big, narrow-striped Grevy zebras, the hardy and courageous beisa oryxes with their lancelike horns and flowing tails, the long-necked gerenuks that stand up on their hind legs to delicately nibble acacia leaves, a few rhinos, some big-tusked elephants, and a surprising number of leopards in the ravines and wooded valleys that tumbled down the sides of Mount Nyiro.

Don Siebern and I (accompanied by my wife and six-month-old baby) camped under the flat-topped thorn trees by the Uaso Rongai stream at the south end of Nyiro, and hung leopard baits all around. While awaiting a nibble, we hunted kudu on the nearer reaches of the mountain and on the nearby hills.

It was again an unusually dry year, even for that semidesert country, and we went several days without seeing much sign. Eventually we found a good bull taking his midday siesta in the shade near the top of Kowop hill. The wind was such that the only possible approach was up a little gully. We ended up crawling on hands and knees, but ran out of cover more than four hundred yards below it. The kudu had noticed something and was staring in our direction, but was still too far off to shoot. So Kinuno, the tracker, and I sat there, talking casually and never looking at the kudu, while Don got down on his belly and, by slithering along like a snake, successfully worked his way to a rocky ledge perhaps sixty yards closer.

He put his hat in a notch in the rock, rested the rifle on it, wriggled around till he was comfortable, took unhurried aim, and fired. But the shot kicked up a puff of dust just under the kudu's brisket, and that was that. We had simply underestimated the actual hold-over required.

A while later Lowell Douglas and I came back, strictly for kudu. This time we camped at Tuum, a one-store trading post on the western side of Nyiro, intending to concentrate our hunting on the mountain. We sought information among the locals, and finally one of the Samburu said that he could show us an area to the north of Tuum where a big bull (he raised both arms high over his head to illustrate) used to live. That country was now uninhabited, he explained, because the previous year a band of renegade Shifta from the north had swept down on it, killed the people, and made off with all their livestock.

At first light next morning Lowell, Kinuno, and I, together with the Samburu guide and a pal of his whom he insisted on having along, left the Toyota at the end of the track and started climbing. We went slowly, because Lowell had two crippled knees that he had injured playing college basketball, and stopped at every suitable point to search the ground with binoculars. Our hearts leaped when we startled a big, gray antelope out of a thicket soon after leaving the truck, but it was only an eland that went away in a smooth, ground-eating trot with its dewlap swinging from side to side.

Toward midday it became obvious that Lowell's knees were giving him considerable pain and that he was about done. I decided we would make one last spy from the next little rise and then turn back. As soon as Kinuno peeked over it, he ducked down and signaled me to come up beside him. A thousand yards away across the valley, on a main ridge of the mountain, a kudu bull lay under a scraggly little thorn tree. How big it was I could not tell, but it had the full two turns of a mature bull, and that was plenty good enough for us.

Unfortunately there was no way to approach it from where we were without being seen. The proper thing to do would have been to go back down the mountain the way we had come, make our way around behind the main ridge, climb it, and come at the kudu from above. But that would have necessitated a hard march of several hours over rough terrain, and Lowell's knees would have given out before we were halfway.

Guns and Hunting

Groups of people walking from hither to yon across country are a common sight in East Africa. So in the end I decided that we would just stroll openly up our ridge, talking and showing no interest in the kudu, until we reached a spot opposite it from which Lowell would have a long but barely feasible shot at it. There he was to drop down behind a tree while the rest of us walked on, and do the best he could.

Of course it did not work, which is just as well. As soon as we came in sight, the kudu rose to its feet. Then it turned and went slowly up the hill, stopping to stare back at us from time to time—a beautiful sight with the sun glinting off those great horns. It disappeared over the top, into what appeared to be a little basin on the crest of the ridge that was overlooked by a rocky knoll.

Our ploy had succeeded to the extent that the kudu had not seemed unduly alarmed, and I thought there was a fair chance that it might stop and bed down again in the basin. I suggested that we continue up our ridge for another half-mile, then cross the valley to the main ridge and come down it until we could look into the basin from the knoll. Lowell was tired and hurting, but gamely assented to give it a whirl.

It took us an hour, but finally we reached the rocky knoll and climbed it. After a break to catch our breath, I put Kinuno in the lead, closely followed by Lowell, who had instructions to be ready to shoot quickly if the kudu broke into view. I followed a little way behind with the Samburu.

Suddenly Kinuno stopped, touched Lowell's arm, and pointed. The two Samburu immediately sprang forward to get a better look, but I was able to grab them in time and force them to sit down. Lowell stared where Kinuno pointed, nodded, moved a step to his right as if to get a clearer view, snugged the .270 into his shoulder, and fired.

"Got him!"

I rushed up, saw the kudu thrashing around on the ground, realized it had dropped out of Lowell's sight, and slapped a .375 bullet into it.

Lowell said the kudu had been standing in the thornbrush about sixty yards away, looking at him. Its chest had been completely obscured, leaving him no option but to shoot it in the neck, which he had done as nicely as you please.

Then came the hard work. We had to cut it up, carry it down off the mountain and about three miles out to the Toyota. But who cared? I was glad to be staggering along with the heavy horns gouging my shoulders, the blood trickling down my back, and the sweat bees swarming around my face!

That kudu was a real trophy, no matter what it measured. (I never did put a tape to it; horn length seemed entirely beside the point.) We had done it right, and Lowell had given it everything he had and then some. He thoroughly deserved his success.

I do not hunt to get my name in a book, or even to acquire a beautiful trophy for my wall. Not really. I hunt for the joy of it, for the sake of testing my paltry skills, and for the satisfaction of playing man's original role in nature. I hunt for the sake of the hunting, and that is why I would as soon hunt the East African greater kudu as any game on earth, except buffalo and, nowadays, perhaps the white-tailed deer.

Rhino!

⊕ **Chapter 4**

Africa's big bruiser adds both spice and comic relief to life in the bush. (American Hunter *magazine, September 1986*)

With none of the usual steam-engine puffing, the rhino came silently and with deadly intent down an aisle in the wait-a-bit thorn. Fritz Walter, hearing the crackling of branches, squatted down to look under the canopy and was shocked to see the brute not twenty feet away, rushing upon him with its horn seemingly aimed directly as his midriff.

He fell back into a sitting position as the Winchester .375 rifle came up and his thumb automatically flicked off the safety. He was hardly conscious of the hazy circle of the thin-rimmed peep rear sight with its large aperture, but the white-enameled bead of the front sight was highlighted against the rhino's reddish, mud-plastered hide.

When it glowed momentarily between neck and shoulder as the armored head swung slightly to the right, Fritz fired and immediately snatched the bolt to ram another round into the chamber. The rhino turned, and as it went past him three steps away, Fritz stood up and slammed a second shot into its shoulder. He got a third one into it as it went away.

The three shots sounded like a burst from a slow-firing machine gun—it is almost incredible to the uninitiated how fast a practiced man will cycle the bolt of even a long magnum action when his blood is up!

In turning from Fritz, the rhino inadvertently pointed itself at Joe Cheffings, who had been in the lead a little way up the buffalo trail we had been following through the thicket. I had yelled a warning, but when Joe turned around to face the excitement, all he could see was brush coming down toward him—so he stuck a .375 solid into the middle of the commotion. As he was reloading, the rhino's head burst out into the open. Joe shoved the barrel of his rifle past the horns and fired with its muzzle almost touching the hide, then stepped aside as the beast staggered by and collapsed a few paces farther on.

From my position between Joe and Fritz, I had a front-row seat to the whole show, but could play no heroic part as I was armed only with a .22 Hornet! My first impulse had been to remove myself expeditiously from the trail to give the rhino room to pass should he need it. But I got not two feet before the fishhook wait-a-bit thorns had me as tightly ensnared as if on barbed wire. There is no outrunning trouble in that stuff; one has to stand fast, face the music, and shoot as hard, as quickly, and as straight as he can.

In those days there were rhinos—Voi and all the Tsavo country swarmed with them; they were plentiful in the Mara Game Reserve, in the Mountain National Parks, along the Athi and Tana Rivers, and all across the vastness of the harsh, heat-shimmering Northern Frontier District. "Gertie," "Gladys," and the rest of their marvelously long-horned kin were the chief attractions at wondrous Amboseli, which lay still pristine at the foot of Kilimanjaro, and rhinos often drove elephants from the water hole at fabulous Treetops.

Even in the hunting areas they were in such numbers that we tended to regard them as a bit of a bloody nuisance. Anywhere in the bush country, or in the forests or wherever there was suitable cover, one could expect to find rhino trails and note their round, dessert-plate-size tracks with the three distinct toes. (Hippos, by the way, have four toes.) On hard ground three ellipses from their toenails might be all that was discernible, but that was sufficient identification. So, too, were the "scrapes" where they deposited their grapefruit-size droppings before kicking and scratching them around with their hind feet, at the same time often raking nearby vegetation with their horns. Rhino droppings, like those of elephants, contain nothing much but the fibrous remnants of twigs and bark and are quite inoffensive.

Every self-respecting rhino had a retinue of red- or yellow-billed tickbirds, relatives of the starlings if you must know. They not only attended to his external parasites but, even more importantly, gave him air cover and early warning of approaching danger. Their high-pitched chattering (which I have been too deaf to hear for many years and which was a real handicap, believe me) was often the first intimation we received that there was a rhino close-by, though they did attend on buffalo, eland, and giraffe as well. Then there might sound a series of sharp snorts, rather like an old-fashioned steam locomotive laboring up a grade, and, Oh, my gawd, here comes trouble again!

Near twenty years ago, on the safari when my wife and I got engaged, Kinuno, Jim Clifton, Berit, and I were tracking up half-a-dozen buffalo bulls from a water hole in the vicinity of Tsavo Park. Eventually we caught up and spotted them grazing along the next rise, perhaps 150 yards away. We were planning a stalk when trouble came in exactly the manner described. I grabbed Berit's arm and hauled her violently off the track, while Jim and Kinuno faded into the shrubbery as the rhino came by, puffing loudly and swinging its head about in apparent bewilderment as to what the dickens was going on.

It did not stop, so presently we emerged and proceeded with the business at hand. The buffalo were still there. But all the pother had alerted them, and they were staring hard in our direction. We decided that Berit and I would remain there as decoys to hold their attention while Jim and Kinuno ducked down and made a fast sneak to reach a spot from which Jim could get a clear shot.

The plan worked, but the bull Jim fired at ran off with the rest. We found a few splashes of blood, whereupon I put Berit up a tree and told her to stay there until I came back for her. A silly old rhino is one thing, but a wounded buffalo is entirely another matter!

Four hours later I told Jim I had to go back and fetch Berit. I suggested that he and Kinuno should stay on the buffalo tracks until they crossed a road a little way ahead, while Berit and I would walk out to the Land Rover and drive around to meet them.

I had to follow the spoor in reverse to find Berit's tree, and when I reached it she was not there. But when I called out in near panic, she replied cheerfully from a different tree close-by. It seemed the tree I had put her up was not good enough for her, so she had climbed down and found a better one. I should have been warned right then, shouldn't I?

We met Jim and Kinuno as specified, and the three of us followed the buffalo until almost dark. The wounded bull had stayed with his mates and had stopped bleeding completely after the first hour. Finally the bulls joined up with a large herd, and we could no longer distinguish their individual tracks.

The evidence suggested that the bull had received only a flesh wound. I am convinced that the rhino incident, and the consequent need to hurry to get a shot before the alerted buffalo moved on, put Jim off his stride and caused him to jerk the trigger.

One of the main problems in dealing with rhinos was that unless one held an expensive and not always obtainable rhino license, they were strictly protected. And the game department was not very sympathetic to claims of self-defense. The chief game wardens of colonial Kenya were generally of the opinion that anyone who called himself a hunter should have enough knowledge and wit to stay clear of rhinos, and that if he got into trouble with them it was almost certainly his own fault, for which he should be held accountable. (Only after a thorough investigation and a personal interview with the chief game warden himself were we cleared in the killing of the rhino that came for Fritz.) I am in thorough agreement with that attitude, and it certainly worked in inducing us by all means to avoid having to shoot a rhino.

Perhaps I should say it nearly always worked. Joe went hunting buffalo at the Seven Forks of the Tana River, accompanied by his newly wedded wife, Simmonne. They found a herd, and Joe hammered a bull. But it did not drop immediately. As they started to follow it up, with Simmonne some way behind, a rhino appeared on a flank, coming at a hard trot. Joe stepped smartly behind a tree but then saw that the rhino was heading directly for Simmonne, who was caught in the open with no cover.

Well, ever since he came to Kenya at the age of seventeen, Joe had itched to bag a rhino, and here was an excuse of sorts. Besides, he really had grown quite fond of Simmonne, so he stepped out and shot the rhino, which went into a spin and hit the ground.

As they approached the animal, Joe was already starting to formulate the justification he would have to present to the game department when, to his incredulous relief, he found a poisoned arrow sticking in its side, with the wound fresh and still bleeding. Obviously it had been running from a Kamba bowman who had just plinked it when they crossed its path.

That put a different aspect on the whole matter. It was no longer a dubious case of self-defense; instead Joe had virtuously and as in duty-bound finished off a wounded, dangerous animal that might otherwise have terrorized the district and spitted who knows how many innocent bush dwellers!

Joe never wanted to shoot another rhino, and I had taken the only one I will ever willingly kill some time previously on a license. So thereafter we did indeed take all necessary evasive action upon encountering them.

It is truly amazing how fast a fellow can shinny up a totally unclimbable, thorn-laden tree when an irate rhino is snorting at his heels! Apart from that, when a rhino was charging blind at a sound or whiff of scent, as was not uncommon, it was sometimes possible to get out of trouble by running around downwind of it—the behemoth would be inclined to keep puffing along in the direction in which it was pointed.

Otherwise, one could often stop a rhino by shouting at it, or by putting a shot in the ground right under its nose. In the national parks, with a Land Rover full of camera tourists, we would on occasion provoke a charge and let the animal come right in while the cameras whirred and clients gasped. At the last second we would turn the rhino by slapping the outside of the door vigorously and screaming at it. The technique was almost, but not quite, infallible.

Joe usually had a rhino dent or two somewhere on his truck, and one that refused to stop for Soren Lindstrom jabbed its horn up along the driver's-side door, neatly hooked Soren's watchband, and tore it off his wrist!

Few rhino charges are really determined attacks. The rhino has keen hearing, with its large, trumpet-shaped ears constantly swiveling around independently to pick up the faintest whisper of sound. And it has an excellent sense of smell. But its eyesight is poor (it appears to be extremely shortsighted), and it is not noted for its quick intelligence. A rhino's characteristic response to danger, real or imagined, is to charge in its general direction, making as much noise as possible in the hope of frightening away whatever it might be.

When that fails, the rhino often turns and flees itself, putting many miles behind it at a springy trot with its tail curling over its back. There is nothing ponderous about rhinos; they are astonishingly light and fast on their feet, and can stop and turn on a dime like a cutting horse.

Most charges may be mere demonstrations, but every now and again one will come on in dead earnest, meaning every bit of it, as my friend Gunnar Lundstam discovered.

Accompanied by a nonhunting companion, Gunnar was hunting waterbuck along the Athi River in hunting Block 29, using factory ammunition with 150-

grain softpoint bullets in a .308 Winchester. They worked their way slowly and painfully through a belt of wait-a-bit thorn. Finally Gunnar broke out into a sort of bay on the far side, while his partner was still struggling through the bush behind him. Gunnar was immediately aware of a rhino in the more open country ahead. It had obviously heard or smelled them and was already launched in full charge.

Hemmed in by thornbrush, Gunnar could not run in any direction, and there were no trees. So he stood and shouted at the animal. It paid not the slightest attention. Then he put a shot in the ground in front of it. Surely that must turn it, thought Gunnar. But no, without hesitation the rhino kept bearing remorselessly down at him, as if directed by radar. Gunnar realized that he would have to try to shoot it.

Even with a suitable heavy rifle, an onrushing rhino presents a man with something of a problem. Its lowered snout covers most of its chest, which is in any case usually obscured by brush or high grass, while its horns shield its brain. With a large-caliber solid full-metal-jacket bullet, one could aim to break a shoulder, causing the rhino to swerve off course to that side. But Gunnar doubted that his little 150-grain softpoint was up to the job, so he went for the spine at the withers instead, holding just over the top of the horn.

The rhino did not even flinch. There was no time for another shot—all that remained was to attempt a desperate dodge to one side at the last possible moment. Perhaps he waited too long. The rhino swung its head in passing; its horn raked up along Gunnar's chest, breaking some ribs, then ripped open the front of his neck and smashed his lower jaw. He was flung to the ground, almost unconscious. He vaguely remembers that the rhino spun around and stood over him for several moments. But luckily he was unable to move, and presently it simply went away.

Gunnar was bleeding like a stuck pig from the wound in his neck. His companion tied something around it, then half led and half carried him the two miles out to the truck. By the greatest of good fortune, Gunnar's wife, who happened to be a registered nurse, was in camp. She was able to bring the bleeding somewhat under control before driving him to the village of Mitito Andei, whence an urgent telephone call to the Flying Doctor Service brought an airplane to carry him to a hospital in Nairobi.

Gunnar worked for some quasi-government outfit that gave him two weeks' sick leave after he got out of the hospital. He spent most of it in one of the better hunting blocks in Masailand, where he promptly got himself well and truly charged by a wounded buffalo. This time, however, he was properly armed with a .458 and was able to stop it in time. Thereafter he never went afield without a first-aid kit containing several military-type field dressings, and was seldom seen with anything smaller than a .375 H&H in his hands!

The only rhino that was native to Kenya in historical times is the so-called black rhinoceros, *Diceros bicornis*. A mature adult stands about five feet high at the shoulders and weighs about 2,500 pounds. They are browsers and have a pointed, prehensile upper lip that is quite adept at stripping leaves and twigs from the thorny vegetation. Their hide is practically hairless, and they love to wallow and luxuriate in dust baths. Consequently black rhinos, together with elephants, warthogs, and to some extent buffalo, tend to take on the color of the soil. In country where the termite mounds are red, so will the rhinos, elephants, and warthogs be; where the anthills are gray, so are they.

The other African rhino is the white (or square-lipped) rhinoceros, *Ceratotherium simum,* which occurs in two widely separated areas, one in South Africa and the other to the west of the Nile in north-central Africa. I have encountered only the northern race of this species, and then only in the Murchison Falls National Park in Uganda. The great beasts grazed placidly on the coarse grasses and did not even bother to raise their heads as we drove in among them. They are of a different shape than the common rhino, particularly their heads, have an odd hump on their necks, and are much larger, weighing perhaps twice as much. They are essentially grazers, and are no more white than the black rhino is black.

How the northern white rhino has fared through the revolutions, blatant poaching, and rampaging armies that have ravaged those parts in recent years is unknown; it might be extinct. In contrast, the southern race has been so well managed by the South African government that a certain number of excess animals can be made available to hunters. The black rhinoceros has gone from being a relatively common animal to near extinction in a scant twenty years. The cause is wholesale, commercialized poaching brought on by a dramatic increase in the price of rhino horn. As if the poor, bumbling beast did not already have sufficient trouble trying to cope with encroaching civilization, the market value of the curious, fibrous, agglutinated, hairlike growths on its snout shot up to very nearly equal that of gold. Poachers will go to any lengths and will run any risks to obtain it; consequently it has proven impossible to give rhinos sufficient protection except in heavily guarded areas in a few national parks.

I have seen a Masai club that was carved from rhino horn. The material was tough and yet so flexible that the shaft could be bent in a semicircle without breaking. Most rhino horn, though, is exported to the Far East, where it is apparently in great demand for making medicines and aphrodisiacs. The Arabs of Yemen took great quantities of it to fabricate handles for the traditional daggers all their men wear, and it was also believed that a cup made of rhino horn would reveal a poisoned drink by causing it to froth and bubble. In the old days the Somali warriors used to make their small, round, heavy shields from rhino (and giraffe) hide, and it could be cut into strips to make the whips the Boers called *sjamboks.* Rhino hide takes on an amberlike, almost translucent appearance when dried and oiled.

For the most part, rhinos are easier to kill than elephants and seldom require as much pounding as buffalo all too often take. Rather than trying to get away, they have a tendency to start spinning around after the first hit, enabling one to pour in a couple more shots in quick succession. In fairly open country they were easy meat. If one paid attention to the wind and went quietly, he could usually get within easy range and kill them with so little trouble that there really was no sport in it.

But tracking a rhino up in dense thorn thickets was quite a different game that could become decidedly hair-raising. Often enough a hunter found himself so close that he could hear the rhino chomping on the vegetation long before he could see any part of it; then would come the realization that the slightest shift in the fitful breeze might bring the monster down on him like a runaway train, brushing the scrubby thorn aside like grass straws. It was not a good way to get a record-book trophy, as one could easily end up having to shoot an inferior specimen (or, much worse, a cow with a calf) simply to keep it out of his lap. On the other hand, it was never boring!

But in truth, most rhino encounters were not very serious, and were often quite hilarious. One I'll never forget involved a pal I will call Mike, who went into the bushes bearing a roll of toilet paper in one hand. Suddenly we heard a series of indignant snorts and a loud yell. A highly outraged rhino burst out of one side of the covert, while a shocked and embarrassed Mike came rushing out the opposite end with the toilet roll still in one hand and holding up his unbuttoned pants with the other.

In those days there were rhinos. And many times I cursed them in exasperation and wished them into perdition. Now they are almost gone, and I am sorry. They added spice and comic relief to life in the bush. They kept us agile and alert. They were an essential part of an innocent and uncomplicated Africa that was still much as the Creator had intended it to be. They belonged there. If the rhinos were to go, Africa would be grievously diminished by the loss. And as no man is an island, so would I be.

The Lion Hunters

$\oplus$ **Chapter 5**

From the manhood rituals of Masai spearmen to the daring practice of "galloping" lions, adventure seekers have dreamed up some fascinating ways to hunt Africa's kingly cat. (American Hunter *magazine, July 1986)*

The first vulture came plummeting out of the hot, steel-gray African sky with legs outstretched and cupped wings desperately backstroking to break its fall. Vultures are superlatively graceful on the wing, consummate soarers, but they are clumsy on the ground. Their landings resemble frantic, semi-controlled crashes.

As it thumped down, the bird craned its neck and nervously twitched its naked head around in all directions. All clear. The vulture hopped awkwardly over to the dead zebra and, after another look around, stabbed its sharp, hooked beak into the soft tissues between the hind legs.

A second vulture landed beside it, and then another. Within seconds the rest of the circling cloud were hurtling down, and the zebra was soon hidden under a heaving, straining mass of frenziedly pecking birds. Tall, grotesquely ugly marabou storks paced around the fringe of the crowd, ready to mug and rob any unfortunate vulture that retired from the fray with a choice portion, while a handsome little silver-backed jackal came sneaking out of the grass to see what he could glean.

Soren Lindstrom, who had been watching the show and the nearby lava flow intently through his binocular, finally stood up and turned to his client.

"It is not going to work this time," Lindstrom sighed. "Those blasted *morani* scared the lions so badly that they will not come out into the open today, not even to save that juicy zebra meat from the birds."

Lions hate vultures. One of my more vivid memories is of a lioness that had just chased a mob of them off her kill, standing up on her hind legs and flailing with her paws in an exasperated attempt to bat one out of the air. On the other hand, the big cats are lazy and unprincipled opportunists that would just as soon pirate someone else's kill as make their own. A gathering of vultures will quite often bring lions hurrying in to see whether there are any morsels left worth appropriating.

We had been hunting these lions for the past few days, but that morning a band of newly fledged *morani* (young Masai warriors) had encountered and speared a couple of juvenile members of the pride, driving the rest to refuge in a rough, brush-covered lava flow.

Every few years all the Masai youths of a suitable age undergo perhaps the most important rite of their lives; after a period of rigorous tutelage and testing, they are circumcised and initiated into the warrior class. They go off to live in a separate young warriors' village—the Masai equivalent of a military barracks—and in former times it was their duty and pride to raid neighboring tribes. Nowadays, spoil-sport authorities frown rather severely on that sort of thing, so lion hunting is one of the few ways left for the *morani* to prove their prowess and manhood, and to earn the adoration of the maidens.

It is by no means unknown for a Masai cattle herder to kill a lion by himself, but the organized hunts are group affairs. Generally scouts are sent out to locate a lion (or a small party of lions), which is then surrounded by the pig-tailed, red-ochre-smeared, ostrich-plumed spearmen, who close in until they are shoulder to shoulder.

Individual lions react differently to this predicament. Some will furiously charge one of the warriors in a bid to break through the circle. The *moran* will crouch under his heavy, buffalo-hide shield and endeavor to spear the lion as it rears up over him, while his neighbors hurl in their spears also. Nevertheless, he most likely ends up on the ground under his shield with the dying lion thrashing around on top of him and usually collects some interesting and highly impressive scars.

On other occasions the lion refuses to charge and stands snarling and uncertain what to do as the men encircle it. Then, if a *moran* wants to earn the highest honor, he dashes in to grab the lion's tail and hold it while his companions spear the beast. I expect he hopes they will be quick about it, though! Everyone is berserk with excitement, spears whistle about madly, and the lion ends up looking like a pincushion.

But the Masai apparently feel that a lion is a lion, and they do not scruple to kill a lioness or cubs if that is what they encounter. When he met them that morning, Soren learned from the *morani* that they had speared two juvenile lions, but that most of the pride, including a mature male, had avoided them and escaped into the lava. Soren took his Toyota hunting car slowly around the lava. When he got a glimpse of the lions he did not alarm them further by stopping but instead drove by and out onto the plain, where he had the client hammer a zebra.

He hitched it to the truck, dragged it back to where they had seen the lions, and dropped it off. He took the Toyota a mile away, and then he and the client sneaked back to discover whether the vultures would bring the lions out.

When it became apparent that the ploy would not succeed, Soren hitched the zebra behind his truck once more and dragged it up and down the length of the lava to leave a scent trail that the lions could not possibly miss when they left their sanctuary that night to go to drink at the water hole out on the plains, as they were bound to do. Desert lions may on occasion go a long time without water, but those of the Masai normally drink every night.

Soren found a suitable tree in which to hang the bait. It stood in a pocket on the edge of the lava where a subsidiary ridge of rock ran out at an angle from the main flow to form a small bay, as it were. On this "headland," which would provide useful cover for the approach, Soren built his blind. Possibly "blind" is too strong a word; he merely cleared sufficient space in a clump of scraggly thorn scrub for four of us to sit and piled the cut vegetation up to form a low wall on the side toward the zebra. Two holes barely large enough to aim through were left in it. He was, however, very careful to clear all leaves, twigs, and loose stones away from the floor of the hide and from the path leading up to it, which he marked with little pieces of toilet paper.

There is an art to hanging a lion bait. Soren put a rope around the zebra's neck and hauled it up into the tree with the Toyota until its hindquarters were four or five feet off the ground, and tied it there, taking care that there were no limbs on which vultures could perch to reach the bait. Hyenas would be able to get at just enough of it to keep them whooping and giggling around it, and if there is anything that attracts lions more surely than vultures, it is the sound of excited hyenas around a kill. A large mob of hyenas can drive one or two lions from a kill, though.

The lions would be able to feed on most of the bait but not quite all of it. Enough would remain tantalizingly just out of reach to keep them there till morning—otherwise a large pride can clean up a zebra and be several miles away by dawn.

Meanwhile, at Soren's request, I was hanging a couple of additional baits around a likely looking swamp down at the far end of the hunting block. But I could find no tracks or any other signs of lions in that vicinity, so I did not expect too much of them, and they remained untouched.

Although it is worthwhile to keep a check on the carcasses of recently killed large animals such as an elephant or buffalo, hanging lion baits at random is usually wasted effort. There are exceptions, but normally a bait is properly used only after the lions have been located and their likely movements have been deduced, merely to entice them out and hold them where one can get at them.

We left the Toyota a good mile from the bait well before daybreak the next morning and made our way on foot toward the blind by the light of a quarter moon.

Excitement began building when a lion suddenly started grunting over yonder toward the bait, proclaiming, "Whose land is this? Mine, mine, mine." But presently, when we were within a hundred yards of it, a lion called between us and the blind and was answered by another far away in the direction of the water hole. There was no future in stumbling over lions in the dark, so we had to wait for it to lighten before we could proceed.

As we reached the blind, a startled lion got up from directly below it and dashed for the lava bed. *Damnation,* I thought, *that blew it.* But then it struck me that the animal had looked small and was likely a half-grown cub whose alarm might not be taken too seriously by the rest of the pride, so we settled into the blind to await developments.

After a while, just as the sun came up, a lioness materialized at the foot of the tree. She studied the remains of the bait, rose up on her hind legs, hooked a front paw into the zebra's shoulder to steady herself, and commenced feeding. Others followed, and for fifteen minutes or so lionesses were moving back and forth between the lava flow and the bait. Now and then we caught a glimpse of a lion with a fairly decent blond mane, but he remained in the background where we could not get a good look at him.

Finally a pretty young lioness left the bait, came toward us, and, after climbing up onto the lava ridge to our right, sat looking straight down at us from a distance of about thirty feet. She had noticed something out of the way, and stared for an eternity trying to make out what it was. She cocked her head first one way and then the other, and then tried the old trick of turning away as if she had lost interest before snapping her gaze back suddenly to catch any movement. We sat still as statues, but I felt her curiosity was such that eventually she would be bound to come down and stick her head into the blind to discover what we were.

Luckily, another lioness distracted her attention by coming up to rub faces with her—just as domestic cats do—before going on to flop down in the sunshine a few yards away. After several other members of the pride had gone by to enjoy the same patch of warmth, she gave up her vigil and joined them.

An older lioness, heavy in milk, took a slightly different route. She came up onto the ridge beside the blind and stopped not ten feet from me, looking out onto the plain beyond. Only a leafless branch or two separated us, so she could hardly have failed to see me if she had glanced in my direction, and to this day I am astounded that she did not hear the pounding of my heart.

I was sitting with a .458 between my knees, my thumb on the safety catch and my finger alongside the trigger guard. Lionesses were strictly protected by the awful authority of a game department that was notoriously skeptical of claims of self-defense. And what mattered even more, she apparently had small cubs hidden away somewhere. Nonetheless, we were probably within her critical distance, so close that she would feel an instant attack was her best hope. I decided that if she did spot us, the moment I saw recognition dawn in her eyes I would whip the rifle up and slam a 510-grain softpoint into her. Though I could hardly have missed, the next few seconds might have been decidedly messy, so I was more than a little relieved when she moved on.

At long last the male lion emerged from the lava flow and started to follow his females. Soren saw that it had enough mane to be a respectable trophy and told his client to shoot it.

At the shot the lion stumbled, recovered, and was immediately gone from the field of view available to Soren and the client. I stood up and saw the lion running toward the blind just to our left. It was not charging, just running blind, but if it had got in among us the distinction would have been inconsequential. So I fired and dropped it with a .458 bullet through the chest at about twenty feet.

Examination showed that the client had hit the lion exactly right, on the point of the shoulder as it came at an angle toward him. He was using an 8x68mm, a European cartridge comparable in power to our .300 Winchester Magnum, with an RWS 224-grain Cone Point softnose bullet at 2,850 FPS. Although they are heavily muscled beasts, it takes an uncommonly heavy lion to weigh 500 pounds, and I doubt that this particular one reached 400. So the 4,000 foot-pounds of muzzle energy developed by the 8x68mm should have been ample. The trouble was that the bullet blew up in the humerus just below the shoulder joint, smashing the bone and itself to smithereens but penetrating no farther.

On dangerous game it is essential to use a bullet that will smash through to the vitals from any reasonable angle, and it is infinitely better to have too much penetration than too little. For this reason I would prefer to rely on Nosler Partition bullets, when they are available, for lion. I would not feel too badly undergunned if I had to hunt lion with a .300 magnum loaded with 200-grain Nosler Partition bullets, but I would prefer a .375 H&H. When it comes to following-up a wounded lion, I am much happier with at least a .458! Because I believe in the efficacy of placing the shot precisely, and because the light is not always the best, I think a lion gun should be fitted with a scope sight of 2½ to 3X.

Be that as it may, all is well that ends well. We strained and grunted and heaved our lion into the safari car and drove back to camp through herds of wildebeest and zebra concentrated here by recent rains that had greened the country and brought out myriad wildflowers. As we drove into camp with the horn blowing, the staff turned out to grab the client and carry him shoulder-high in the exultant lion dance.

Soon some Masai drifted in to look at the lion. The women *oohed* and *aahed* and clapped their hands, but the warriors stood silent and aloof. They probably felt that *real* men used spears.

Although most lions are bagged by baiting, there are other methods that may sometimes be used. An acquaintance of my father, who fifty years ago ranched in what was then a wild and remote area at the junction of the Thika and Tana Rivers in Kenya, felt that it was unfair to shoot lions in the open with a rifle—"Not quite cricket, what?" He maintained that the only sporting way was to follow them into cover, provoke a charge, and stop them at arm's length with a shotgun.

Actually a 12-gauge loaded with buckshot is often used when following-up a wounded lion. I have not tried it myself because I always felt more comfortable with my familiar .458. But there is no doubt that at short range a smoothbore has awesome stopping power. One must be close, however. When I patterned the modified-choke barrel of my 12-gauge with 00 buckshot, it was still putting all nine pellets into about a six-inch circle at 15 yards; but it spread them out over 12 inches at 20 paces, and beyond that, forget it!

Before World War I the wilder spirits among the white settlers in Kenya delighted in "galloping" lions on the Athi plains—chasing them on horseback until they turned at bay, when a charge was almost inevitable. The plan then, according to Blayney Percival in his *A Game Ranger's Notebook,* was to wheel the horse around and get a hundred yards or so ahead of the angry cat before jumping out of the saddle to face it with rifle in hand. Percival said that the horse had not been foaled that could escape a lion from a standing start within twenty-five yards, but that the lion did not live who could catch it once the horse was in its stride.

Several men were mauled or killed while galloping lions, including one poor fellow whose saddle girth broke when his horse swerved violently to avoid a charge. The most famous casualty was George Grey, the brother of a noted British statesman, who was killed in 1911 when he failed to stop a lion that turned on him after he had pressed it too close. He leaped from his pony, fired once at twenty-five yards and again at five yards, and then the lion hurled him to the ground and shook him like a terrier with a rat. His companions galloped up and shot the lion off him, but he died a few days later.

Grey was using the newfangled .280 Ross cartridge with 140-grain bullets at the phenomenal—for that era—muzzle velocity of 2,900 FPS. It is said that the bullets blew up on the muscles of the lion's chest and failed to give the required penetration. Big-bore enthusiasts have used this incident as a horrifying example ever since.

The Portuguese hunters in Mozambique used to bring in lions with a call fashioned from a large can. Although calling certainly ought to work with animals that are as social, as territorial, and as vocal as lions are, I have not heard of the technique being used elsewhere in Africa. I did see Syd Downey, the dean of East

Guns and Hunting

African professional hunters, bring two big-maned lions in on the dead run by playing a tape of hyenas squabbling over a kill, but that was in the Mara Game Reserve several years after he had retired from hunting.

Perhaps the most sporting way of hunting a lion is to track it down. Because its soft pads leave little impression, this is seldom feasible in Masailand, but the method is used in sandy terrain in the Kalahari. I am told that often the lion is pushed from one cover to the next until it refuses to be pushed anymore, which should make for interesting encounters if one is afoot. It seems, however, that many so-called "hunters" shoot lions from a hunting car these days.

I fail to understand what pleasure or sense of achievement can be gained by shooting any game from a vehicle, but the fellow who shoots a lion or other dangerous game from the safety of a truck is a double cheat. Mostly he is cheating himself, denying himself the satisfaction of knowing that he has what it takes to handle the moment of truth.

Which is the most dangerous game? I do not know. But it might be worth considering that there are a number of men alive today who have taken one thousand elephants; indeed a friend of mine who was involved in elephant cropping accomplished that feat while still in his early twenties. In eight years of control work for the Kenya Forest Department, Ken Clark killed some three thousand buffaloes. I believe that he was run over once or twice, but he was never seriously hurt. John Hunter killed a thousand rhinos without trouble in the late 1940s, to open some country to settlement by the Kamba tribe.

Yet I know of no one who has even come close to those figures with lions. I think it extremely unlikely that anyone could bag even five hundred lions under similar circumstances without being severely mauled several times or, more likely, killed. So from the African hunter's point of view, it could well be that the lion really is the "King of Beasts."

Lion Hunters II

 **Chapter 6**

A tale of two maulings and a look at the big cat's awesome power and predatory instinct leave no doubt about who is the king of beasts. (American Hunter *magazine, November 1986*)

There is a wise and ancient African proverb that says, "Without luck there is no hunting." Actually, Joe Cheffings invented it, but nonetheless there is much truth in it. Some would dispute it, of course, insisting that a competent hunter can make his own luck. That is also true up to a point, but there is no denying that blind luck or chance—if you prefer—often influences the outcome of a hunt.

To illustrate: Soren Lindstrom and his client spent the afternoon in a leopard blind on the edge of the Loita plains in Kenya's Masailand. The leopard came quite early while the light was still good and posed as nicely as one could wish, standing broadside on the feeding branch contemplating the bait. At the shot it fell and hit the ground with a thump like a sack of corn. Lovely—no nasty follow-up would be necessary.

As they were examining the cat with jubilant admiration, Soren heard a lion calling a short distance away. He hushed everyone up, and when it grunted again it sounded like a male; so he told the client to pick up his rifle and come along. They walked over there, found a big lion with a handsome mane, and shot it.

I do not know how the rest of the safari went, but after bagging a leopard and a lion within thirty minutes of each other, it was probably anticlimactic. And if that lion was not the product of pure good luck, I don't know what you would call it. In fact, it could be argued that much of the skill of a hunter lies in being able to recognize and take full advantage of a chance opportunity when it occurs.

In any case, Soren was both a skillful hunter and a very fortunate one, until the day his luck ran out quite spectacularly—or did it? It happened this way:

After hunting was closed in Kenya, Soren moved to Botswana and eventually joined Safari South, a major hunting concern. Some time later he had out a party consisting of a lady with her grown son and daughter, and a friend of the son. They were all through hunting and were just driving around enjoying the country and the animals, and maybe shooting a few birds.

The young people were riding in the back of the Toyota pickup together with the two gunbearers when they came across a fine, big-maned lion all on its own. It promptly charged and was trying to clamber up into the bed of the truck with them before Soren could accelerate away. When he circled it, it persisted in making furious rushes at them.

Because this extraordinary behavior might have been the result of a wound or other injury, Soren approached the lion once more to have a good look at it. He told the son, who had a .375 H&H rifle in his hands, that if the lion tried to climb into the Toyota again, he was to shoot it. But the excited young man fired immediately when he saw the lion crouch, while they were still some way off.

The lion spun around, growling and biting at its foreleg, and then ran into cover. Now Soren had a wounded lion on his hands for certain.

I gather that it was fairly open country with islands of thick brush. They cruised around for a while trying to find the lion, until eventually it broke cover and made a dash into a large patch of trees and bush. Soren drove half a mile away to leave the ladies and the son's friend safely ensconced on a large termite hill, and then returned with the son and the two gunbearers.

Soren and the two Africans got out of the truck to look for sign. Presently they found a good blood trail that led past a fallen tree trunk overgrown with tall grass and on into the bush. Soren decided they would be able to follow it in the Toyota.

He had barely turned around to walk back to the vehicle when the lion roared, shockingly close-by. Soren swung back in time to see the lion burst out from under the fallen tree, but was able to get off only one hurried, unaimed shot from his double-barrel .458 before he was knocked to the ground.

The lion caught him by the right arm and shook him as a bull terrier shakes a rat or another dog, tearing out the biceps muscle. Things got a little hazy after that, but at one stage the lion chewed on Soren's left arm as well. Then it picked him up by a shoulder and started to drag him away. Soren thought it meant to take him into cover and eat him.

One of the gunbearers had found a tree, but the other had just flung himself flat in the grass. Now, when the lion happened to drag Soren toward him, he leaped up in panic and ran. The lion forthwith dropped Soren and went after the gunbearer. (Don't ever run from one of the big cats!) It bowled him over, caught him by a leg and shook him, and then remained standing menacingly over him. Apparently the man was knocked out and unable to move, which most likely saved him from a worse mauling.

Soren got up and looked around for his rifle, meaning to shoot the lion and save his gunbearer. But when he found it, he was appalled to discover that with both arms bitten through he was unable to raise it. He had to get back to the truck, but the lion was between him and the vehicle. So he staggered slowly around it, dragging his rifle by its muzzle. The lion watched him intently every step of the way. Soren was certain that it would attack him again before he reached the Toyota, but by some miracle it did not and at long last he was able to climb into the safety of the cab.

With the young fellow driving, they were able to push the lion sufficiently far from the injured African to enable them to hurriedly lift him into the back of the truck. Then they fetched the two ladies and the other young man from their perch on the anthill.

Soren instructed them how to work the radio to call headquarters for medical aid and an aircraft, and then directed the search for a clear strip where a plane could land. Very luckily they found a suitable one—Soren could never have survived the six-hour drive back to their camp, where lay the nearest prepared landing strip.

As it was, the two women had to take turns applying finger pressure on a spurting artery in his torn right arm to prevent him bleeding to death before the plane came. Soren says that toward the end he could feel their hands trembling with fatigue and, no doubt, shock. But they stuck it out and, in a nightmare situation, did everything that needed to be done, which is a pretty good definition of courage.

Soren spent weeks in a hospital in Johannesburg. They were able to save his ruined right arm but had to fuse the elbow joint. He will never have full use of it. Luckily he is left-handed. He can already handle a shotgun fairly well and is determined that in time he will be able to use a heavy rifle again also.

All in all, though, I must say that Soren's luck really remained amazingly good even when it ran out!

When Soren arrived back at Safari South headquarters in Maun after his release from hospital, Tony Henley, another ex-Kenya professional hunter, greeted him. "Welcome to the club, Soren," Tony said quietly. You see, Tony had himself survived a close and intimate encounter with an angry lion.

Several years before, Henley had been following the spoor of one that had been wounded by his client, when a large lion got up from cover and went slowly away from him. He was on the point of shooting it when he realized that it was not the wounded one and lowered his rifle.

At that exact moment there was a lot of noise and commotion as the wounded lion got up in some brush nearby. Tony fired at it; still the lion came hard and fast, low to the ground. Tony worked the bolt with desperate speed and slammed a shot into its chest. To his surprised consternation the lion did not even flinch, but leaped up, put its paws around his shoulders, and brought him facedown to the ground. The lion had some trouble with the thick woolen sweater Tony was wearing but finally got a good grip on his back and shook him. Tony tried to reach his sheath knife but could not. Then the lion shifted its grip to his right arm and shook him some more. Tony realized that his only hope was to play dead, so he forced himself to relax and go limp, whereupon the lion dropped him and then lay down on top of him.

The lion perched on Henley for about twenty minutes—which must have seemed an awfully long time—before Henley heard the Land Rover with his client coming to look for him. Instead of being relieved, Tony was horrified, fearing that in the excitement someone would shoot through the lion and hit him also. He shouted at them to shoot only at its head. The client, who understood the danger, kept cool and finished the lion with a precisely placed brain shot. (The lion was pretty far gone from its wounds by this time.)

Actually, shooting an animal while it is attacking someone is a risky business; several hunters have been killed or seriously injured by their would-be saviors in those circumstances.

When one considers that a lion is a large, wonderfully fast, and tremendously powerful predator whose chief business is killing, it is remarkable how many people have survived a lion attack. Even in the old days many casualties survived the actual mauling, only to die later from "blood poisoning."

Tony Henley suggests that while lions are used to dealing with four-footed animals, they may simply not know how best to set about dealing with a two-legged, upright beast, and that flapping clothes and the strange human odor may further confuse them.

It is not uncommon, in the national parks of East Africa, to watch a lion making a kill. To be successful the lion must normally get to within about twenty yards of its intended prey, either by stalking or by lying in ambush. Then comes a sudden rush from cover, and before the surprised quarry can get into its stride, the lion rears up to place one paw on its withers and another on its neck or face, and pulls it down. As the dust clears, one sees that the lion has a stranglehold on the neck, or sometimes over the mouth and nose.

It used to be thought that lions killed by breaking the animal's neck, but that is rarely the case. They kill large prey by strangulation, and smaller ones such as young warthogs—which they apparently find very succulent and will spend much time and effort trying to catch or extract from their holes—by simply biting them through the chest.

"Nature fakers," as Theodore Roosevelt called them, like to claim that vile and depraved Man is the only animal that hunts for sport, and that "natural" predators kill only when they are hungry. This is utterly a fallacy; lions often kill in what can only be described as sport.

One wet afternoon my wife and I took the kids for a drive in Kenya's Nairobi National Park. Not five miles from the Hilton Hotel tower in downtown Nairobi we came on a couple of lionesses beside a freshly killed wildebeest. After waiting a while for them to start feeding, which they did not do, we went on in search of the rest of the pride. Half a mile away we found six or seven lionesses and juveniles lying in the rain below a little ridge, looking just as thoroughly uncomfortable as any wet cats would.

Suddenly a herd of wildebeests came pouring along the ridge above the lions. What they were running from or where they were going no one could tell; most likely the gnus themselves did not know. Instantly the lions threw off their miserable lethargy and stared at them with quickening interest. A big lioness sprang to her feet and started running along the foot of the ridge, with the rest following her. They got in front of the wildebeests, then cut up the ridge and over the crest to intercept them. There was a mad melee as the startled antelopes jinked and ran in every direction. Then we saw that the big lioness had a kicking wildebeest calf by the throat.

Soon it went limp, and the lioness dropped it and stood panting. But the calf revived. It scrambled to its feet and, with an outraged bellow, promptly charged the lioness, which leaped aside in surprise. For a few seconds the lions stood as if nonplussed while the little wildebeest shook its head belligerently at them. Then they closed in on it. One grabbed it by the muzzle, another by a hind leg, and they pulled in different directions. Then they played with it as a cat plays with a mouse, until at last one of the lionesses took a proper stranglehold and finished it. Then, without making any attempt to feed on it, the lions sauntered off, leaving the calf to the vultures. When we returned to the first kill, we found that it had been abandoned and was lying untouched also.

A quickie visit to an African national park all too often leaves a tourist with a one-sided and Disneyesque impression of lions. He encounters them flopped out in the shade of a tree, the big black-maned fellow asleep on his back with all four paws in the air and a cub playing with the twitching tuft of his tail, while two lionesses rub faces and lick each other affectionately.

Seeing them thus, lady tourists used to irritate my wife by declaring that the animals were just like their darling little tabby cats back home. How ridiculous, Berit thought, to compare a silly, spoiled, pink-bowed house pet to our magnificent wild lions. But then, years later, I brought home two kittens that someone had dumped out on a country road, and we have since learned that the tourist ladies were quite right: Domestic cats do move and play and greet each other and flop down and stalk and pounce just like lions.

No matter how well-fed it may be, a cat is a hunter at heart, and given the opportunity it will stalk and kill a songbird, or play with a mouse up and down the hallway until the mouse can play no more. Except for size, lions are not very different. It is commonly believed that lions always kill quickly and painlessly. Obviously this is untrue, and in fact the only reason a lion kills its prey is to immobilize it so that it may be eaten.

In the Serengeti Joe Cheffings and his clients were watching and photographing a herd of zebras grazing in open, parklike country amid a scattering of yellow-barked, flat-topped acacia trees, the whole scene lit by the slanting rays of the evening sun. It was an idyllic scene until eight lean and ravenous lions rose out of the tall grass, pulled down one of the zebras, and immediately started to feed on it. Their combined weight sufficed to hold the zebra down, so none of them bothered to kill it.

In areas where they are hunted, lions have generally learned to avoid all contact with humans, but in national parks, where they have been protected for several generations, they can be exceedingly dangerous to a man on foot, having no reason to regard him as anything but another potential meal. There exists a rumor about a Volkswagen tourist bus that got hopelessly stuck in a *korongo* (dry wash) in the Serengeti some years ago. The driver and the unarmed national parks guide decided to walk out a mile or so to the main road to get help, but they never reached it. Lions are supposed to have caught and eaten both of them. The story is most likely apocryphal, but it certainly could have happened.

John Kingsley-Heath, a well-known professional hunter who made Safari South one of Africa's leading safari outfitting firms, and who is himself a member of the lion club, put matters in their proper perspective quite succinctly on a radio talk show when he was asked how lions regarded people.

"It is my opinion," John replied, "that lions look on humans as nothing more than mobile hamburgers!"

Nyati!

 **Chapter 7**

Close calls from the author's African hunting journal reveal Cape buffaloes are never boring and sometimes deadly. (American Hunter *magazine, December 1984*)

If you asked him, young Ronnie Berman, who runs one of Houston's best restaurants, would probably tell you that there is nothing much to hunting buffalo—just go a little way out of camp and shoot one. When Ronnie came on safari in 1976, he had never fired a shot at any sort of four-footed game whatsoever. But his mentor and companion, Leonard Burke, had taken him out to the range many times and had so drilled and practiced him that he handled a rifle safely and very competently. Ronnie could even shoot Len's .375 H&H Magnum calmly and quite well.

Our first camp was at about seven thousand feet elevation in the cool forest of Masailand's rolling Loita Hills. We got in during the afternoon after the 150-mile drive from Nairobi. By 5 PM we were all settled in, so I suggested we take a drive around to get the feel of the country and perhaps find tracks or some other indicators that could suggest where we should start hunting on the morrow. Almost as an afterthought, I added that we might as well take the guns along.

Kinuno, the tracker, stood in the back of the Land Rover station wagon with his head out of the roof hatch. But the rest of us were not paying much attention as Len and I reminisced, for Ronnie's benefit, about our first hunt together some five years previously. That time, it had been Len who was the neophyte, and the smallish zebra we bagged the first morning was the very first game animal he had ever taken. But by the end of a wonderful three-week safari, he was a veteran with two buffaloes and an elephant to his credit, and both he and his vivacious wife, Connie, had fallen so much in love with Africa that they had come back to some part of it every year since.

Len had by now hunted all over the continent and had collected almost every trophy he had ever wanted. Now he had reached the stage where it was more fun to introduce a novice to the sport and to go along and watch him experience it all rather than to do it himself.

"*Sumama, Bwana. Nyati!*"

Kinuno urgently and accusingly broke in on our yakking, commanding me to stop because he had seen a buffalo. Sure enough. A patch of forest grew along the crest of the otherwise open ridge across the valley, and out of the trees came a huge and grizzled old solitary buffalo bull to graze in the open during the cool of the evening. The massiveness of his head was quite apparent even to the naked eye, so I did not have to study him very long through the binocular before reaching a decision.

"Normally one likes to start a beginner on an impala, a Grant gazelle, or other such innocuous beast," I told Ronnie. "But that fellow is much too good to pass up. Take the .375 and come along."

Luckily, our side of the valley was timbered, so we just went straight down under cover and started up the other side. Though it was open grassland, the opposite slope was so convex that one could not see more than about thirty yards ahead. Nearing the top, we went very slowly until I caught a flicker of movement as the bull's tail swished at a fly. I grabbed Ronnie's arm and motioned him to imitate my crouch as we duck-walked forward another twenty feet. Then we stood up quickly while, with practiced swiftness, Kinuno planted the crossed shooting sticks in front of the client and indicated that he should lay the rifle in the crotch. The surprised bull raised its head to stare and, startled into a momentary immobility, stood with its body almost, but not quite, dead on to us. I touched Ronnie on the collarbone between neck and shoulder. "Hit him right there," I whispered urgently. "Shoot now!"

I hardly heard the roar of the .375, but as the 300-grain Winchester full-metal-jacket solid thumped home, the bull simply collapsed and rolled over until all four feet came up in the air. It was so unexpected—buff never drop in their tracks—that I must have stood there with my jaw dropped for a good second before remembering to tell Ronnie to shoot it once more, as is customary and wise. It was no doubt redundant in this ease, but old pros don't attain that status by taking unnecessary chances!

The whole thing was utterly incredible. Here this kid, on his first afternoon out of Nairobi, walks half a mile and clobbers a monstrous old bull, which just rolls over in its tracks as dead as the proverbial kippered herring. Not only was it the first game of any sort that he had ever taken, but it was also a tremendous trophy with massive bosses and deep curls that swept around to give a 43½-inch spread. Many a man has spent weary weeks of travail on several different safaris looking for a decent buff without getting anything near as nice.

Later in the hunt, though, we spent two whole days trying to put the whammy on a certain handsome impala. So Ronnie might tell you that buffs are a piece of cake but now impalas—they are a real challenge! Not everyone would agree with him, of course; in fact, hardly anyone. Len certainly knew better because we had had a certain trifling amount of excitement with his two buffaloes on that original safari.

We had encountered the first one halfway down into the gorge of the Siapei stream. Len shot it well with my .375, and I put a .458 slug into its departing backside. But it got into a thicket nevertheless, and we had a slightly hair-raising ten minutes of follow-up before we heard its death bellows.

Then we moved most of the way across Kenya to the hot, dry, low-altitude thorn scrub of the Galana country that reminds me somewhat of west Texas. Mainly we were after elephant, lesser kudu, and oryx, but one evening we spotted three big buffalo bulls wandering along a *lugga* (dry wash or arroyo). One of them at least looked to be significantly better than our first one, so we made a fast stalk to get in front of them. Our timing was perfect: As we reached the *lugga*, we met them browsing slowly toward us. They were only intermittently visible through the brush, but eventually the big fellow, accompanied by one of the lesser bulls, came into the clear quite close, not twenty-five yards from us.

Len hit it on the point of the shoulder. The Kynoch 300-grain solid went clear through to break the last rib on the far side, but the bull's reaction was to break into a hard run in the direction it was pointed—which was toward us. I slammed a 500-grain solid into it, which turned it enough that Len's second shot took it through the chest close behind the shoulders. That slowed it down visibly, so I was able to divert my attention to the second bull, which was circling behind us, head high and with a wild look about its eyes. For a second I thought I might have to shoot it, which I was loath to do because—apart from any other consideration—

we were now out of buffalo tags. But when I shouted at it, using rather uncouth language, I'm afraid, it fortunately took the hint and went away.

Bulls are commonly encountered in small bachelor groups, the members of which are usually quite obviously buddies. My brother-in-law saw and photographed an incident where a buffalo bull charged and drove off (temporarily) a pack of a dozen lions that was attacking another bull.

I experienced much the same thing in the Mara Game Reserve. We watched five young adult lions harassing a lone buffalo. While a lioness feinted at its head, the others sneaked around behind and apparently attempted to hamstring it. Though they had not yet succeeded in crippling the bull, they had bitten its tail almost off and had ripped the hide on its haunches into bloody shreds when another bull appeared on the scene. It immediately went for the big cats and chased them off. They withdrew to the shade of a big tree half a mile away and flopped down in the shade while the two buffaloes took refuge in a thicket. For the rest of the day, the unhurt bull remained with its companion, charging out furiously at any car or tourist bus that came too close.

I have not yet been charged by a buddy of a bull we had just shot. But on several occasions it has seemed that one of them might seriously have been considering doing so, and I have no doubt at all that it could happen.

In fact, it happened to professional hunter Boet Dannhauser in 1970, according to a yellowing cutting from the *East African Standard* that I found in my journal. It seems that local tribesmen had asked Dannhauser and his hunting partner, Doug Coetzee, to deal with a group of several buffalo bulls that was raiding their cornfields every night. They tracked the buffaloes to the patch of brush where they were lying up, and then had the tribesmen throw stones into the thicket to drive them out.

One bull came rushing out by Coetzee, who bowled it over with a fine shot. Nothing further developed, so Dannhauser entered the brush, walking along a little stream to find out whether the others had cleared off. Rounding a bend, he came face to face with a great bull, which immediately charged him. Boetie gave it both loads from his double-barrel .458, then tried to leap aside, but the buff hit his knee and knocked him down. As he fell, the bull hooked a horn under his belt and tossed him into the air, ripping off both his shorts and his underpants and leaving Boetie in an embarrassing state of dishabille, as if he'd had time to worry about it.

Dannhauser had been wearing a revolver. Somehow he managed to grab it before he lost his belt, and landed on his feet with the handgun in his fist. The bull charged in again. Boetie shot in desperation with the handgun. The bull knocked him down into the stream and held him underwater until Boetie managed to wriggle free enough to drive it off by shooting it again with the revolver.

The newspaper reported that Dannhauser said, "The revolver saved me—and the fact that if I laid still, the buffalo would do the same. When I moved, he would charge . . ."

This happened several times, and Boetie was down to his last cartridge before Coetzee was able, at long bloody last, to arrive on the scene and shoot the beast off him. Incredibly, Boetie sustained no worse damage than a couple of broken ribs, and the thing that impressed him most about the encounter was that the bull had "de-bagged" him!

Normally, however, one would not expect any trouble until he was following up a beast that had been bashed, but not too well. My tracker, Kinuno, almost met bad trouble once under those circumstances. Matters started to go wrong right from the beginning when, through a misunderstanding, the client shot at the wrong bull in a bunch—a smaller one.

The animal wheeled around and went lumbering off after the others in that ponderous, rocking-horse canter of theirs, heading for the nearest thicket. I managed to get a .458 bullet into its midsection somewhere, then the brush closed around the animal. For a few minutes we could hear the buffalo crashing through the thicket, then all was quiet. We waited, hoping to hear the mournful bellows a dying buff often emits, but there was only an ominous silence. So presently it became obvious that we would have to go poke around in that nasty thick stuff to discover whether it was dead or merely very vexed.

We started to follow the spoor in, but something suggested that might be stupid. Instead, we skirted around the thicket and entered it fifty yards downwind from the trail. Proceeding very slowly and alertly, pausing every few feet to listen and to duck down to look under the brush in the hope of spotting legs, we eventually came out into a tiny glade. I was by then convinced that the wounded bull must have gone on with the herd, so I suggested to Kinuno that he circle the edge of the glade to pick up the tracks while Ed, the client, and I stayed back out of his way. All at once there was a furious grunting, and Kinuno came flying back toward us, hurdling low bushes and fallen limbs in best Olympic style, with the buffalo close behind and gaining.

Ed and I raised our rifles, but Kinuno and the bull were in line. For a few everlasting, horrifying moments, it seemed that we would be forced to watch helplessly while the buffalo caught and tossed him. But fortunately Kinuno grasped the situation and abruptly swerved to his left. At a range of ten feet, Ed and I fired together into the bull's shoulder, just looking over the top of our sights, not through them. The animal went down as if under a pile driver, but I emptied the two shots remaining in the .458's magazine into it anyway.

We got away with it that time, but I believe that close to half of all the professional hunters in Kenya have been pounded on by a buffalo at one time or another. Surprisingly enough, though, I can remember only one fatality, Tony Catchpole.

Tony was Kenya born and raised. After serving some time in the British army, where he attained the rank of major, he decided to go into the safari business. He was hunting buffalo near Lolgorien, in the western Masai, to gain the necessary experience to qualify for a professional's license. Exactly what happened is uncertain, but I gather that when they spotted a large, solitary buffalo bull that was a known rogue, Catchpole jumped out of the Land Rover and went after it, carrying a double rifle—but no spare ammo. He fired his two shots, and then the bull caught him. . . .

In truth, however, charges are rare, and very few visiting hunters ever experience a genuine, deadly serious charge *à outrance* [to excess]. Mostly buffalo hunts are, well, perhaps not exactly routine but relatively uneventful, one might say.

Take Bill Keith's buffalo as an example. In the Loita forest, again, sunrise found us working our way along the crest of a high ridge when a large and handsome, dark-pelted forest leopard crossed an open saddle a hundred yards in front of us. He stopped to snarl his resentment at our intrusion while the sun low behind us spotlighted him against the bright-green, dew-wet grass—a gorgeous sight! Not a quarter of a mile farther on, we caught a glimpse of some buffalo moving around just beyond the next little rise. We made a rapid sneak up to a small clump of trees, and there they were, six or seven buffalo bulls moving slowly past us at about fifty yards, disappearing one by one into the black shadows of the forest to our right.

Bill already had a fairly decent buffalo, so we were only interested in an exceptional head. But when the second from last came by, I did not hesitate:

"That's a good one. Shoot it, Bill!"

Inevitably, the bull plunged into the thick stuff. But I had seen the bullet strike, and it had looked good. A few minutes later, confirmation came in the guise of a few low, moaning bellows.

"I believe that you killed it," I told Bill. "But we can't be absolutely certain, so we will proceed as if we knew it was just wounded."

It took us a tense thirty minutes or more to cover the sixty yards the creature had run. It was quite dead, which was probably just as well, given that it was so awfully thick there that I almost trod on the bull's tail before I saw it.

And then there was the Wild Kongoni Gang. This consisted of Frank Kongoni himself, aided and abetted by Wild Bill Warthog. (When they flew F4 Phantom reconnaissance planes for the U.S. Air Force, they were also known as Captain John McCoy and Major William B. Adams, respectively.) The gang had harried far and wide in the land, successfully making off with many a fine trophy, until the last day found us up on top of the Siria escarpment with one unfilled buffalo tag.

It was beautiful country—a high plateau overlooking the Mara Game Reserve with thick forest along the valleys, open ridgetops, and grassy plains sprinkled with small stands of trees and clumps of brush. A splendid hunting ground: open enough to see, yet with plenty of cover for stalking; cool because of its 6,000-foot elevation; always green because the escarpment caught the rain; and with lots and lots of buffaloes!

We soon found a herd of about fifty moving slowly up a valley in the forest edge, got ahead of it, and waited in the cover of some brush. A buffalo cow presently emerged into the open about ten yards in front of us, closely followed by a bull with sex on his mind. He sniffed and nudged her, but she would have none of it. Nor was he big enough to interest us. All at once the cow lifted her nose suspiciously, then turned and bolted for the forest. Next, we heard the whole herd stampeding down the valley. The trees ended a quarter-mile down that way, so we cut out into the open and hurried after them.

Suddenly, another bunch of buffaloes appeared about seventy yards above us on the open ridge, walking up the valley. They had not seen us, so Wild Bill put his .375 up on the crossed sticks and waited till I told him to take the last bull in the band. The rifle crashed, the buffalo bucked as the bullet told, then it ran. In my usual fashion, I managed to get a .458 slug into its rear end, which slewed around its hindquarters. But it disappeared into cover nonetheless.

The herd went over the ridge. We reloaded and were about to follow when the bull burst out of the brush and came thundering down the slope straight at us. I do not think he was charging; he was just taking the most direct route toward the sanctuary of the forest behind us—though that distinction might have seemed somewhat academic to a chap who got in its way.

Everyone opened rapid fire. It must have sounded like the battle of Rorke's Drift all over again. But three-quarters of a ton of determined buffalo coming downhill as hard as it can go is awesomely difficult to stop, and it took nine or ten hits before it swerved aside and dropped twenty paces to our left. Even Kinuno got in two shots with my .375, which absolutely made his day!

The Cape or, better, African buffalo is not a rare species. In fact, they are by far the most common of the Big Five and must still number several million. They are not difficult to find. In good buffalo country it is no big deal to see several hundred in a day. Nor are they usually very difficult to approach, despite having excellent vision and good noses. They are not even very pretty; in fact, they are downright ugly. On the other hand, however, buffaloes are never boring, which is why I'd rather hunt them than any other game on earth!

The .470 Nitro Express

 Chapter 8

Though little but nostalgia and the Cape buffalo may warrant its continued existence, this yesteryear big-bore hangs on. (American Rifleman *magazine,* July 1991)

A round the turn of the century, English big-game hunters were almost to a man discarding their old black-powder rifles in favor of the latest small-bore arms that used the newfangled smokeless nitro powders to drive long, jacketed bullets of great sectional density to previously unheard of velocities. Their flatter trajectories extended the distance out to where vital hits could be obtained with certainty, and their enhanced energies allowed the 6.5mm, 7mm, and .303-inch bores to do the work of the .450 black-powder expresses.

John Rigby's .450 Nitro Express (NE), with its 480-grain jacketed bullet at 2,150 FPS, proved to give better penetration and to be a more reliable stopper of aggrieved behemoths than the elephantine 8- and 4-bore black-powder cannons. It made for a more portable and much faster-handling rifle, too, because a double .450 NE did not need to weigh more than 10 to 11 pounds, while the 8- and 4-bores went from 16 to over 20 pounds.

Then the British government, apparently as knowledgeable about firearms as ours is presently, threw cold water on the euphoria by banning the possession of .450 and other military-caliber ammunition in India and the Sudan. It seems that the natives were restless, and the measure was designed to deprive them of ammunition that could be used in the obsolete .577/.450 Martini-Henry rifles still common among them.

The notion that rebels might be able to harass the servants of the Raj by cramming the long .450 Nitro Express 3¼-inch cartridge into a chamber cut for the 2¼-inch case of the Martini-Henry round seems a little far-fetched. And I have no doubt the ordinance was as effective in keeping arms out of the wrong hands as are all the useless prohibitions the hoplophobes (those afraid of weapons) try to impose on us nowadays.

Be that as it may, a replacement was needed for the .450 Nitro Express, and every other British gunmaker, almost, came out with his own creation. They were for the most part based on the .450 straight-taper brass or a .500 case given a slight bottleneck, and included the .500/.465 H&H, three different .475s, the .476 Westley Richards, and, destined to be the most popular of them all, the .470 Nitro Express.

Joseph Lang is usually credited with designing the .470 Nitro Express in about 1907, but most of the other makers eventually chambered rifles for it, and Rigby virtually adopted it as its own.

The .470 Nitro Express uses a rimmed, slightly bottleneck case that is 3¼ inches in length with a total case capacity (to its mouth) of about 156 grains of water, compared to about 145 grains for the .460 Weatherby Magnum. It was originally loaded with 75 grains of cordite to propel a 500-grain bullet to a listed 2,125 FPS, yielding just over 5,000 foot-pounds of energy. In *African Rifles & Cartridges,* John Taylor gives its bullet diameter as .483 inch, a figure repeated by John J. Donnelly in *The Handloader's Manual of Cartridge Conversions* and by Michael McIntosh in his recent and most interesting work, *The Big-Bore Rifle.* They are no doubt mistaken, for, although one of the .475 No. 2 cartridges did use bullets of that diameter, everyone else, including with one exception all the bullet makers, insists that .475 inch is the proper diameter for .470 Nitro Express bullets. Woodleigh of Australia makes its .470 bullets in .474-inch diameter, according to its literature.

Theoretically the .470's greater bullet diameter should give it an advantage over the .450 Nitro Express and the .458 Winchester Magnum, particularly with solid nonexpanding bullets. But in practice the effect of its approximately 8 percent greater cross-sectional area (0.7088 square inches versus 0.6590 square inches for the .458) is indiscernible.

In common with the other British cordite cartridges designed for double (and single-shot) rifles, the .470 Nitro Express operates at quite modest pressures. Taylor lists its chamber pressure as 14 (British) tons, which works out to 31,360 PSI compared to the 50,000 PSI or more maximum permissible working pressure for the .458 Winchester Magnum and other modern cartridges. (We should note, however, that the British used a slightly different procedure to measure pressures, and their figures are not strictly comparable with ours.) Modest pressures put less strain on the actions of break-open double rifles and ensured against extraction difficulties, particularly in the heat of the tropics, and, in the absence of any sort of repeating mechanism, using a cartridge half as long as a maiden's arm was no disadvantage.

When Imperial Chemical Industries (ICI) ceased production of Kynoch centerfire sporting rifle ammunition during the 1960s, it seemed that the .470 and all the other great Nitro Express cartridges had been made obsolete, and that they would be replaced by modern rounds like the .458 Winchester Magnum. A good many African resident and professional hunters did indeed adopt bolt guns in .458 Winchester, but others clung to their .470 and other Nitro Express doubles and carefully hoarded their supplies of ammo.

Many of the double rifles ended up in this country as collectors' items, while others, especially those from India, went to Australia. Their new owners wanted to shoot them, if only out of curiosity, and so there arose a demand for, at the least, reloadable cases and bullets. The demand was met by small manufacturers in both countries, and now both components and loaded ammunition are available from several foreign and domestic sources for most of the Nitro Express rounds, from the .375 2½-inch round up to the .600.

Barnes Bullets of American Fork, Utah, has been supplying bullets suitable for most calibers up to .600 Nitro Express, in both softpoint and in homogenous solid form, for many years. Swift Bullet Company of Quinter, Kansas, makes its fine partition-type A-frame bullets with bonded front cores (which Remington uses in the .416 Remington Magnum factory ammunition) only in calibers up to .458, but that could change.

Trophy Bonded Bullets of Houston, Texas, can provide its extraordinary Sledgehammer solids and bonded-core Bearclaw softpoints in diameters up to .475 inch, and Woodleigh Gunsmithing in Victoria, Australia, manufactures solid and bonded-core softpoints in calibers up to the .600 Nitro Express.

Suitable cases from which many of the Nitro Express cartridges can be formed are listed by Eldorado Cartridge Corporation's Custom Shop of Boulder City, Nevada, while C.H.A.A. of Howell, Michigan, offers loaded ammunition for most of them, again including the .600 Nitro, using Barnes and in some cases Trophy

Bonded or CorBon bullets. From A-Square Company of Madison, Indiana, one can obtain it all—bullets, brass, dies, and loaded ammo—for most of the Nitro Expresses up to .577 but excluding the .600 NE, and for a whole host of other standard, classical, and wildcat cartridges as well. RCBS loading dies for the .470 Nitro Express may be ordered from Huntington in Oroville, California, and, far from least, Federal Cartridge Co. is offering .470 Nitro ammunition loaded with Woodleigh solid and softnose bullets. Velocity is listed as 2,150 FPS, for 5,130 foot-pounds of muzzle energy. Of course, the .470 Nitro Express is not exactly a plinker's delight—most of the loaded ammunition carries a retail price of around $8 to $12 per shot.

The huge .470 cartridge is not suitable for use in bolt-actions. It was most likely chambered in some of the big British falling-block rifles built on the Farquharson and other single-shot actions, but if so, I have never encountered them, nor can I recollect having even heard of one. In any case, they were rendered obsolescent soon after the .470's birth, when powerful large-game cartridges for Mauser magazine rifles such as the .425 Westley Richards, .404 Jeffery, and .416 Rigby appeared on the scene. Thus the .470 Nitro Express has always been primarily a cartridge for heavy, double-barrel "stopping" rifles, and remains so today.

Nevertheless, single-loaders are available. J. D. Jones's SSK Industries of Wintersville, Ohio, accepts orders for .470 Nitro Express rifles built on the Thompson/Center TCR break-open single-shot action, or on the Ruger No. 1 falling-block action that is an improved close relative of the famous Farquharson. The well-known Heym gunmaking concern of Germany also offers single-shot rifles based on the Ruger No. 1 in .470 Nitro, in addition to double rifles and a combination rifle/shotgun buchsflinte so chambered.

Double rifles in .470 Nitro Express may be ordered from (among others) Heym and possibly other German and Austrian makers, from Beretta in Italy, soon from Chapuis in France, and from several British gunmakers, including Purdey, Westley Richards, John Wilkes, Rigby, and, no doubt, Holland & Holland, though the latter might prefer that a shopper choose its own .465 Nitro Express instead.

In addition, exceptional best-quality double rifles in .470 Nitro (and other calibers) may be ordered from the noted house of Auguste Francotte in Liege, Belgium, through Armes de Chasse in Chadds Ford, Pennsylvania, which, incidentally, also imports the Chapuis double rifles from France.

Armes de Chasse's affable and knowledgeable Art Foley offered us the loan of an Auguste Francotte double .470 Nitro Express, and I was vouchsafed the privilege of test-firing it. The rifle's arrival was announced by the wife of Joe Sherrod, our local gunsmith and FFL dealer, who called to say that a rifle insured for $17,000 had arrived for me, a single shallow-V standard (or "standing bar") with no silly flip-up leaves. However, its rather shiny rear face sloped forward and bore no white or platinum centerline, and altogether I found it difficult to get as clear a sight picture as I needed for precision shooting.

For close-up, fast work when the rifle is pointed as much as it is aimed, it would not matter that much. Nevertheless, for my own use I would have had the rifle fitted with a generous "ghost-ring" aperture sight mounted on the breech end of the rib. The upper surfaces of the front ramp and of the quarter rib were finely checkered, but the rear face of the ramp was not so. (I should note that Francotte doubles are individually custom built to the client's specifications in all these matters.)

The rifle measured 42¾ inches in overall length and weighed 10 pounds loaded, when its balance point was just at the front of the hinge-pin, about 6 inches ahead of the rear trigger and 20 inches in front of the rear surface of the butt pad. One of my .458 Winchester bolt guns, a 22-inch-barrel post-'64 Model 70 that is standard except for its Lyman 48 aperture rear sight, is exactly the same length but weighs 9 pounds, 2 ounces with three cartridges. Its balance point, with one round in the chamber and two in the magazine, is remarkably similar to that of the double, coming right at the hinge of the magazine floor plate, 6½ inches forward of the trigger and 20 inches in front of the butt pad.

A letter accompanying the Francotte stated, "Regulation of this rifle was made with Federal softpoint ammunition. It was regulated at 60 yards, to be fired in 5 to 7 seconds between each shot. Fired at a shorter interval it will cross up to about 2 inches." Because the barrels of a side-by-side double lie on either side of the centerline, their recoil tends to throw the shots at an angle to the right or left of the line of sight.

Consequently, rather than being parallel, they must be set to converge sufficiently to overcome this recoil-induced dispersion. The exact amount of convergence depends on the individual rifle, can be found only by trial and error, and applies only to the load for which it is regulated. (With over-under rifles, the dispersion tends to be more vertical than horizontal, but it must still be compensated for.)

Among the disadvantages of double rifles is that they are generally limited to the one load for which they were regulated, and that any change to the rifle, such as the addition of a scope or alteration to its weight or to the length of pull, may destroy the regulation and thus cause an unacceptably wide dispersion between points of impact of the two barrels.

Since Federal had kindly provided 20 rounds of its softnose .470 Nitro ammo, I tried the rifle at 60 yards from the bench, holding it firmly with both hands as one would in the field, with a sandbag under the forward hand but no support under the butt. Because of the inadequacies of the sights where my eyes are concerned, I got a vertical dispersion of 5¼ inches, with three shots high out of the group, but the horizontal dispersion was only 1¾ inches and the remaining five shots formed a round 2-inch group with no indication of any cross-firing. Four shots, two from each barrel, fired at 100 yards revealed no crossing either, and though vertical dispersion was again marked, the high and the low shots came from the same barrel.

I am quite satisfied that the rifle shoots both barrels to the same point of impact with Federal ammunition at 60 yards, and practically so out to at least 100 yards and most likely quite a bit farther. Velocities were taken with the Oehler Model 35P chronograph. At 15 feet they averaged 2,156 FPS, but there was a distinct discrepancy between the two barrels. The left barrel recorded an average of 2,186 FPS, with an extreme spread of 124 FPS, while the right averaged 2,126 FPS, with a spread of only 39 FPS. However, no great significance can be attached to figures obtained with only six shots per barrel, although one might wish the extreme spread had been a little less.

While it might be hard for those who seldom shoot anything more powerful than a .30-06 to accept, the kick of a well-stocked .470 fitted with an effective recoil pad is quite bearable for a dozen shots or so, even from the bench. In the field, provided one was holding the thing with the requisite firmness, the recoil would hardly be noticed at all in the excitement of shooting at dangerous game.

The primary mission of a double .470 Nitro Express is fast, close-range shooting, so I used up the remaining ammunition comparing it to the .458 Winchester for two quick shots at gallon milk jugs at 30 feet, timed with a stopwatch by one of my sons. The double was still very stiff to open, and would need to be worked quite a lot before it was fit to be taken after dangerous game, but it fit me nicely and came to the shoulder with the sights pretty much on the target.

Nevertheless, I am not a double-rifle man; the only double I own is a shotgun I have not fired in two or three years, and I am not in practice with them. Thus, starting with the butt at my hip, I got my first hit $^1/_{10}$ of a second faster on average with the familiar old Model 70 .458 than with the .470, but the interval between hits with the double was 1.3 seconds compared to two seconds with the bolt gun. If this sounds slow, be assured that it is—I am slow. But to date I have always been both fast and accurate enough when it really mattered.

The point, though, is that even for one who is not practiced with it, the double proved significantly faster for two shots than the bolt-action. But then the "magazine" rifle will deliver the third and fourth shots with much greater celerity—and there has been more than one occasion in Africa with buffalo when I was quite glad to have them quickly available.

While acknowledging the irony of the revival of interest in heavy double-barrel rifles in the face of the waning of much African heavy-game hunting, this Francotte in .470 Nitro Express is a classic example of an African professional's stopping rifle, and it would serve that purpose to perfection even today.

The "Keneyathlon" Challenge

⊕ **Chapter 9**

A sort of sporting clays for the rifleman, this inaugural event pitted hunters against unknown-distance targets in the natural terrain of the NRA Whittington Center in New Mexico. (American Rifleman *magazine, November 1990)*

The Keneyathlon? What in the heck is a Keneyathlon? The name derives from the classic Greek *keneyous,* meaning a hunter, and *athlon,* meaning a test; thus, it is a "hunter's test." It was conceived by Dr. David Kahn, a physician who chooses to live in Casper, Wyoming.

Besides having an interest in sports medicine, Dr. Kahn is a runner, a hunter, a shooter, and a practical pistol aficionado who has attended Jeff Cooper's American Pistol Institute. His intent was to devise a competition that in addition to testing shooting skills would allow side-by-side comparison and evaluation of rifles, equipment, and techniques under field conditions, just as practical pistol contests were originally supposed to do.

A participant should discover what works and why, and be able to gather more data from a few competitions than from several seasons of hunting, given today's restricted bag limits. But even more, the Keneyathlon is meant to be fun, a sporting endeavor and training aid that even those hunters and shooters who are not particularly enthralled by the more formal kinds of paper-punching competition will be able to enjoy.

It is, in effect, a rifleman's version of the sporting clays game.

Essentially the Keneyathlon demands that the competitor cover a course laid out in natural terrain within a time limit, while stopping at several designated points to shoot—or not to shoot, as he may decide—at one or more targets. The time limit is unknown to the competitor, but is designed to put him under a certain amount of physical pressure. An allowance is made for age: 4 percent is added for every decade over 29 years up to 49, and 3 percent for every decade thereafter. But women compete on an equal footing with men, given that male and female endurance is in fact very similar. A bonus target is offered to those who save their time.

The first Keneyathlon was run at the NRA Whittington Center near Raton, New Mexico, this past May [1990]. The center comprises 33,000 acres of plains and foothill mountains and supports thriving wildlife populations. Elk, mule deer, and turkeys are to be seen almost any evening, and black bear sightings are common. A certain number of permits for these species are available every year to NRA members by drawing. Mountain lions roam the ridges but are not normally hunted. In addition to a 1,000-yard high-power rifle range with firing points for up to 100 shooters, there are various silhouette, pistol, PPC, small-bore rifle, black-powder, trap, skeet, and international skeet ranges and a sighting-in range.

Accommodation for ninety competitors is offered in double rooms with shared bathroom and kitchen facilities. There are campgrounds for recreational vehicles and tents, and a dining hall serves simple but excellent fare at very reasonable prices. Everything seems to have been solidly built and is well maintained, and every member of the staff I met was friendly and helpful—they actually seemed to enjoy their work.

Any NRA member who finds himself in that vicinity ought to take a look at this New Mexico property. He will be welcome and will, I suspect, be as favorably impressed as I was. (NRA Whittington Center, P. O. Box 700, Raton, NM 87740)

To keep the competitors to a manageable number for the initial trial, the prototypal Keneyathlon was not widely advertised, and just eleven of us ran it. The rules were simple. The .243 Winchester was the minimum cartridge, and to save the targets, belted magnum rounds were prohibited. Otherwise one could use any legal centerfire rifle, any sights, and any equipment he cared to carry. Eye and hearing protection were mandatory, as was a blaze-orange vest while running the course.

Between firing points the rifle had to be carried with the striker down on an empty chamber. We were told that the targets would be twelve-inch steel gongs placed next to "life-size" NRA deer targets, which could be used as an aid to judging the range. The NRA paper deer are obviously of the stunted central-Texas variety—they measure only about a foot deep through the chest.

At each firing point there would be a proctor (umpire) to point out the targets and the marked area from within which we had to shoot, to inform us of the drill for that stage, and to record our scores. Hits would score one point, but misses would cost two points each. On the other hand, we could decline any target (before we had started firing from that point) without being penalized. The rationale for this is valid. In big-game hunting a miss is an abomination—anytime one misses he could just as easily have wounded the beast. A responsible hunter will therefore refuse to shoot when he is not absolutely certain of making a killing hit.

I expect we were all wondering what we had let ourselves in for as we gathered at the start of the first run. We were a diverse bunch. There were two or three instructors from the American Pistol Institute and the Department of Energy's shooting academy; two gunmakers, Bill Dowtin and Bruce Russell; Brent Clifton, who manufactures the well-known Clifton fiberglass stocks with built-in bipods; several other young fellows; and Ron Troyer, who is in charge of construction at the Whittington Center.

I was the oldest competitor by several years, and some of the young chaps looked to be disgustingly fit. I immediately decided that I would not try to compete with them in speed, but would just endeavor to hit every target and let the time take care of itself. I was using a post-'64 Winchester Model 70 .243 Winchester with an old Weaver K4 scope. My handloads for it pushed the accurate 100-grain Nosler Solid Base bullets to 2,775 FPS, the same velocity that Winchester Supreme factory ammunition yields. The rifle can be relied on to hold five shots inside 1½ inches at 100 yards, and I had it sighted to strike 3.3 inches high at that range, which would put it on at 250 yards and only 4 inches low at 300. That meant that even allowing for some shooter error, I should be able to get solid hits with a center hold out to 300 yards. At 400 yards the bullet would be about 18 inches below the point of aim, and beyond that I really did not care.

I had a military-style loop shooting sling on the rifle, but dispensed with the keepers that are used to tighten the loop around the upper arm in target shooting. The rig weighed 9 pounds, which is on the heavy side for a .243, but I reckoned that would help it settle down when I was breathing hard. Also, recoil would be minimal, which could matter if I had to fire all the 200 rounds Dr. Kahn had advised us to bring (in fact I used a total of 64 cartridges).

Bruce Russell was using a heavy, target-grade Springfield Armory MIA (semiauto version of the M14) fitted with a Leupold 3–9X scope and a Harris bipod. It weighed close to 14 pounds.

Clifton had a .308 HVA (Husqvarna) -barreled action in one of his own stocks, with a 2X intermediate-eye-relief scope mounted ahead of the receiver in Jeff Cooper's "scout rifle" style.

One of the shooting school instructors had one of Cooper's own scout rifles, a .30-06 with a 19½-inch-barrel on a '03 Springfield action. However, he was unfamiliar with the piece, whose stock was too short for him, and did not do well with it.

Bill Dowtin used a pre-'64 Model 70 in a synthetic stock, and another chap had a .308 silhouette rifle with a 10X scope. There was an ordinary Remington Model 700 sporter and a Remington Model 742 autoloader in .243 Winchester. Ron Troyer had his standard-grade pre-'64 Winchester Model 70 in .270 Winchester, fitted with a shooting sling and an old Unertl 6X with a 1-MOA dot in the reticle.

We were sent off at ten-minute intervals.

Dr. Kahn told me: "Follow this road for about a quarter-mile to where a little creek crosses it. Turn left up the creek bed until you come to yellow flagging. Follow the flagging up out of the creek to a fence. Cross the fence, and then you will see the proctor, who will instruct you further. GO!"

I trotted down the road and around the bend, but had not gone 100 yards before realizing that I was not going to make it that way. I hate running, I have always hated it, and I never do it. But I can walk. I settled into a fast, long-stride, ground-eating walking pace that I can keep up for hours. If that pace was not fast enough, so be it, but I would at least get to shoot at all the targets.

I came to the fence, laid the rifle down, and climbed over. The proctor showed me an area a few yards square marked with blue tape and told me I could shoot from anywhere within it. Then he pointed out three widely separated targets on the face of a slope across the way and directed me to take them from left to right, one shot at each. The farthest looked to be a little over 200 yards out, while the closest was perhaps 150 yards. I got into prone with the sling, took a few deep breaths, and rang all three easily.

That stage was a gift. The next one presented three gongs down in a creek bed at not more than 100 yards. We had six seconds from our first shot to hit all three. There was some brush, but after a little searching I found a spot from which I could see all three from prone, and then it was easy.

Next, after panting up a long, steep slope, I located four targets, one at about 275 yards. Three were visible from prone, but one would necessitate going to sitting, so that is how I took them, changing my position when I had to, despite the extra time it took. Then came three targets in the brush, the farthest at such a distance that I held on its upper half. The shooting point was beside a large boulder that tempted me to use it for support, but the position would still have been awkward, so I again preferred to shoot prone with the sling.

At the next point, the proctor halted me before I reached him. He explained that there would be a target visible over there (he pointed) as soon as I entered the marked-off shooting area, and that I would then have ten seconds to fire one shot at it. It was a gong at fifty paces. I dropped into kneeling but could not see it over the intervening brush. It had to be taken from standing. All the while the proctor was counting steadily, but I could not hear the numbers through the earplugs.

Time was passing; any time now he would call "stop." I jerked the trigger in an attempt to catch the gong as the cross hairs slid across it and of course pulled the shot wild. Fool, I know better than that! It turned out he had counted only to six, and in fact I had plenty of time.

Three more targets and a brisk hike back to the starting point finished the timed portion of the course. It had covered about 2½ miles, had presented seventeen targets, and had a par time allowance of fifty minutes. I was relieved to find I had saved my time handily, despite my refusal to run. The bonus was a gong at perhaps 150 yards, at which we were required to fire five rounds from any position, with no time limit—this was a bonus indeed.

The second course—tackled after lunch—was much shorter, only a mile, and offered twelve targets. One lot was best taken with the rifle supported on a big fallen tree, and another four required going from sitting to prone and then back to sitting for the last two. I missed my first go at one, which was a long way off and partially obscured in the brush, but luckily three tries were allowed at it. The bonus was again five shots at a gong, but this time there was a time limit of ten seconds, starting from standing with the butt at one's hip.

I slipped into the sling as I went to prone and just barely got in my fifth hit at the count of ten.

We ran the last course the next morning. It was somewhere between the first two in length, with a par time of forty-five minutes and sixteen targets. It offered the most difficult shooting of the three, necessitating some rather awkward shooting positions—look out for that cactus!—and presenting the longest shot of the match.

I would never have attempted it at game, but as steel does not bleed or hurt, I had a go. Three shots were allowed. The first kicked up dust a foot below the gong, so I held that much over it and thought that I'd touched it, but the proctor said no.

On my third shot there was no doubt: The steel rang like a bell. Jolly good show, but unfortunately I had missed the previous target, which was somewhat closer, three times in a row. It was in the brush, and I could not see where my bullets were landing. Then I wobbled off another gong from sitting—I simply could not hold steady on it.

The last bonus shoot was a beauty. The contestant stood his rifle against a bench, placed two rounds beside it, and sat down fifteen yards away. On the signal he had fifteen seconds to dash over to the rifle, load it, and hit a gong twice (without using the bench for support). The gong was 100 yards or so away, and a berm made hitting it from prone doubtful. One chap who tried it that way bounced his bullets off the top of the berm. Others tried it offhand or sitting, but no one had hit it when it came to my turn.

I grabbed the rifle and ammo, put my arm through the sling as I slid into sitting, fumbled getting the rounds into the magazine, missed my first shot, and then time was up. I fired the second round anyway and had the satisfaction of ringing the pesky target even though it did not count. Bill Dowtin followed me. He shot from offhand, a position he likes, and obtained one hit.

Ron Troyer was the last man to go. He is an NRA high-power rifle shooter who has won the national high-power match rifle championship four times and the open championship three times (1970–1973). He has shot on U.S. Palma Teams half-a-dozen times and has hunted all over North America.

Troyer scooped up his rifle and two rounds, acquired the sling, and dropped into sitting in one smooth motion, loaded, and hit the gong twice, with the two shots coming closer together than most fellows can achieve with an autoloader. Anyone who believes the bolt-action is slow, or that it takes too long to get into a shooting sling, would have learned otherwise from that demonstration. It was as nice a display of superb rifle handling as I have seen in a long while.

After the scores had been computed, it was announced that Bruce Russell and I were tied for first place, with most of the others close behind. Dr. Kahn remarked that Troyer had trounced us by eight points but was ineligible because he had helped set up the course. We immediately rejected that ruling, recognizing that any advantage he may thus have gained was minimal, and could certainly not account for an eight-point lead.

Besides, we felt that he had clearly demonstrated his superiority with the last shoot, of whose form he had no prior knowledge. Despite his protests, we therefore unanimously voted Ron Troyer winner of the first Keneyathlon.

It had all gone remarkably smoothly; everyone had thoroughly enjoyed it and was full of enthusiasm for the concept. There was much discussion about possible developments and improvements. It was suggested that where space was a limitation, it could be run with .22 rimfire sporters, or with bows, hunting pistols, shotguns, or muzzleloaders.

Someone proposed using Comstock scoring, in which the score is divided by the time. I totally opposed the notion on the grounds that speed must not be allowed to compensate for missing; after all, in big-game hunting nothing makes up for a miss. Someone else argued that the time allowance should be known beforehand. I am against that also. Time is always a factor—no live game animal is going to remain in the same spot forever. The hunter is aware he has a limited time in which to make his stalk or get off his shot, but he seldom knows exactly how long he has.

Granted, one does not dog-trot much in hunting; mostly he moves slowly or often not at all. On the other hand it is not uncommon for a fellow to be short of breath and suffering from a pounding heart while hunting in the mountains, and sometimes he does have to scramble to reach a ridgetop or other point from which he can shoot before his quarry has moved out.

It is interesting that two of the top scorers—Ron Troyer and myself—were using absolutely standard bolt-action hunting rifles with fixed-power scope sights and no gimmicks, except for the old-fashioned loop shooting sling. To my mind the sling has the advantage over the bipod in that it can be used in any position. (I get no help from the so-called hasty sling.) Bruce Russell found the 14-pound

MIA to be too much of a good thing, but he is sold on the large-capacity detachable box magazine and used the Harris bipod whenever he could. He intends to put together a bolt-action 6mm Remington Improved, adapted to use the MIA magazine and fitted with bipod and laminated stock, for the next Keneyathlon. It will have a 6X fixed-power scope and will weigh 8 to 9 pounds.

When I asked about a muzzle brake, he said it would kick up too much dust when shooting from prone unless it vented all the gas upward, as Mag-Na-Porting does.

In contrast, Brent Clifton finds much merit in Cooper's light scout rifle idea (see September 1985, p. 44). He thinks having the scope mounted ahead of the action port is a worthwhile scheme. It allows easy access to the action, permits the use of stripper clips (not important in hunting), and precludes bruising one's hand against the scope when manipulating the bolt in a hurry.

Clifton used his retractable bipod from prone and Cooper's two-point "CW" sling (see July 1984, p. 28) from the other positions. He would have preferred more magnification for the farthest targets, and will replace the 2X scope with a 2¾X Burris, but otherwise is satisfied with his rifle.

As for me, unless the rules are drastically changed, the next time around I will use the same rifle and load with 4X scope and a shooting sling; hopefully, I will just practice more with it. I will also rely on the same tactics: While traversing the course as expeditiously as possible, I will take the necessary time to make sure of hitting every target I fire at. If I was set on winning, I would decline to shoot at those I was not absolutely sure of, but since I am more interested in learning my own capabilities, I will probably have a go at all of them.

There is no way that a trial of this sort can test every hunting skill, but all those this competition does test are of significant value to a big-game hunter, and any rifle that serves well in it should make an excellent all-round big-game hunting arm. Above all, though, the Keneyathlon is an interesting, challenging, and most enjoyable sporting contest—a heck of a lot of fun.

John Rigby & Company, London

⊕ **Chapter 10**

More than 250 years since its founding in Dublin, this prestigious gunmaker still crafts fine arms for those who demand best-quality "business" guns. (American Rifleman *magazine, April 1990*)

What is in a name? For all of this century, at least, the inscription "J. Rigby & Co." on the barrel of a sporting rifle has inspired confidence, assuring the big-game hunter that he held in his hands as fine an arm of the chase as was obtainable. Other firms might turn out flossier and more ornamental pieces, but no one surpassed Rigby when it came to producing best-quality but practical and utterly reliable "business" guns.

Rigby rifles were meant to be used, and used hard. They were designed to stand up to whatever rough conditions they might be subjected to in the field, particularly in Africa, and they are still built that way today.

When Rigby offered me the loan of one of its latest .275 High Velocity "magazine" rifles, I accepted with alacrity. Identical to the 7x57mm Mauser, a cartridge that has likely brought to bag every big-game animal on this globe, the .275 Rigby has been used successfully by all sorts of hunters all over the world. In its Mauser form it was greatly favored by many settlers in Africa, including my father.

Rigby was founded in Dublin in 1735, some forty years before the American Revolution. Gunmaker John Rigby was awarded a silver medal in 1781 for being "The Best Shot in the Grenadier Company of Independent Dublin Volunteers." Upon his death in 1819 he was succeeded by two sons, William and John. When John died in 1850, William continued the business on his own and in due course passed it on to his son, John (III), who was later appointed superintendent of the Royal Small Arms Factory at Enfield Lock in Middlesex. A London branch was opened in 1865, and the Dublin premises were closed in about 1898.

During Rigby's tenure at the Royal Small Arms Factory, his sons Ernest John and Theodore continued the business on his behalf. A private limited-liability company, John Rigby & Company (Gunmakers) Ltd., was formed in 1900. Both John Rigby and his eldest son died in 1916, but Theodore Rigby continued with the firm until 1934. Thereafter it remained in the hands of a number of private shareholders until Paul Roberts, himself a sportsman who has hunted in Africa every year since 1970, acquired a controlling interest in 1984.

John Rigby's .450 Nitro Express, adapted from a black-powder cartridge in 1897, is generally held to have been the first of the big classic English cordite dangerous-game cartridges. In the introduction to his 1901 catalog, Rigby describes the difficulties encountered when smokeless (nitro) powders were first substituted for black powder in the "express" cartridges of the day: "Dangerous irregularities of pressure while miss fires, hang fires, and occasional wild shots, due to stripping, were but too frequent . . . occasionally rifles of sufficient strength for black powder were bulged or burst in such experiments."

Rigby was able to overcome these problems by using a "special cap" (primer) to ensure proper ignition and by building rifles strong enough to withstand the pressures generated by smokeless powders such as cordite. The old black-powder express rifles mostly employed hollow lead bullets, light in weight for their diameter and therefore of poor sectional density. The bullet for the .450 black-powder express, for instance, weighed but 270 grains and was started at 1,900 FPS. It was usually recommended only for the small and medium-size varieties of big game, while even the black-powder .577 was considered too light for elephants, rhinos, and such, which were better left to the monstrous 10-, 8-, and 4-bore rifles.

The British .303 service round had been successfully converted to cordite (though loaded at first with black powder, it had probably been designed with smokeless powder in mind), so Rigby applied its principles—namely a jacketed bullet of good sectional density shoved along to something over 2,000 FPS—to the .450 bore. The resulting .450 Nitro Express used a 480-grain softnose or "solid" (full-metal-jacket) bullet at a claimed 2,150 FPS to produce 4,950 foot-pounds of energy and immediately proved itself superior to the black-powder 8- and 4-bores in both penetration and stopping power, and in a lighter and handier arm with less recoil.

Shortly thereafter the British authorities prohibited the importation of any .450-caliber ammunition into India and the Sudan in a fatuous attempt to deny rebellious natives ammunition for their appropriated Martini-Henry rifles and carbines. A superfluity of similar cartridges was quickly introduced to avoid this restriction, including Holland's .500/.465. Rigby adopted the .470 Nitro Express, originally designed by Joseph Lang, as its own, and probably produced more rifles for it than did any other gunmaker.

Two years after the .450 Nitro Express came the .350 "Special" (also known as the .400/.350 Nitro Express because it was based on a necked-down .400 case), which was in effect a scaled-down .450 (despite its bottleneck case) or a scaled-up .303. It drove a 310-grain bullet of great sectional density (.347) to 2,050 FPS and gained a reputation for being an utterly reliable killer on almost anything. Despite its rimmed case, it was later chambered in bolt-action rifles (or "magazine" rifles as the British prefer it).

Fritz Walter, a young Dane who during the 1950s managed the neighboring ranch to ours in Kenya, was given a scarred old Rigby Mauser .400/.350 by his employer. It was his only rifle, and he used it on everything from tiny dik-dik and deer-size impala to buffalo, and he swore by it. It was with great reluctance that he finally augmented it with a .375 H&H when the latter was made the legal minimum for dangerous game, and he was never fully persuaded that the Holland's cartridge actually killed anything better than his beloved Rigby.

About 1908 Rigby introduced a rimless .35-caliber cartridge better suited to magazine rifles. It was called the .350 Rigby Magnum and used 225-grain softnose and solid bullets with 2,600-FPS muzzle velocity. The steel-jacketed solid had a round nose, but the softnose was of semi-spitzer form. The case had a very abrupt shoulder and a head diameter of .519 of an inch, a length of 2.74 inches, and a full case capacity of about 91 grains of water, compared to a .470-inch head diameter, 2.494-inch case length, and 72 grains of water capacity for our .35 Whelen. Yet today's Whelen can achieve the identical ballistics with either the Sierra or the Nosler Partition 225-grain bullets.

At the same time, for use in double rifles, Rigby loaded the .400/.350 case with the lighter bullet and renamed it the .350 No. 2. It remained obscure enough, however, that it does not rate description in *Barnes's Cartridges of the World*.

One of the most famous big-game cartridges of all time, the .416 Rigby, was introduced in 1911. It looks like a grown-up version of the .350 Remington Magnum, but its case is significantly larger in most dimensions than the standard belted magnum case (the cavernous .460, .416, and .378 Weatherby Magnum cases are derived from it), and its full-case capacity is a generous 132 grains of water. It operates at a comparatively moderate chamber pressure to drive a 410-grain bullet to 2,370 FPS, which yields 5,100 foot-pounds of muzzle energy. The performance of this cartridge in the field, particularly with its steel-jacketed solid bullet, is legendary (see December 1988, p. 26). Suffice it to say that I have never heard or read a single word in criticism of it, which is well nigh incredible.

For use on the lighter species of big game, including the red deer of Scotland, Rigby chambered bolt-action rifles to the 7x57mm Mauser round. Eventually Rigby introduced its ".275 Rigby High Velocity," which was the 7x57 loaded with a 140-grain bullet. Rigby's 1924 catalog claimed 3,000 FPS for it, which it might have achieved in a 28-inch or 30-inch barrel. This catalog offered both a "Model No. 1" rifle for the standard 7x57 ammunition with a 175-grain bullet at 2,300 FPS and a "Model No. 2 High Velocity," which appears identical except that it is sighted for Rigby's High Velocity load.

Rigby has never made rifle ammunition, and its .275 High Velocity loads were manufactured for it by Eley-Kynoch and have always been completely interchangeable with the 7x57mm Mauser cartridge. (A rimmed .275 Rigby No. 2—sometimes called the 7mm Rigby Magnum—was introduced in 1927. It has been obsolete for many years.) The .275 Rigby has thoroughly proved its worth on animals tougher than Scottish deer. The famous D. W. M. "Karamojo" Bell used a .275 Rigby rifle to take many hundreds of bull elephants, mostly with brain shots, though he employed German DWM 7x57 ammo with 173-grain solid bullets almost exclusively (he once wrote that the barrel of this rifle had never been polluted with a softnose bullet).

Jim Corbett of *Man-eaters of Kumaon* fame also had a .275 Rigby. He put paid to most of his man-eating tigers with a double .450/.400, but thought that the fact that he was carrying the .275 on one occasion helped save his life. While looking for one of the Chowgarh man-eaters, he came on a nightjar's nest containing eggs of an unusual shape, which he decided to add to his collection. He still had them in his left hand when he passed a large rock and, looking behind it, saw the tigress eight feet away to his right rear, gazing at him with a pleased expression. She had him cold.

Corbett realized that she would react to any sudden movement with a spring that would have her on him before he could do anything. He was holding the

Rigby across his chest with the safety catch off and the muzzle pointing to his left. Very slowly he swung it one-handed through three-quarters of a circle until, after an eternity, it was pointing at the tigress; then he pressed the trigger. For a long fraction of a second nothing happened; then the beast's head slowly sank onto its paws. The 7mm bullet had injured its spine and destroyed the upper portion of its heart. Corbett believed that he could not have accomplished the maneuver with the heavier double rifle.

I was glad to note that the Rigby rifle I received for testing was built on a proper, traditional Mauser Model 98 action complete with thumb slot, and with the magazine floor plate release catch in the trigger guard bow. The right side of the receiver ring was marked ".275 Rigby High Velocity" and the left side "Made in England," both within engraved rectangles or cartouches. The barrel reinforce bore the nitro-proof marks of the London house, 18 tons, and the date, "89." In fancy script on the barrel was "J. Rigby & Co. London." The knob of the gracefully formed bolt handle bore five panels of fine checkering.

The serial number was in gold on the trigger guard, and "Rigby .275," also in gold, appeared on the magazine floor plate, together with two areas of scroll engraving. The borders of the trigger guard, the front and rear trigger-guard tangs, and the heads of the action screws were also engraved. The front action screw had its slot aligned fore and aft, but the rear one did not. Aligning the slots is nonsense anyway because the screws are bound to need tightening as the action settles into its stock with use and compresses the wood, and also if the stock dries out over the years.

The bolt sleeve was fitted with a side-swinging safety somewhat resembling that of the Winchester Model 70 except that it was two-position only. I found it dangerous in that it swung through a very small arc, moving so easily that the slightest contact with brush or what-have-you could—and did—move it to "Fire." Of course, a minor adjustment would rectify the problem. The inside of the action, including the lug raceways and the extraction and cocking cams, had been polished very smooth, and the bolt operated beautifully. The locking lugs appeared to bear evenly and with contact over the greater part of their rear surfaces. The extractor would snap over the rim of a chambered round without too much effort. The trigger seemed to be an adjustable one of the Canjar type. It had just the faintest trace of creep and was a hair heavier than I like, but it is adjustable.

The barrel measured $22^{13}/_{16}$ inches long from the bolt face and was fairly heavy, with a diameter of about .615 inch at the muzzle. The medium-dark walnut stock had attractive fancy grain in the butt but was plainer through the fore-end. It was fitted with a black rubber butt pad with a hard plastic (possibly horn) insert at the heel, just to make sure it would not slip or clink on a stone if set down on its butt. There was a light gray translucent horn grip cap and a gold initial plate, but no useless contrasting fore-end tip and no cheekpiece. The comb was thick and straight, and so high that the bottom of the cocking piece just barely kissed it when the bolt was withdrawn.

The rifle fit me to perfection for scope use. The slender, comfortably rounded pistol grip had a good open curve measuring about 4 inches from the center of the trigger to the front of the grip cap; consequently I found the 14⅛-inch length of pull quite usable, though 13¾ inches would have suited me better. The checkering ran 20 lines to the inch, about as fine as one wants on a working gun. A generously long area of checkering wrapped completely around the fore-end, and the pistol-grip panels were separated by about a ¼-inch ribbon top and bottom. The finish was quite glossy, obviously not the traditional old London oil finish (which frankly was a pain). More likely it was a modern synthetic.

The front sling-swivel eye was on a barrel band, and the 1½-inch-wide carrying strap had a foot-long piece of suede sewn to it to prevent it from slipping off the shoulder. It was nondetachable except with a screwdriver, and a little spring washer was provided to take up any slack and prevent the swivel from rattling against its eye.

The rifle had no open sights. It was fitted only with a Swarovski Habicht 4X32 Nova scope in top mounts specially made for Rigby in Germany. The scope was absolutely superb, as clear as rainwater used to be, with outstanding resolution and no discernible distortion even at the edge of the field. It had a soft "rubber" recoil ring around the eyepiece (which all scopes should have), and furthermore the eyepiece was spring-loaded so as to give if one's forehead should impact it.

The rifle weighed 8 pounds 10 ounces unloaded, which is heavy for a 7x57mm by today's standards. But it was very nicely balanced, handled splendidly, and was apparently extremely accurate. It came with two of the maker's targets shot at 100 yards. The first showed four shots with Hirtenberger 140-grain ammo that made a single hole 1 inch above the point of aim and grouped, as near as I could measure, into about .35 of an inch. When it was arranged to send the rifle over here, the company thought Hirtenberger ammo would be difficult for us to obtain, so they re-zeroed it for the Federal Premium load with the 140-grain Nosler Partition bullet. The second target was shot with this ammo and has three shots clustered into less than ½ inch, and another, the first one from the clean barrel, an inch below them.

I could not match the Rigby tester's shooting. The day I put a boxful of the Federal ammo through the Rigby from the bench, I was even more unsteady than usual. Every group showed four shots inside an inch or less and one flyer. Two of the flyers were so wide that they were easily called "out" before I looked at the target. Disregarding them, the rifle put 18 out of 20 consecutive shots into a single group measuring less than 2 inches, which is all the accuracy the great majority of us can make any use of in big-game hunting. Nevertheless, I am convinced that this rifle is capable of consistently shooting 1 inch, five-shot groups at 100 yards, given the right loads—and the right shooter. (The Federal ammunition gave an average instrumental velocity of 2,518 FPS at 15 feet for the 20 rounds, with the temperature at 50 F.)

I had hoped to take the Rigby .275 on a Wyoming antelope hunt, but it did not arrive in time. So I used my own 7x57mm Brno, with a handloaded version of the Rigby .275 High Velocity load—the Nosler 140-grain Solid-Base bullet propelled to 2,800 FPS with 48 grains of IMR 4350, a nicely accurate load in my rifle. I chose a buck with a deformed head, one horn stuck out at near 90 degrees, because I was after meat and it was a good one to remove from the gene pool. I spent the morning stalking it. The High Velocity load dropped it cleanly within 30 paces with a shot through the lungs at a range that was barely 100 yards. (I find far more thrill and satisfaction in sneaking in close than in sniping at them at excessively long range.)

I did hunt whitetails one day with the Rigby here in Texas, using a very gentle handload that propelled the 139-grain Hornady bullet to 2,550 FPS. I was still-hunting along the bed of a little draw when I spotted deer on the edge of the brush across a wide glade. I crawled on hands and knees, and finally on my belly, out to a persimmon bush, fearful the whole time that the rifle would get banged up or scratched on the rocky ground. Again, I was out for venison.

I saw a couple of yearling does that I preferred to leave alone, and a big doe that I would have taken except that her fawn was awfully small. I lay there watching for a long time, until at last a little buck emerged into the glade. Normally I would have let it go, but it was becoming a strain to hunt with the Rigby—I was concentrating more on not marring its finish than I was on finding deer. (If it had been mine I would not have cared—I hold with Rigby's Paul Roberts that a rifle is a tool to be used, and feel that such dings as it may accumulate are but honorable scars attesting that it has served its proper purpose.)

Then I noticed that the buck's antlers were rather uneven, with three points on one side and four on the other, so I decided to take it. I shot from prone with the buck turned half away from me, at a range of 120 paces. The bullet ranged forward from the rear ribs, passed through the lungs, and exited. The buck dashed out of my sight behind some brush, but I found it dead some twenty paces from where it had stood. No great trophy, but an interesting and enjoyable little hunt, a clean kill, and meat in the freezer—not a bad beginning to the Rigby's career.

I liked the rifle very well, though for my own use I would have preferred to have it at least three-quarters of a pound lighter. But then John Rigby & Company Ltd., (formerly at 66 Great Suffolk St., Southwark, London SEI OBU, England) is essentially a custom gunmaker. I do not suppose it would be happy to make a Weatherby-style stock, and I did not dare to even mention synthetics, but within reason the company will give the customer what he wants. Rigby currently makes thirty to forty magazine rifles a year, of which about half are in .416 Rigby.

The company has a good supply of Mauser actions for the standard, .30-06-length cartridges, but has of late mostly used the Brno action for the .416, unless a magnum Mauser became available. Jeremy Clowes, marketing adviser to Rigby, informed me that the firm is "pleased with both the new Heym action, which has a five-shot box, and the Hartmann and Weiss Magnum Mauser copy, and Paul Roberts is reluctant to make a .416 that will not hold four rounds in the magazine." Rigby continues to build double-barrel rifles and in 1989 delivered them in calibers from .577 to .22 Long Rifle, including several .416s (with rimless ejectors) and is currently making .600s. Last year's price was £25,000. In addition, Rigby still produces gorgeous double-barrel shotguns on its true sidelock action, which has rather distinctively shaped side plates.

The basic price for a Rigby "magazine" rifle such as the .275 I tested is £3,500 [in 1990], sans scope. (Delivery time is presently eight to twelve months.) To arrive at the total cost in this country, one has to add shipping and import duty to that figure. The exchange rate fluctuates but at this writing runs about $1.75 to the pound; thus the London price would be $6,125, and the total cost delivered in this country would probably amount to $7,500. That is a lot of money, and to be brutally honest I must say that one could obtain as fine a rifle, one exhibiting every bit as good craftsmanship, from several of our better custom gunmakers at somewhat less expense. But it would not bear the "J. Rigby & Co London" inscription on its barrel.

The .416 Remington Magnum

$\bigoplus$ **Chapter 11**

Ascribing the concept to professional hunter George Hoffman, the author pronounces Remington's new round a worthy claimant as the premier all-round heavy/dangerous-game cartridge. (American Rifleman *magazine, December 1989*)

There is no need to beat about the bush: Everything considered, Remington's new .416 Magnum is the finest standard-production cartridge ever developed in this country and, quite arguably, in the world for all-round use on dangerous game and the largest beasts.

The concept owes more than a little to George Hoffman, who lives in Sonora, Texas, but has worked many seasons as a professional hunter (guide) in Africa. He started with the .375 Weatherby Magnum case somewhat modified and necked out to hold .416-inch-diameter bullets and found that the resulting .416 Hoffman would push 400-grain bullets to velocities of 2,400–2,450 FPS with chamber pressures that were mild enough that they gave no hard extraction or other problems, even in the searing noonday heat of the Sudan.

Hoffman and many others have given his cartridge a thorough testing in the African game fields over the last decade, and the round has gained a considerable following among those who have custom and semi-custom rifles built for dangerous game. Its ballistics easily surpass those of the factory-loaded .416 Rigby of legendary repute (December 1988, p. 20), despite the latter's much larger case (the parent of the huge .378 and .460 Weatherby Magnum cases). A problem with the .416 Rigby is that it was designed to operate at comparatively low chamber pressures. Out of deference to old rifles proofed only for those pressures, manufacturers may not be able to load the round up to its modern potential. Federal lists its newly introduced .416 Rigby ammunition as giving a 410-grain bullet only 2,370 FPS from a 24-inch barrel, for instance, whereas the also spanking-new .416 Weatherby Magnum produces about 2,700 FPS from a case of only slightly greater capacity, and the wildcat .416 Taylor can easily yield 2,350 FPS from a short magnum case.

The Rigby case is too large to fit satisfactorily in most normal actions; it requires a special action such as the magnum Mauser, the Weatherby, the Brevex, the Magnum Brno, an altered P17 Enfield, an expensive custom action, or the new Kimber and incipient Ruger Magnum actions. But the .416 Hoffman and the .416 Remington Magnum work perfectly in the Remington Model 700 action and in any other that is suitable for the old .375 H&H Magnum cartridge.

The .416 Remington is based on the 8mm Remington Magnum case necked out, but with most other dimensions the same. Maximum case length is 2.850 inches, base to shoulder is 2.389 inches, shoulder angle is 25 degrees, and the maximum overall cartridge length is 3.6 inches. While both cases have the same overall length, the Remington has the greater taper and is shorter to the shoulder than the Hoffman, and consequently has about 2.4 grains of water less case capacity, according to Hoffman. The Hoffman cartridge will not fit in a .416 Remington rifle, but the Remington round will enter a .416 Hoffman chamber, and as headspace is controlled by the belt, it could probably be safely fired in such a rifle, though the practice would have nothing to recommend it.

Very wisely, I think, Remington chose premium bullets for its .416 ammunition. That does make it quite expensive, but then the cost of ammunition is not a significant factor in the sort of hunting for which a .416 is appropriate, whereas bullet performance most certainly is so. The softpoint is the 400-grain Swift A-Frame bullet, which employs a partition and has the lead of its front core bonded to the jacket to ensure great weight retention and a good expanded frontal area. It is an outstanding bullet.

The "solid," nonexpanding bullet, meant to give the deepest possible penetration for use on elephant, hippo, and sometimes buffalo, is exactly that. It is the 400-grain Barnes Super Solid, which contains no lead at all but is made of a homogenous bronzelike alloy. The theory is that normal steel-jacketed, lead-core solids may become deformed or bent upon striking massive, hard bones, and that they will then start to tumble or be deflected off course. Perhaps so, but I have recovered solids from elephants and buffalo that had tumbled or swerved considerably despite being completely undeformed except by the rifling. It also seems to me that a force sufficient to bend, say, a Hornady 500-grain steel-jacketed solid would be enough to cause any bullet to deflect, whether it was deformed or not. The homogenous bullets, being made of a lighter material, must necessarily be longer than lead-core bullets of the same weight and are therefore less well stabilized by the spin imparted by the rifling. Barrels in which they are to be used might with advantage be given a faster-than-standard rifling twist.

Actually, my impression is that the shape of the nose of a solid bullet may make a bigger difference. In my testing I have invariably gotten the straightest and deepest penetration with Jack Carter's Trophy Bonded "Sledgehammer" solid bullets. They have lead cores encased in very thick jackets machined from naval bronze, and bear wide, flat meplats (points). The idea originated with barrelmaker John Buhmiller, who spent many months in Africa testing all sorts of bullets and cartridges while doing control work on buffalo and some elephants. He reported that flatnose solids generally seemed to hold their course better after impact than did roundnose ones. Carter tests his solids in Uniseal, a dense duct-sealing compound, packets of which he stacks in a plywood box about six inches wide. That width has always been sufficient to contain his bullets, so he was quite astonished to find that, when I started testing conventional and homogenous roundnose solids in it, they would tumble and exit through the side of the box as often as not. It seems likely that Buhmiller was right—"solid" bullets should have flat noses. (Plywood, by the way, is too kind to solids when used as a test medium—it does not allow them to tumble the way they often do in flesh.)

Both bullets are listed at 2,400 FPS from 24-inch barrels in Remington data, but in fact they achieved almost exactly that from the 22-inch barrel of the test rifle, albeit at ambient temperatures of 80–95 degrees F. Consequently they develop more energy at any range than does the .458 Winchester Magnum. I pulled the bullets from a couple of .416 Remington cartridges and found that the powder charge under both the softpoint and the solid bullet consisted of an extruded powder of a similar grain size to IMR 4320 (though it was almost certainly not the canistered version of that powder available to handloaders) and weighed 79.5 grains in both cases. The charges appeared to have been slightly compressed, especially that under the long Barnes solid bullet.

Besides Barnes, Swift, Trophy Bonded, and perhaps some other smaller bullet makers, Hornady is also supplying 400-grain, .416-inch bullets in both softpoint and solid roundnose form. In addition to the 400-grainers, Barnes has 300-grain and 350-grain spitzer softpoints, while Trophy Bonded Bullets offers a solid-shank spitzer of 335 grains These may be useful for the larger varieties of nondangerous game at long range, and might do well on leopards and perhaps even lions. I have tried only the 335-grain Trophy Bonded, but because a perusal of the ballistic data for the velocity I was able to achieve with it showed only a trifling gain in trajectory flatness compared to the 400-grain Swift bullet, and a marked loss in energy delivery past 100 yards, I believe that I personally would just stick with 400-grain bullets.

At this writing neither Hornady nor any of the powder manufacturers has been able to supply me with pressure-tested loading data. Wolfe Publishing's *Handloader* magazine for May/June 1989 (No. 139) published some of George Hoffman's reloading data for the .416 Remington, and the results of the very limited amount of loading I have so far ventured agree quite well with his. I was able to achieve 2,380 FPS with the 400-grain Hornady RNSP using both IMR 4320 and Hercules Reloader 15, and 2,637 FPS for the 335-grain Trophy Bonded bullet with Reloader 15. By all indications the chamber pressures were well within bounds, but until I have access to pressure-tested data, I cannot recommend any handloads for the .416 Remington Magnum.

The capacity of the .416 Remington Magnum with a 400-grain Swift bullet seated is about 85 grains of water, compared to 107 grains for the Rigby case, 80 grains for the .375 H&H, 75 grains for the .416 Taylor, and 63 grains for the .30-06 with a 180-grain Speer spitzer bullet. With 24-inch barrels, their expansion ratios (comparison of capacity of the powder chamber to that of the barrel and powder chamber combined) run 9.7, 7.8, 8.5, 10.9, and 7.4 respectively. The higher the ratio (up to a limit), the more efficient use the gun can make of its powder charge, thus the comparatively good expansion ratio of the .416 Remington suggests that it might not lose a great deal of velocity when its barrel is shortened to 22 inches.

The test rifle, a Remington Model 700 KS Safari grade, has a gray Kevlar stock with molded-in checkering (made by McMillan, I believe) and a heavy 22-inch barrel with a diameter of .835 inch at the muzzle. It has a blind magazine that holds three cartridges and is fitted with a large, white-painted bead front sight and an adjustable U-notch backsight. The front sling swivel eye is on a clamp-on half-band on the barrel, an unsatisfactory arrangement because it can be moved by heavy thumb pressure. A full barrel band sweated in place would be much better.

The benefits of a blind magazine are moot. There is no floor plate to come unlatched under recoil and spill the magazine's contents into the grass or snow at an inopportune moment. On the other hand, I have, quite rarely, seen a magazine become so tightly jammed by clumsy attempts to recharge it in a tense situation that it could not be cleared with the fingers. Then a magazine that can be opened from the bottom is rather convenient, else one would have to try to dig the cartridges out with his knife, or might perhaps have to take the rifle out of its stock.

I fitted the rifle with a Burris Fullfield 3¾X scope, a strong, high-quality instrument that suits the purpose of a .416 perfectly, in my opinion. With its wide field of view it is an extremely fast sight at close range (for me, distinctly faster than open sights), while it has ample magnification for the sort of animals for which the cartridge is appropriate, out to the longest distance at which one has any business shooting at them.

The rifle weighed 8 pounds 1½ ounces bare, 8 pounds 15 ounces with the scope mounted, and 9 pounds 4 ounces with the scope and a full magazine, when its balance point was about ½ inch ahead of the forward action screw. I like a trace of muzzle-heaviness, and for me the rifle handled superbly. It came up fast, with the sights closely aligned to the target, and settled down nicely in more deliberate shooting. The comb was the right height for me, the length of pull spot-on, the pistol grip and fore-end were comfortable, and altogether it just felt right in my hands. There is a walnut-stocked version with a 24-inch barrel available, but I would prefer this practical, shorter-barreled, synthetic-stocked model myself; I think it would prove handier and more reliable under exacting conditions in the field.

At 9¼ pounds it is certainly not overweight for its power, but it wears an excellent Pachmayr pad, and its recoil is surprisingly mild—relatively speaking, that is. Compared to a .243 Winchester or even a .30-06, it kicks hard—there is no doubt about that. But it does not seem to hurt any more than my 9½-pound .375 H&H does, though it may shove me back a trifle more, and it is less obnoxious than my 9-pound .458 Winchester Magnum. Good stock design undoubtedly has a lot to do with it, but the fact is that I have been able to fire 20 rounds with it from the bench, in five-shot strings, without suffering a bruised shoulder or anything like that. Admittedly that was about enough for one session, but then the .416 Remington is not a benchrest or varmint gun, or any sort of deer rifle. It really bothered me only when I held it too loosely on the sandbags, when it would slam my middle finger against the trigger guard. As I have a touch of gout in that knuckle, that hurt. For two or three shots at a time from the standing, kneeling, or sitting positions one normally uses in the field, it is not too bad, and even from prone I found its recoil entirely tolerable. It does require a firm grip.

And the gun will shoot. It seems to be capable of consistently placing five shots with both types of Remington ammunition into not much over 1½ inches at 100 yards and showed promise of doing even better with some handloads. Using the Remington load with the Swift bullet, I fired one shot on the same target from various distances. The 25-yard shot hit virtually dead center, those fired from 50 and 150 yards landed about 1½ inches high, that from 175 yards went 1¼ inches high, and the 200-yard shot struck 1 inch below point of aim. All five were in a group measuring extreme spread.

The ballistic tables indicate that when sighted for 200 yards, the Swift bullet will strike 4.7 inches low at 250 yards and a foot below point of aim at 300 yards. Its trajectory is similar within ½ minute of angle to that of the .375 H&H with Winchester's 300-grain Silvertip bullet and should allow a killing hit to be obtained on all but the smallest big game with a center-of-the-chest aim out to 250 yards, and a lot farther on a big elk or moose. At 300 yards a hold at the top of the shoulder ought to work perfectly even on a mule deer. In contrast, the .458 Winchester Magnum shows more than twice as much bullet drop at ranges beyond 200 yards.

Dangerous game is generally taken at quite close range—within 100 yards or, preferably, half that distance. But on occasion a good opportunity presents itself at a somewhat greater range, and when there is no possibility of getting closer, there is no reason a decent shot should not avail himself of it, if his rifle and cartridge are up to the job. Also, it is sometimes necessary to try to stop a fleeing wounded bear, lion, or buffalo at quite a considerable distance, before it disappears into that horrible thick vegetation.

There are more powerful cartridges than the .416 Remington, but they also kick more, whereas I believe that (as with the .375) almost anyone who really wants to can learn to tolerate its recoil sufficiently to do good work with it in the field. For those few hunters who can thoroughly dominate them, cartridges such as the .460 and .416 Weatherby Magnum will outdo the Remington by a small margin. If I had to follow a sick buffalo into the thorn, I might still prefer my .458, because when all is said and done it does make bigger holes. A fellow who wants to take just one rifle to Africa for a mixed-bag hunt where he will be tackling only one buffalo and perhaps a lion might be better served by a .375 H&H, and for most guided Alaskan bear hunters a .338 Winchester Magnum or a .300 magnum would likely be preferable.

But as a cartridge for hunting all sorts of dangerous game under a variety of different conditions, one that can be used for elk and moose without it being entirely ridiculous, and that will work just fine on the smaller stuff when necessary and has tolerable recoil withal, I cannot think of anything better than Remington's new .416 magnum. It hits harder than the .458 while matching the trajectory and accuracy of the great old .375 H&H, and that combination is going to be awfully difficult to beat.

Which Is Faster, Scope or Irons?

$\bigoplus$ **Chapter 12**

The author field-tests a variety of sights in an effort to answer that often asked question. (American Rifleman *magazine, July 1987*)

T here is not much controversy about the best type of sight to use for taking big game at long range. Obviously a telescopic sight of 4X magnification or more is the proper choice.

But when it comes to fast, close-range shooting at a deer tearing away out of its bed, say, or at a lion, buffalo, or bear coming the other way, or at an elk almost completely obscured in the black timber, there is no such consensus, because the requirements are more complicated.

The close-range sight must have a wide enough field of view to enable the shooter to find and catch up with a fast-moving animal before it gets out of sight (or worse). This calls for a low-magnification sight usable in poor light. But at the same time it should allow precise aim to be taken at a vital spot seen through a hand's-breadth opening in the cover, and it would be nice if it permitted the user to take advantage of the 150- to 200-yard opportunities that are occasionally presented even in thickly wooded country.

Until about fifty years ago open iron sights were almost universally employed for all big-game hunting, and they are still preferred by most African professional hunters for use on heavy, close-range, stopping rifles. The best combination is held to be a large, easily seen gold-, silver-, or ivory-colored front bead in conjunction with a wide, shallow-V back sight that usually has an inlaid platinum centerline. Aim is taken with the bead nestled into the bottom of the V, and the rule is: "See the bead, the whole bead, and nothing but the bead."

I have tried various open back sights, including a form of the buckhorn with its useless wings, the shallow V with an additional U-notch (forge it), the barleycorn front/V-notch rear combination found on Mauser military rifles, the Patridge with its rectangular notch and post front sight, and the common flat-topped European rear sight with its U-notch into which the front bead fits neatly. I prefer this last at longer ranges and when I can take my time, but I find the shallow-V English express sight to be better suited for fast shooting.

Express-type open sights are simple and sturdy. Not very much is apt to go wrong with them. Even the fragile-looking bead front sights are surprisingly strong, and I have managed to break only two of them in almost forty years of hunting.

But they do have disadvantages. For one thing, the blade of the back sight hides the lower half of the target. For another, a bead large enough to be readily seen under adverse light conditions obscures too much of it at any sort of distance. But the worst drawback is the necessity of bringing into focus and lining up three widely separated objects—back sight, front sight, and target. Young eyes normally have the accommodation to handle this problem fairly satisfactorily, but it becomes progressively more difficult to accomplish as the years slip by.

The same problem occurs in pistol shooting, in which one is advised to focus on the front sight and let the target blur. In much hunting, though, the target is small, far away, or so poorly defined that if the shooter let it blur he would lose it altogether. Furthermore, the natural thing to do is to focus on the target, and in an urgent situation it is unlikely that one would be inclined to do otherwise.

This makes it essential that the front sight be highly visible. In target shooting, when there is good light and a pale background, dead-black sights stand out well, but those conditions do not often prevail in hunting. What works best for me under the greatest variety of conditions is a white bead with a flat face that slopes at about 45 degrees to catch whatever overhead light there may be.

Sometimes, particularly when it has a contrasting centerline, the rear sight blade may slope forward for the same reason. Alternatively, it may slope back toward the eye so as to reflect no light and appear dead black, or it may be vertical. I have never been able to decide which scheme is best. Regardless of what form it takes, when one is in a hurry there is a distinct tendency with any open back sight to see too much of the front sight and to shoot high. Hence the old maxim that one should always hold low on a deer.

The best type of metallic rear sight for fast shooting is generally misunderstood, little appreciated, and seldom used anymore. In truth, it has never been very popular.

It is the receiver-mounted "peep" sight with a large aperture at least .20 of an inch in diameter, surrounded by a narrow rim of metal that becomes practically invisible in use. It is, therefore, most aptly designated the "ghost-ring" aperture sight.

The old Lyman 48 and the present Williams Foolproof and 5-D receiver sights function as ghost-ring apertures when their sighting discs with the tiny peepholes are screwed out and discarded.

The beauty of the aperture sight is that one does not have to line up two sights; he just places the front bead on what he wants to hit, and shoots. There is no need to try deliberately to center the front sight in the aperture; in fact, it is counterproductive to do so. The eye is the rear sight, and it is lined up accurately enough because it will quite unconsciously look through the center of the hole.

For target and other long-range shooting in good light, a smaller aperture is more accurate. But for fast shooting out to 100 or perhaps 150 yards, the large aperture is much quicker, covers up none of the target, and has an unrestricted field of view. It is faster than any open sight, including the express, but at ranges of 100 yards and beyond I find the open sight to be slightly more accurate when I take care to ensure that everything is lined up properly.

Receiver-mounted aperture sights are a little more delicate than a sturdy open sight. Once, a client was carrying my .458 down a wet forest game trail (because my tracker and I were laden down with the skull and cape of his buffalo) when his feet went out from under him and he came down hard, slamming the rifle against a rock. The aperture of the Lyman 48 was broken clean off, so for the rest of that safari I had to rely on my scope-sighted .375 for backup work, and learned a few things thereby.

A scope has certain advantages over all iron sights, the chief of which is that it puts the aiming point—the reticle—and the target in the same focal plane so that both can be in perfect focus simultaneously. Also, most scopes "gather light" and can still be used when it is too dark for iron sights. The magnified image they provide aids accuracy at the greater distances, but is not usually significant at ranges of under 100 yards on deer and larger game.

The brush-gun scope should have a wide field of view—not less than 35 feet at 100 yards, and 40 feet is better. It needs at least 3½ inches of eye relief to reduce the likelihood of the rim of the eyepiece cutting one's forehead when he is shooting in a hurry with the rifle perhaps not perfectly mounted. And it should allow some latitude in eye placement without the image blacking out or any noticeable decrease in the field of view. Scopes of less than 4X normally come closer to meeting these requirements than those of higher power.

The disadvantages of scope sights are that their fields of view have some limitations, they are a little more likely to go wrong or be damaged than iron sights, they can become unusable in very heavy rain, they add ¾ pound or more to the weight of the rifle, and that attaching them solidly enough so that they do not work loose can be difficult. The integral mounting bases found on Brno, Sako, and Ruger rifles go a long way toward resolving the last problem and should be standard on all big-game rifles, I believe.

Normally, riflescopes are mounted over the ejection port of bolt-action rifles, where they may hinder the loading of Mauser-type magazines and necessitate bent-down bolt handles, low safeties, and side ejection.

There are alternatives, however. Jeff Cooper is renowned for his prowess with the defensive handgun and for originating the modern sport of practical pistol shooting. But he is also a purposeful scholar of the practical rifle whose studies of the subject have culminated in the Scout Rifle concept. This is a light, handy rifle that he feels should make the ideal general-purpose arm for hunters of medium game, in addition to whatever application it may have in combat.

An essential constituent of the design is a compact scope with about 9 inches of eye relief mounted just forward of the magazine well and as low down upon the barrel as possible. Cooper avers that such a "scoutscope" permits extraordinary speed without any loss of precision, that it puts the glass out of the way of the action to facilitate hand carry and instant loading, that it does not clutter the forward vision of the shooter, and that it allows him to easily see around it so that he can keep track of the target with his left eye while the right eye simultaneously picks up the cross wire.

Ordinary pistol scopes could serve, but they tend to have such long eye relief that they must be mounted farther forward than Cooper stipulates. Lately, though, Burris has started making a scope that meets Cooper's specifications. It is the 2¾X "Gunsite Scout" scope that weighs less than half a pound and has 7 to 14 inches of usable eye relief. Suitable mounts, however, are something of a problem.

Another fairly recent development is the Swedish electronic Aimpoint sight in which a battery-powered light-emitting diode generates a bright red dot that is used as the aiming device. There is no parallax, so the dot does not have to be centered, nor is there any magnification to limit the field of view (except when the optional 3X eyepiece is screwed on).

The latest Aimpoint 1000 is lighter and shorter than most scopes, is adapted to Weaver-type bases, and has unlimited eye relief, so it can be mounted over the action or forward of it, as desired. It employs readily obtainable batteries that are said to provide 100 hours of use. The intensity of the red dot can be varied to suit the light conditions. It appears to fall in the focal plane of the target, and is so visible that it can be much smaller than the normal bead front sight, thus permitting more accurate aiming. It has the advantage over iron sights in dim light, and it can be used under almost any conditions where the target can be discerned with the naked eye. But it does not gather light the way even a 1½X scope seems to do. In failing light one loses sight of the target a few minutes earlier with the Aimpoint than he does with a low-power scope sight.

A possible disadvantage of the Aimpoint is that it does depend on batteries, which could run out of power at an awkward moment.

I have had some little experience with both open and aperture iron sights on game, and with low-power scopes. But I had never used the Aimpoint or the forward-mounted Burris Scout, so I decided on a little test shooting in an attempt to get some idea of just how well they might compare.

I have a very accurate .308 Winchester sporter that was originally an Israeli M98k service rifle. It has a B-Square one-piece base that fits over the unmodified clip guides. This permits some latitude in the spacing of the scope rings. I also obtained the B-Square M98 base that replaces the military rear sight leaf and allows a scope to be mounted forward of the action. Then I drilled and tapped the receiver for a Williams 5-D receiver sight, so as to be able to interchange and use all the different types of sights on the same rifle.

I borrowed a variety of fixed and variable low-power scopes from Leupold, Weaver (Omark), Redfield, and Burris. Then in a brilliant flash of inspiration I asked Redfield for the loan of a collimator with a .30-caliber spud as well.

The collimator proved a tremendous boon that saved me much time and ammunition. I zeroed the rifle at the outset with the Redfield 5-Star 1–4X scope, then stuck the collimator in the muzzle and noted where the cross hairs rested on its grid. Every time I changed sights thereafter, I just adjusted them to the same spot on the collimator grid, and found that even the iron sights were then quite close to the proper zero at 100 yards.

The collimator may not always come back to exactly the same point when it is removed and replaced in a rifle's barrel, but it is close. It's close enough, certainly, to indicate whether there has been any serious shift in zero after the scope has been knocked about in a fall, for instance. In addition, it can be used to see whether there is any alteration in point of impact as the power of a variable scope is changed, and to check the value of the windage and elevation adjustments. It also revealed that with the ordinary Weaver top-mount rings, the scope may be removed and replaced without causing any great change in the rifle's zero, provided the two retaining nuts are tightened evenly and by the same amount every time.

I tried all the sights from the bench at 100 yards and from prone with a fore-end rest at 200 yards, shooting a five-shot group with each at both distances. Animals don't come with aiming marks (except leopards), so I shot at a plain piece of 8½x11-inch typing paper at 100 yards, and at a tan-colored 16-inch deep by 36-inch long cardboard box placed in the shade of a tree (with a safe backstop) at 200 yards. I decided that the box was facing to the left, and endeavored to place all my shots in its "chest."

The results suggest that at 100 yards group size was dictated mostly by my ability to judge where the center of the paper lay, but that at 200 yards magnification was starting to become a factor. They also suggest very strongly that I ought to consider 100 yards to be my maximum iron-sight range. The Aimpoint gave much better accuracy than the iron sights, and it seems to be entirely suitable for deer-size game under reasonable conditions out to 200 yards, as were all the scopes tested, even at 1X.

All the sights were then tested for speed on an 8½x11-inch plain target at 20 and 45 feet. I started facing 90 degrees away from the target with the rifle loaded and the safety applied. On the word GO, I swung on the target and put a shot into it as quickly as I could while being sure not to miss. The time was taken with a stopwatch. Three live shots and 10 dry-firings were timed with each sight at both ranges. The times obtained when shooting live ammunition were entirely comparable to those recorded while dry-firing.

I still had eight rounds left when I was through, so I tried five of them at 20 feet and three at 45 feet using the front sight only, with no rear sight at all.

All eight shots were on the paper, and the average time recorded at 20 feet was the fastest of any. Next fastest were the 1X scope (actual magnification 1.3X) and the ghost-ring aperture, while both the 2.5X scope and the Aimpoint proved quicker for me than the open V back sight. Even the 4X scope was only fractionally slower. (The times are listed as the stopwatch recorded them, to $1/100^{th}$ second. But I doubt that anything less than $1/10^{th}$ second is of any significance.) It should be noted that the forward-mounted Burris Scout was at something of a disadvantage in these tests because the B-Square base put it much too high in relation to the comb of the stock.

Finally, I mounted the different sights on various rifles and took them, with the bolts removed, into a pasture full of cattle to try them for the "all I could see in the scope was hair" syndrome, and in particular to compare the Scout to conventionally mounted scopes.

In the end I came to the conclusion that because of the 2¾X Scout's very narrow field of view that subtends only 15 feet at 100 yards—which is less than that of a standard Burris mini-6X scope—I still preferred the use of conventionally mounted scopes.

When shooting with both eyes open, as I do, one can indeed see around the Scout scope, but not much more easily than the left eye can see around a normal scope. Actually, in moments of fear or excitement one tends to concentrate on the source of the agitation with such tunnel vision that it is doubtful how much he would then see around any scope. Personally, I feel I would be better served by the wider field of view of a conventional scope, such as the 55 feet at 100 yards of the standard Burris 2½X, just for example.

The choice of sights for fast and close-range shooting is to some degree a subjective matter, given the fact that in practice traditional open express sights, ghost-ring apertures, newfangled electronic sights like the Aimpoint, and various scope sights with up to 4X magnification can all serve the purpose quite well.

During a decade as a safari outfitter and guide in Kenya I used the ghost-ring aperture almost exclusively on my .458 stopping rifle, and might still prefer it for that purpose today. But during the same period my .375 H&H, which was borrowed by many clients to use on dangerous game, was fitted with a Weaver K2.5 scope that is still on the gun. It has been used to stop an elephant charge at 14 steps, on several buffalo at about 10 feet, and on much other game at short range.

On none of these occasions did we find the low-power scope to be any hindrance. I have also used that rifle and scope on a lot of plains game at 200 yards, and in a few instances out to 300 yards.

I like the ghost-ring aperture for its unobtrusiveness, its simplicity, and its reliability under all weather conditions (except in the poorest light). The Aimpoint was nearly as fast as iron sights, is more accurate, and is usable under worse light conditions. It should make a great brush-gun sight for those who do not mind depending on a battery-operated device. But, everything considered, I believe that the optimum sight for big-game hunting in the thick stuff, where ranges can vary from arms' length to medium-long, is a low-power scope.

Any of the 1½ to 3X fixed powers would be good. I prefer a 1½X like the new Burris shotgun scope for dangerous game, but think that 2 or 3X makes a fine sight for a general-purpose rifle to be used both in close cover and in fairly open country. I have used a 3X scope on pronghorns in Wyoming without feeling unduly handicapped.

Nevertheless, although I do not altogether trust them, I cannot avoid concluding that the best choice of all is most likely one of the low-power variables such as the new Omark Weaver 1–3X, the Redfield 5-Star 1–4X, the Burris Fullfield 1¾–5X, and the Leupold Vari-X III 1½–5X. In fact, they are probably the best all-round sights available for most big-game hunting.

The .338 Winchester Magnum

 **Chapter 13**

An imposing performer when the game is heavy or the distances long, this belted magnum has earned its following. (American Rifleman *magazine, April 1987*)

O f all the belted magnum cartridges that have appeared since WWII, the 7mm Remington Magnum is undoubtedly the most popular. The most useful of them, however, might well be the .338 Winchester Magnum, which, excepting the phenomenal .458 Winchester Magnum and the semiproprietary Weatherby cartridges, is also the only postwar magnum cartridge over .30 caliber that is still a going concern.

The failure of the potentially great .358 Norma Magnum, the 8mm Remington Magnum, or even the little nonmagnum .350 Remington Magnum may puzzle and sadden us, but there are good reasons for the modest success the .338 magnum has enjoyed. One may guess that the Winchester creation filled the slot between the .30-caliber magnums and the ancient but still renowned .375 H&H so adequately that there simply was no room for another cartridge to grow there. For all big-game hunting purposes, the .338 magnum matches anything its competitors could do, and it was there first.

Winchester developed the cartridge by necking down its 2½-inch-long .458 magnum case to hold .338-inch-diameter bullets. The company gave it the same 25-degree shoulder angle that was subsequently employed by the .264 Winchester and 7mm Remington Magnum. Why Winchester chose .33 caliber rather than .35 is unknown to me, but possibly the excellent reputation held by the wildcat .333 OKH Belted in those days had something to do with it. Also, .338 bullets have better sectional densities than those of the same weight in .358-inch diameter. To equal the 250-grain .338 bullet's sectional density of .313, a .358 bullet would have to weigh 281 grains, for example. All else being equal, the heavier the bullet, the greater the recoil.

The only other standard American .33-caliber cartridge was the rimmed .33 Winchester designed early in the century for the 1886 lever-action rifle. It used bullets of .338-inch diameter, rather than the .333 inch common to the OKH cartridges and the British .333 Jeffery, and the .338 Winchester Magnum followed suit. The .338 magnum was first available with a 200-grain Power-Point bullet at a listed 3,000 FPS muzzle velocity and a 250-grain Silvertip at 2,700 FPS. Later, a 300-grain Power-Point at a claimed 2,450 FPS was added. In its 1986 catalog, Winchester listed only the 200-grain Power-Point at 2,960 FPS and a 225-grain spitzer softpoint bullet at 2,780 FPS.

Remington has offered neither rifles nor ammunition in .338 until this year [1987]. Not only is the annual limited-edition Model 700 Classic being made for 1987 in .338 Winchester, but Remington's Custom Shop is also now chambering for the round. Additionally, Remington is offering two .338 loads, one with a 225-grain Hornady bullet that starts at 2,780 FPS, and a 250-grain Speer Grand Slam bullet load with an initial velocity of 2,660 FPS.

Until recently Federal had only one loading, with the 210-grain Nosler Partition bullet at 2,830 FPS. Recently, though, Federal announced the addition of a load employing the 250-grain Nosler Partition bullet at 2,660 FPS.

Besides Nosler, all our other major bullet makers also offer .338 bullets. Hornady has 200- and 225-grain Spire-Points—a flatnose 200-grain softpoint for the .33 Winchester, and a roundnose 250-grain softpoint. Hornady once made 250-grain roundnose, full-metal-jacket solids for use on thick-skinned African heavyweights like elephant and rhino, but it no longer does so. Sierra makes only one .338 bullet, a superbly shaped 250-grain spitzer boattail. Speer has a conventional 200-grain spitzer and the premium-grade 250-grain Grand Slam. It also offers the 275-grain semispitzer with a sectional density of .348 that used to be Elmer Keith's favorite bullet in this caliber. In addition to 210- and 250-grain bullets, Barnes Bullets has 300-grain roundnose softpoints and solids (sectional density .375!), and can provide .333-inch bullets as well.

Col. Charles Askins, our senior field editor, took a pre-production .338 Winchester Magnum to East Africa in 1957 or '58. He wrote for the 1959 *Gun Digest* a most interesting account of its performance with 250-grain Silvertips on nineteen animals ranging in size from dinky little gazelles and a leopard, to tough and hardy zebras and oryxes, and up to a moose-size eland. Thirteen of them required only one shot apiece, and Askins declared that the new cartridge "performed admirably."

The .338 Winchester Magnum

In the 1962 *Gun Digest* Kenneth Waters reported shooting a whitetail buck at 110 paces with the 200-grain Winchester factory load. Despite passing through a 1½-inch-thick tree limb before reaching the deer, the bullet did not expand too violently, and it dropped the animal where it stood with less meat damage than a .270 Winchester round might have caused.

The .338 magnum was soon hailed by many as the best all-round cartridge for this continent's larger beasts—just the thing for elk, moose, and big grizzly bears. I was curious to watch one do its stuff, but because Kenya's game regulations declared that nothing less than a .375 H&H was legal on dangerous game, most of my clients chose to bring the old Holland's cartridge to Africa instead.

Finally, in 1976, Bill Zybura came on a two-week hunt with just one rifle, a .338 Winchester Magnum. His ammunition was handloaded with 250-grain Nosler Partition bullets, and I agreed to let him use it on buffalo, provided I could collaborate with a .458 as backup.

We started the safari in the high, cool forest of the Loita Hills, which are full of buffaloes, colobus monkeys, bushbucks, turacos (African birds), and stinging nettles. Walking back along a ridgetop toward the Toyota right at dusk the first evening, I saw a bushbuck. As soon as I had glimpsed its horns I commanded: "Shoot that bushbuck! No, not the one against the sky on top of the rock, the one in the shadows below it."

Zybura was not too sure which end was which, so he shot it more or less in the middle. I don't recommend that, but the big bullet put it down well enough this time. The horns were long enough to have qualified for Rowland Ward's *Records of Big Game.*

Several days later we ambushed a small herd of buffalo as they came out into a glade. Zybura shot a fair-average sort of bull, the best in the bunch. He hit it three times in the chest from about fifty yards, the first shot having pretty much anchored it. We discovered that the first shot had entered just behind one shoulder, where it broke the very heavy upper leg bone just below the shoulder joint. I was impressed! None of the Noslers exited. We found them all just under the skin on the far side, expanded back to the partition.

The next morning we came upon a very big lone buffalo bull in thick timber. Zybura had a second buffalo tag, so he decided to take it. The bull was turned partly away from us, so he shot it some way behind the near shoulder. It immediately swung around to face us, as if it meant to come over and flatten us for our impudence. I slammed a .458 bullet into it, which stopped it long enough to allow Zybura to finish it off. We were not able to ascertain exactly what Zybura's first shot had done, and one cannot reach any firm conclusions from the taking of just two animals. But my impression was that the .338 magnum seemed to thump the buffalo only a little less hard than a .375 would have.

Zybura took eight other gazelles and antelope with the 250-grain Noslers, and as Askins had found with Silvertips of a like weight, they performed admirably in the field.

Some months later, during the same year, Dunlop Farren also brought a .338 to Kenya for his safari. He had hunted with the rifle for 16 years, and, in addition to probably 40 whitetails and seven or eight mule deer, he had used it to take a huge 52-inch 7x7 trophy elk at extremely long range across an open "park" in Alberta. Shooting from prone, he tried to hold 18 inches over its back. The bull stumbled forward one step and then stood, so he gave it another, at which it turned to face him. He put his third shot into the center of its chest, and that was it.

Farren was using 210-grain Nosler Partition bullets. The first two wrecked the elk's lungs and penetrated through the far-side ribs, while the path of the third was traced into the paunch, where it was lost. The range? Well, the rifle was sighted for 300 yards, and the bullets had dropped at least 30 inches below the point of aim, so it was a considerable distance. Too far, it may be said, but Farren is one of the best game shots I know.

He used a .416 on his buffalo, but took nine head of lesser game, including a Grant gazelle, an ostrich, another record-book bushbuck, an oryx, and an eland with the .338 Winchester Magnum. We recovered only one of his 210-grain Noslers, from a coup de grâce shot on the oryx. All the rest gave complete penetration, even on the eland.

A few years ago I put together a .338 Winchester Magnum for myself, using a Mauser M98 action and a 24-inch Douglas barrel. For a long time it had one of Fajen's inexpensive Rebel walnut stocks, but eventually I decided that a serious, rough-country big-game rifle such as this one needed a fiberglass stock. Steve Sharpe, who operates Bear Creek Custom Rifles of Grapevine, Texas, claims to put a superior finish on his stocks, so I sent the rifle to him.

Many replacement fiberglass stocks have a wrinkle spray-can paint job that is easily scraped off and needs to be redone after every hunt. Sharpe says he textures his stocks with epoxy before applying a superior-quality paint, and thus gets a very durable finish. His stocks are foam-filled in the fore-end and buttstock, but are solid fiberglass through the action area, so that the receiver is firmly supported without any tendency to bend or twist as the action screws are drawn up. It should be an extremely stable stock that will promote good accuracy and help the rifle maintain its zero.

I ordered Sharpe's classic stock, which, with its trim lines, its slender pistol grip with quite an open curve, and its high, straight comb handles very nicely for me. It was painted a light gray (camouflage and other colors are available) over a textured finish that gave a good grip without being overdone. Apart from the free-floated barrel, the stock fits the metal closely with no visible gaps, and the bedding is precisely done.

With a matte-finish Leupold 4X scope and three rounds in its magazine, the rifle weighs a very portable 8 pounds. It kicks more than, say, a .30-06, but when it is held as firmly as a rifle of this nature should be held, its recoil is entirely innocuous in the field and is quite tolerable for five-shot strings at the shooting bench.

I loaned the .338 magnum to Ron Murdock for our elk hunting this past season. It came through a wet hunt on foot in quite rugged country, where it was dragged through the alders, banged against branches, and rubbed against backpacks without suffering a single blemish to the stock finish.

Murdock used 250-grain Nosler Partition bullets loaded up to about 2,680 FPS. He was in thick stuff near the bottom of a deep canyon when a glint of ivory caught his eye, and he saw a 5x4 bull 40 yards away, standing on a trail and swinging its head about. Murdock shot it close behind the shoulder. The Nosler put a 3-inch hole into the rib cage, a much larger one through the lungs, tore open the top of the heart, and went out just in front of the opposite shoulder. The bull ran perhaps 20 yards the way it was pointed, turned downhill, fell, and slid down the steep slope until it came to rest against a tree with all four feet in the air, ready to be field-dressed.

Another friend had previously taken two Canadian moose with this rifle, and I have used it on a 6x6 bull elk and on two white-tailed deer. I killed one of the deer with a .33 Winchester-equivalent load, using Hornady's 200-grain flatnose bullet at approximately 2,200 FPS. The small spike buck was hit a touch far back from about 80 yards, but the slow-moving bullet still made a mess of the rear lobes of both lungs. The buck ran 60 paces, but left a good blood trail and was dead when he was found.

Everything else killed with this rifle has been taken with Nosler 250-grain Partition bullets at about 2,700 FPS, which is my standard use-it-on-anything load in the .338 Winchester Magnum.

A lot of fellows, including Dunlop Farren, have enjoyed great success with 200-grain or 210-grain bullets and see no need for heavier projectiles. My own feeling is that if I am going to use 200-grain bullets, I would prefer to do so in a .300 magnum, where they will have a greater sectional density and a far better ballistic coefficient to allow them to deliver more energy at long range.

The only reason for choosing a .338-caliber cartridge over a .300 magnum is to obtain the enhanced stopping power its heavier bullets are thought to provide on the largest game. When it comes to lighter bullets, most of the advantages lie with the smaller caliber.

Nevertheless, if a .338 is one's only big rifle, then there are many situations where 200- or 210-grain bullets might be the optimum choice. I have no experience on game with 225-grain bullets, but they could well be the best compromise for an all-round load in this cartridge.

Formerly the 250-grain Nosler Partition bullet had a round nose, causing it to lose velocity rather quickly and giving it quite a curved trajectory compared to the 210-grain Nosler. This is no longer the case; the present 250-grain Partition bullet is of spitzer form and has as flat a trajectory for all practical purposes as the lighter one. The prime projectile for long-range shooting with a .338 magnum is most likely Sierra's streamlined 250-grain spitzer boattail.

The capacity of the .338 Winchester Magnum case is such that powders like IMR 4350 and IMR 4831 give good results with most bullet weights. Hodgdon's H4831 is a touch on the slow side—I could not get enough of it into the case to produce other than modest velocities, even with the 275-grain bullet. Du Pont's IMR 4831 did well with this heavy Speer bullet, but otherwise I got the best accuracy with IMR 4350 powder. A very accurate load in my rifle is the 250-grain Nosler with 70 grains of IMR 4350. It averages close to 1¼ inches in extreme spread for five-shot groups at 100 yards from the bench. (Warning: This load is close to maximum, and it may be excessive in some rifles.)

Debating the best all-round single cartridge for American big game is a favorite pastime of gunwriters. It allows us to display our erudition with soaring arguments that need seldom touch down on the hard ground of reality. Although great fun, it is rather a silly game.

Nevertheless, I'll play it briefly. If I could have but one rifle for all my big-game hunting, it would not, under my present circumstances, be a .338 magnum. The great preponderance of my hunting involves deer, pronghorns, hogs, and exotic game of similar size, with only an occasional foray for elk and possibly for moose and caribou. Thus a .30-06 with suitable handloads would be sufficient.

But if I lived where I could hunt elk and moose as often as deer, or where grizzly or brown bears were definitely a factor to be reckoned with, then a .338 Winchester Magnum would be my choice. I would most probably load 200-grain bullets down to around 2,300 to 2,400 FPS for whitetails in the brush. I might use 220- or 225-grain spitzers at full velocity for pronghorns and open-country mule deer, but in practice I believe I would tend to use 250-grain Partition bullets on everything.

A superior, but expensive, alternative to the Noslers for some purposes would be the Trophy Bonded Core bullets that Jack Carter turns out. They expand to a greater diameter than any other bullets I am familiar with, but typically retain 90 percent of their original weight and give deep penetration (though not quite as deep as do Noslers).

In any event, a two-rifle battery for all North American big game is a much more realistic concept. Two rifles could indeed handle it all. The smaller one might be anything from a 6mm or a .257 Roberts on up to a 7mm magnum or a .30-06. I would take a 7x57mm Mauser or a 7mm-08 myself, but from a purely pragmatic point of view the .270 Winchester would seem to be the best choice. A lightweight .270 with a 22-inch barrel works as well in deer cover as it does on a pronghorn prairie or a sheep mountain, and it's plenty enough gun for anything up to and including caribou (and the medium-size African antelope and zebra).

For the very largest game, cartridges like the .375 H&H and the .340 Weatherby Magnum do have advantages. Brown bear guides like them, I am told, though some of them prefer the .458 Winchester Magnum. But these are generally large and heavy pieces, and they do kick. In contrast, it is my observation that after a little practice the majority of hunters can become well enough accustomed to the recoil of a .338 magnum to do good work with it.

Stopping power on large or dangerous game derives far more from bullet placement than from any other factor—hitting the right spot is the secret to staying out of trouble. Therefore the old axiom that for such beasts one should use the most powerful rifle he can shoot well is still sound advice. For most of us, the .338 probably comes closer to the ideal than any other cartridge.

The 9.3x62 Cartridge

$\bigoplus$ **Chapter 14**

Despite its long and successful use in both Europe and Africa, this very practical medium-bore round is little known among American hunters. (American Rifleman magazine, January 1987)

Although .35- and .375-caliber cartridges are well known and fairly popular in America, those employing 9.3mm (.366-inch)-diameter bullets are less familiar. Indeed, many hunters and shooters in this country have never heard of them. This is perhaps surprising, as a great many different 9.3mm cartridges were developed in Europe, and two of these saw widespread use in Africa and earned reputations as thoroughly sound and reliable medium-bore cartridges fit for taking even the greatest game if used with a little skill and some common sense.

There were a slew of straight, rimmed, black-powder 9.3mm cartridges with cases of varying lengths, of which the most common was the 9.3x72R (rimmed), a cartridge that is still quite often encountered in drillings (three-barrel guns).

The British .360 Nitro Express No. 2 and the .400/.360 Westley Richards Nitro Express both used .367-inch-diameter 300- to 320-grain bullets at 1,950 to 2,200 FPS, according to Frank Barnes's *Cartridges of the World*. They have been obsolete for many years, but the quite similar German 9.3x74R is in good fettle. It looks old-fashioned with its long, slender, slightly bottlenecked rimmed case designed for the break-open single- and multibarrel arms that are still being chambered to it. Nonetheless, it is a very capable cartridge for which RWS offers a variety of bullet weights ranging from a 247-grain Cone-Point at 2,460 FPS to a 293-grain TUG at a listed 2,280 FPS.

Many years ago a Kenyan chum of mine had a Swedish Husqvarna double rifle in the 9.3x72R caliber. He was more interested in tennis than in hunting and never killed anything but a few impala with it. His father, however, had used it well on a lot of African big game, including some Cape buffalo.

Around the turn of the century a 9.3x57mm rimless cartridge for bolt-action rifles was devised by necking up the 8x57mm Mauser case. It is close to the .358 Winchester in performance, and it apparently became so popular for moose in Sweden that Norma still finds it worthwhile to manufacture it.

The best-known—or perhaps simply the best—of all the 9.3mm rounds was developed about 1905 by the Berlin gunmaker Otto Bock. It has been suggested that it was designed to provide settlers in Germany's African colonies with an adequate cartridge that could be made available in comparatively inexpensive Mauser sporting rifles. If that was the intention, it succeeded admirably. The 9.3x62mm quickly became by far the most popular medium bore among the resident African hunters, and held that position at least up to the 1950s, when the .375 H&H Magnum may have begun to overtake it. (There is also a magnum-class, though beltless, 9.3mm, the 9.3x64mm Brenneke. I have no experience with it, not even at secondhand, and have never seen one. It is said to equal or surpass the .375 H&H in stopping power.)

The 9.3mm Mauser is not a glamorous round and never received the paeans bestowed on more romantic and patrician cartridges such as the .350 Rigby Magnum, the .333 Jeffery, or the lauded .318 Westley Richards. With its 285-grain roundnose softpoint and solid bullets at a nominal 2,360 FPS, it was simply the better cartridge, a plebeian workhorse that got the job done with thoroughgoing reliability under almost any circumstances.

Several of my buddies employed the 9.3x62mm. Joe Cheffmgs had a Belgian FN Mauser sporter chambered to it that he used for several years in conjunction with a double .500/.450. He killed any amount of plains game with it, also one or two buffalo, and found that it performed adequately on all of it, both large and small. The 285-grain softpoint had plenty of lead showing at the nose. It would start to expand quite readily; but with its moderate velocity and good sectional density (.304), it generally retained enough weight to drive in deeply. Cheffings did have one of them blow up on a zebra's shoulder; apparently this failure was due to a faulty bullet jacket, and it is the only failure of this bullet that I can remember hearing about.

A buffalo-hunting enthusiast I was acquainted with was another 9.3mm fancier. He bagged a score or two of the black bulls with it, and he claimed that it did for them so efficaciously that he could see no real purpose in using heavier and harder-kicking artillery.

The 285-grain full-metal-jacket solid did give satisfactory penetration. I still vividly remember a wounded, running zebra that collapsed in midstride when Cheffings smacked it in the stern with a 9.3mm solid from his Belgian Mauser. The bullet had raked it all the way through to the lungs and finished up in front of a shoulder blade.

Cheffings's .500/.450 3¼-inch Nitro Express, for which no fresh ammunition was available even then, began to misfire, making the hunting of dangerous game with it a decidedly sporting caper. After it misfired twice in a row on the same buffalo, he hied himself off to Shaw & Hunter in Nairobi, where he traded both the .450 and the 9.3x62mm for an almost new Winchester Model 70 in .375 H&H. He used the .375 for years on everything from dik-dik to elephant, and finally—when he started guiding hunters professionally—added a .458 Winchester Magnum to complete his battery.

Comparing the 9.3x62mm and the .375 H&H, Cheffings said he knew the Hollands had to be the superior cartridge, but added that it would be awfully difficult to prove it from his experiences with the two on game. I agree. As far as we could tell, the 9.3x62mm apparently killed just as well as the .375 under most circumstances. Only at long range, where its somewhat flatter trajectory told in its favor, did the .375 H&H have any very evident advantage.

Even the conservative and very English Kenya Game Department of the time acknowledged the worth of the 9.3mm Mauser, albeit with reluctance. In 1958 the department gazetted new regulations that made the .375 H&H the minimum cartridge permitted for taking dangerous game; but at the same time it stipulated that experienced hunters who had habitually relied on the 9.3mm could continue to use it.

(Jack O'Connor once wrote that .400 was the minimum legal caliber for dangerous game in Kenya. He was mistaken. At one time the game department recommended nothing less than .400 for such use, but the .375 caliber was always legally permissible.)

I have always had a liking for the 9.3mm Mauser and believe that it would make a superb elk, bear, and moose cartridge. So when Gun South of Trussville, Alabama, asked me to evaluate the Steyr-Mannlicher rifles it imports from Austria, I requested one in 9.3x62mm if possible. They shipped me a Model M Professional in that caliber, and I was delighted until it struck me that now I had to figure out a way to feed it. Ammunition for the 9.3mm is not commonly stocked by gun stores.

According to *Cartridges of the World*, the 9.3x62mm case has the same 0.470-inch rim diameter and 0.473-inch base diameter as the .30-06 but is slightly shorter, with a maximum length of 2.42-inches as against 2.494 inches for the Springfield case. Its neck is much shorter, being only 0.27-inch long on an RWS case I measured, while its body to the shoulder is longer, giving it a somewhat greater powder capacity.

Dies for the 9.3x62mm are available from RCBS, Hornady, and maybe some others. Cases can be made from .30-06 brass, but this does entail necking out and fire-forming. Tapered expander plugs that will expand a .30-caliber neck out to 9.3mm in one smooth pass may be had on special order. But I just spun the expander-decapping rod from my RCBS 9.3x62mm sizing die in an electric drill and tapered the chamfer of its expander button with a diamond hone until it would do the same thing.

To prepare them for fire-forming, the cases should be necked out to a larger diameter, .375 inch or .411 inch, say, and then should be run back into the 9.3mm sizing die. This will leave a little ledge bearing against the shoulder of the chamber to maintain the proper headspace. I omitted this step, and instead achieved the same end by seating Speer 270-grain bullets out to be in very firm contact with the rifling, so that it took some effort to close the bolt, and then fire-formed the cases with about 40 grains of IMR 3031.

This case-forming method worked fine, but it is hardly worthwhile since 9.3x62mm ammunition and components are imported by FFV Norma of Springfield, Missouri, and in RWS brand by Dynamit Nobel of America of Northvale, New Jersey.

I obtained RWS ammo in three different bullet weights, RWS cases, and both RWS and Norma 9.3mm bullets from the Old Western Scrounger of Montague, California. Apart from quite a complete line of both RWS and Norma ammunition and components, this firm's amusing and informative catalog contains fascinating lists of obsolete cartridges from the .600 Nitro Express and the .50-140-600 (3¼-inch) Sharps to the 9mm rimfire BB cap. For information, send a self-addressed, stamped, legal-size envelope.

Barnes Bullets has 250- and 300-grain spitzer bullets in .366-inch diameter to fit 9.3mm cartridges, while Speer has recently introduced a 270-grain semispitzer

9.3mm bullet that resembles its excellent 250-grain .35-caliber projectile. It is very likely the best all-round bullet presently available for the 9.3x62mm, and for the 9.3x74R if both barrels of a double rifle in that caliber can be persuaded to shoot usefully close together with it.

A 270-grain .366-inch bullet has a sectional density of .288, about the same as a 190-grain .308 or a 285-grain .375-caliber bullet. It can attain 2,500 FPS (and 3,747 foot-pounds of energy) in a 9.3x62mm. I do not have its ballistic coefficient, but I expect it should be about .450 for the Speer semispitzer. If so, when the rifle is sighted to hit 3 inches high at 100 yards, it will be on at a little beyond 200 yards and should have a point-blank range of a good 250 yards. Out to that distance, no allowances for bullet drop would be necessary on deer-size game with a center-of-the-chest hold. In the past 10 years I have not fired a single shot at game at over 250 yards.

The present RWS catalog lists 9.3x62mm ammunition with a 258-grain H-Mantel bullet at 2,560 FPS, the 285-grain roundnose in both solid and softpoint form at 2,280 FPS, and a 293-grain Torpedo-Universal-Geschoss (Boattail-Universal-Bullet) at a claimed 2,430 FPS.

The 285-grain softpoints I tested exceeded specifications and gave an average reading of 2,282 FPS at 15 feet on the Oehler M33 chronograph. Both the 258-grain H-Mantel and the 293-grain TUG were slower than the factory claimed, at 2,490 FPS and 2,270 FPS, respectively.

The H-Mantel has a folded jacket that divides the bullet into two sections. The front half has a hollowpoint protected by a copper cap and is meant to fragment violently after impact, while the rear section remains intact and penetrates deeply. The Wilhem Brenneke-designed 293-grain TUG is also a fairly complicated bullet. It has a dual core, with the rear portion of harder lead than the front part.

I have had no experience with either of these in the 9.3mm. I have used H-Mantel bullets with fine results in a 7x64mm, but I am a touch suspicious of the TUG because I once had one in .375 caliber blow up in a buffalo's shoulder joint. Nonetheless, the TUG has enjoyed decades of use.

In actual test, at the velocities generated by the 9.3x62mm, the old-fashioned, simple, roundnose 285-grain softnose and the 270-grain Speer semispitzer will most likely perform just as reliably as the more sophisticated bullets.

The Speer bullets measured exactly .366 inch at the base and carried that diameter forward to the beginning of the ogive. The RWS and Norma bullets were slightly undersize, as I believe is common European practice. They went about .3657 inch at the base and maintained that measurement for a shorter distance along the shank. Consequently, when they were seated out to give an overall cartridge length of 3.30 inches, the maximum length that would function reliably through the Mannlicher's magazine, they had approximately 0.20 inch of free travel before they engaged the rifling (RWS-loaded ammo had the bullets seated even deeper). In contrast, the Speer 270-grain semispitzers had only 0.50 inch free travel when they were seated to an overall cartridge length of 3.26 inches.

Excessive free bullet travel is said to be bad for accuracy, but I could not demonstrate that in this case—the European bullets seemed to shoot just as nicely as the Speer.

The rifle came with a test target fired at 100 meters with RWS 285-grain loads. The three holes cut each other and spanned about 0.40 inch center to center. For me, shooting from the sandbags at 100 yards, the rifle would nearly always put three shots into 1 inch or a trifle less with suitable ammunition. Most five-shot groups went into less than 1½ inches.

The 9.3x62mm case does not have quite enough capacity to develop top velocities with IMR 4350 powder. IMR 4320 works well, as does H380, Winchester's 760, and IMR 4064, though the last two may have to be moderately compressed. In the test rifle, Winchester 760 gave the best accuracy with all the bullets tried.

The Steyr concern has been making quality firearms ever since Josef Werndl founded it in 1864 and Chief Engineer Ferdinand Mannlicher designed the firm's first repeating rifle a year later. Steyr's most famous products were the Mannlicher-Schoenauer rifles and carbines with rotary magazines that were known the world over for their beautifully finished and extremely smooth-working actions. They are no longer in production. In their place Steyr-Daimler-Puch AG offers several versions of its very modern Steyr-Mannlicher bolt-action sporting rifles.

The Steyr-Mannlicher action locks up at the rear via six lugs arranged in three rows, which results in a 60-degree bolt rotation rather than 90-degree rotation of the usual two-lug actions. The rear lockup gives a slightly shorter throw than with front-locking bolts, which, together with the lessened bolt-handle lift, should theoretically make the action quicker to operate.

In practice, the slightest hint of stickiness can make it difficult to raise the bolt handle on multi-lug actions. Several times after firing an RWS factory round, I was unable to work the action with the rifle at my shoulder, but had to lower it to be able to apply sufficient force to open the bolt. In this respect, the "lower gearing" of the two-lug bolt with its 90-degree bolt-handle lift is of some advantage.

The rotary magazine, which holds five standard or four magnum cartridges, is made of a synthetic called Makrolon, has a transparent back so its contents can be noted, and is easily detachable by pressing in catches on either side as one grasps it naturally between the thumb and two fingers. Detachable magazines are a convenience when one has to load and unload the rifle frequently, and this one is a good one. It worked perfectly, and it did not rattle. But with any detachable magazine, one has to be sure to seat it all the way home, even when his mind is on other and possibly urgent matters. The magazine must be removed from the rifle to recharge it.

The trigger guard is also of black plastic, which may look odd to Americans but not to Europeans, who are familiar with the horn trigger guards that were used on some of their best-quality firearms. Adjustable double-set or single shotgun-type triggers are available, and the rifles can be had chambered for a wide range of cartridges from .222 Remington up to .375 H&H and .458 Winchester Magnum. European calibers such as 5.6x50 magnum, 6.5x57, 7x64, 7.5mm Swiss, 8x68, 9.3x62, and 9.3x64mm are also offered, of course.

Half-stock rifles with 23.6-inch barrels and full-stock (or "Mannlicher") carbines with 20-inch barrels are available in standard calibers, but the magnums are chambered only in half-stock rifles with 25.6-inch barrels. Most of the stocks are of walnut, but the Professional, the SSG sniper rifles, and one of the target-type Sport models come with stocks of Cycolac, a synthetic material. There is a deluxe Luxus version with a single-set trigger and a three-shot steel detachable magazine that permits a slimmer stock, and various grades of engraving and stock carving can be ordered—at extra cost, naturally.

An unusual feature is that the recoil lug is not in the normal position under the receiver ring but is instead at the rear of the action, where it bears against the front end of the pistol grip. This means that the recoil forces do not have to be transmitted through the thin sections of the stock surrounding the magazine well.

Complete with a Weaver K4 scope sight, a nylon sling, and five rounds of 9.3x62mm ammo, my Professional test rifle weighed 8.6 pounds, which is not too much for a rifle of this power. When fired from the shooting bench, its recoil was quite noticeable.

I believe this is partly due to the design of the stock, which has a lot of drop at the heel and a quite narrow, sloping Monte Carlo comb. In addition, the Steyr detachable mounts raise the scope so high that I cannot get the firm contact I like to have between cheek and stock. When I throw this rifle to the shoulder for a quick shot, I invariably find myself trying to look beneath the scope.

The high mounts are no doubt necessary for the scopes with very large objective lenses that are often used in Europe for shooting at night. But it would be nice if they would also offer us lower mounts that would put American scopes just high enough to clear the bolt handle. The scope is detachable by releasing a catch on the rear mount, swiveling the scope 45 degrees to the right, and then lifting it off. Steyr urges that the mount and its bases be fitted by a gunsmith.

I shot one four-shot group with the Steyr-Mannlicher while detaching and replacing the scope before every shot. Two bullets went exactly where they should, while the two others were apparently displaced about 1 inch to the right, which would hardly cause one to miss the vital area of a deer within normal range.

Then I tried the same thing for five shots with a .223 Kimber Model 84 that is fitted with a Leupold 3–9X scope in Kimber's Lenard Brownell-designed quick-detachable lever mounts. I got four shots in a group measuring about 0.85 inch and one I know I wobbled out about an inch. Although it was too abbreviated a test to prove anything, it does suggest that Brownell's simple and straightforward design can serve the purpose as well as any more complicated system.

Actually, I have yet to discover any reason I would want to remove and replace the scopes on my rifles as a regular thing—I think it is a sour idea. Normally, I attach them as firmly as may be and leave them permanently in place.

The truth is that I am not overly fond of European hunting rifles in general. Although the workmanship in them is often superb, they tend to be needlessly complicated and over-engineered. To my mind, quick-detachable scopes and magazines; multi-lug, rear-locking bolts; and 60-degree bolt-handle lifts are ingenious answers to rather non-existent problems.

That, however, is only my own personal, subjective, and highly prejudiced opinion. It does not alter the fact that the Steyr-Mannlicher appears to be a very strong and well-made rifle of the highest quality that can take hard usage and is fully deserving of its Professional designation. Hunters who like the European style in firearms will undoubtedly find it to be a thoroughly dependable rifle that should give them years of good service, and outstanding accuracy to boot.

As for the 9.3x62mm cartridge, reliability is its middle name, and that is a virtue I value above most others, in cartridges and rifles as in dogs and people. It is very likely the best nonmagnum medium-bore cartridge of them all.

Does Energy Equal Killing Power?

⊕ **Chapter 15**

It's not an easy question to answer. Though it's easy to turn to tables and formulae in search of a simple solution, this experienced guide says practical field experience is the best teacher. (American Rifleman *magazine, January 1983*)

Americans are a pragmatic folk who, disliking mysteries, feel that it should be possible to reduce any phenomenon to cut-and-dried formulae and a list of figures. Among the beliefs most firmly held by American hunters is that the energy developed by a rifle bullet is a direct measure of its killing power.

Great credence is given to tables purporting to show the minimum impact energies necessary to slay various unfortunate beasts. Generally they read something like this: 1,000 foot-pounds for antelope and deer, 2,000 foot-pounds for elk and moose, and upwards of 2,500 foot-pounds for brown and polar bears. Is the .297 Nonesuch Magnum suitable for elk? Just look up its remaining energy at the expected range and compare that with the minimum recommended in the tables, right?

Wrong! There are many factors involved in killing power, of which energy is not the most important.

Kinetic energy (calculated by multiplying half the mass of the bullet by the square of its velocity, and expressed in foot-pounds) is the capacity to do work. A bullet works by utilizing its energy to destroy tissue. A full-metal-jacket bullet tends to zip right through all but the largest game, expending little energy and thus destroying little tissue.

Consequently, most hunting bullets are designed to expand and be slowed down by the resistance of the animal's body, thereby transferring their energy to the game. Ideally, they should remain in the animal, thus transferring all their energy.

By using fragmenting bullets and energy on the order of 100 foot-pounds per pound of the target's live weight, varmint cartridges give instantaneous kills on the smaller pest species with a hit anywhere in the body.

Though I have seen a 10-pound dik-dik (one of the smallest African antelope) dissolve into a red mist when struck in the shoulder with a 270-grain softpoint from a .375 magnum (and, conversely, know of one that escaped when hit too far back with a .375 solid!), it is not usually possible or desirable to use that proportion of power on big game. From 2 to 10 foot-pounds per pound of live weight is more like it.

Therefore, to produce humanely fast kills, the bullet must disrupt tissue that is immediately vital to life. This includes the brain, the spinal cord forward of the diaphragm (spinal hits farther back paralyze but usually require a finishing shot), the lungs, the heart and its great blood vessels, and often the liver.

A minimal amount of energy—the .22 rimfire has enough close up—will kill the largest beast instantly if applied to the brain or front half of the spinal cord. The problem lies in delivering it there!

The theory that shooting for the brain or neck will always result in either a clean kill or a clean miss is totally fallacious. Both are small marks surrounded by not immediately vital areas. A slightly miscued attempt at the brain all too often results in a broken jaw and an animal that escapes to die slowly of thirst and starvation. The same thing can happen when a too-low neck shot merely severs the windpipe and esophagus.

Brain and neck shots can be taken responsibly only at close, dead-sure ranges, so the suitability of a cartridge cannot be judged by them but must be predicated on its performance on chest-cavity shots.

Theoretically, all of the bullet's kinetic energy should be expended in a vital area. A high-velocity bullet that fragments in the lungs, forming a huge wound cavity while splinters of bone and pieces of bullet jacket fly off in all directions to cut up organs, nerves, and blood vessels far from the bullet's path, is spectacularly lethal. The animal is almost always dumped in its track so fast that the hunter does not see it fall. Such performance will sometimes produce instant kills with shots in the guts, hams, or other nonvital areas.

This is usually ascribed to shock, whatever that may be. Some refer to hydrostatic shock and demonstrate it by exploding milk jugs full of water. Besides being fun, shooting up gallon milk jugs does indeed provide a dramatic illustration of energy at work. The trouble is that the body of an animal really does not very closely resemble a vessel full of a homogeneous, incompressible liquid.

Nevertheless, it can't be denied that something of this nature does quite often happen when a fast-opening bullet impacts at high velocity. But it is a sometime thing, it does not always occur, and the hunter should not rely on it.

While expansion is desirable, penetration is imperative. Whatever else it does, the bullet must be able to reach a vital area. On elephant and rhino we are even willing to do without any expansion at all, using full-metal-jacket "solids" to get the requisite penetration. There is no need to go to that extreme on any American game, but, particularly on the larger animals, some compromise is necessary. The bullet that performs perfectly by exploding in the lungs on a hit through the ribs would blow up prematurely if it struck heavier bone. More penetration is expedient.

The bullet should be able to smash through the head of the humerus at the shoulder joint—about the most solid bone in the body—and still penetrate the chest cavity. Then it will also have the ability to reach the lungs through the paunch on a quartering shot from the rear, but will inevitably exit on broadside hits through the ribs. This means that a part of its energy is used up in reaching the vitals, or is wasted on the ground beyond. Not ideal, but unavoidable unless one is willing to forgo all but broadside shots.

Considered alone, kinetic energy can be most misleading. Smack a moose in the shoulder blade with a 125-grain bullet driven at 3,500 FPS out of a .300 magnum, and you would be hitting him with 2,800 foot-pounds at 100 yards—plenty even for a brown bear according to the tables—but the bullet would almost certainly blow up on the bone and fail to penetrate. The 180-grain bullet from a .300 Savage would have substantially more killing power under those circumstances despite delivering 1,000 foot-pounds less energy.

Selecting a cartridge by its energy figures is putting the cart before the horse. On the other hand, if one chooses a load that will reliably smash through the shoulder joint while giving a reasonable amount of bullet expansion on broadside shots through the ribs, I guarantee that it will have more than ample energy!

Information on how any given cartridge and bullet are likely to perform at various ranges cannot, unfortunately, be gleaned from tables or formulae but must be learned by experience. Reports by other hunters, including writers, can be valuable if they are specific (does "shoulder" refer to the joint, the shoulder blade, or just the general area?). So can comparative tests in a recovery medium such as damp newsprint. But the hunter who does not dig around in his game to note exactly what his bullet did or did not do is missing an important bet. A point worth remembering is that increasing the impact velocity of a bullet sometimes decreases its penetration by causing it to set up violently and expend its energy faster. This means that a certain bullet could have less reliable killing power on large game at medium range when used in a .300 magnum than when used in a .30-06!

Effectively utilized, energy kills. But it also destroys, and on edible animals (as distinct from dangerous game) it is possible to have too much of it which—is why squirrels and rabbits are not generally hunted with a .22-250. Here a sufficiency is plenty, and any excess merely serves to ruin good meat. Can you imagine the outcome of expending the full 8,000 foot-pounds of a .460 Weatherby Magnum in a 150-pound deer? Distasteful, to say the least, and not much left for the freezer.

If one has to hunt with "too much gun"—say, deer in the brush with a .300 magnum—the trick is to ensure that not all its available energy is used. This can be done by handloading it down to the equivalent of a .308 Winchester or by employing a heavy, stoutly constructed bullet that will give but moderate expansion and thus use only a portion of its overabundant energy.

When I used a 7mm Remington Magnum to take two 100-pound whitetails, I chose the 175-grain factory load for this reason. The Remington Core-Lokt bullets penetrated completely though, including a shoulder blade in one case, while disrupting the lungs enough to drop both animals within 20 feet of where they stood. The exit holes were 1 to 1½ inches in diameter, and very little edible meat was damaged. That was exactly the performance I was looking for—yet this same load would have been perfect on a 1,000-pound elk!

Consideration of energy alone would have indicated that the cartridge's 2,500 foot-pounds at 150 yards was grossly excessive, but the choice of a bullet with suitable post-impact characteristics made it into a fine whitetail cartridge.

This tale also illustrates the little-appreciated fact that a bullet designed for the larger game will often work creditably on the lesser as well. Which is not to say that I recommend using the heaviest bullets on everything—far from it. It does mean that for a mixed-bag hunt, one could judiciously select a load for the biggest beasties that would also do excellently on the smaller animals.

As Jack O'Connor once wrote, kinetic energy per se has little to do with killing power. How the bullet's energy is put to work, and where, are the important things. And that is governed by how fast it expands and how deep it penetrates. If it meets those requirements, it will also have sufficient energy.

Many very experienced hunters, including Elmer Keith and John "Pondoro" Taylor, feel that kinetic energy lays too much stress on velocity at the expense of bullet weight. When it comes to bone-breaking ability and "stopping power" on the big stuff, they feel that momentum (the product of mass and velocity, rather than mass x velocity squared, as with energy) is a truer measure.

Taylor formulated a table of "Knock-Out Blows" to compare the stopping power of various cartridges on dangerous game such as buffalo, rhino, and elephant. The table appears in his *African Rifles and Cartridges.* He used this equation:

$$\text{K.O. value} = \frac{\text{Velocity (FPS) x bullet weight (grain) x caliber (inches)}}{7000}$$

I suspect that he should have included the constant for the acceleration due to gravity in there somewhere, but then Taylor was no mathematician, ballistician, or theoretician of any breed. He was a simple hunter who, through having been in on the taking of a lot of game, had some idea of what actually worked in the hunting field. Even so, his formula still fails to give that vital piece of information: how the bullet will perform on impact.

I seldom look at energy figures, and prefer to select cartridges and loads empirically, based on experience and common sense. My conclusions at present (I'm still learning) are:

The .243 Winchester and 6mm Remington do a beautiful job on small deer and like-size African gazelles of up to 150 pounds in weight, but on beasts much over 200 pounds I want more bone-smashing penetration than even their heaviest bullets provide. For the same reason—lack of bullet weight—I would hesitate to use the .25 calibers on anything larger than caribou.

I have no experience with the .30-30 and .35 Remington, but don't know why they should not live up to their reputations as perfectly adequate short-range deer cartridges.

Out to my personal maximum range of 300 yards, I would be content to tackle most American nondangerous game with a suitably loaded 7x57mm, .308, .270, 7mm Express, or .30-06. This includes elk and moose, but here I would not trust any bullet of less than 160 grains to get through their heavy shoulder bones, would prefer even more weight of lead on the latter, and would in either case tend to use Nosler Partition bullets.

The 7mm and .300 magnums deliver more energy at any range, should one feel the need, and perform at 400 yards about as their lesser brethren do at 300—if the shot is equally well placed.

On large, dangerous game that could take a bite out of me, I would settle for nothing less than a .338 magnum, mostly because its big slug is quite comforting. In practice the .300 and 8mm magnums would likely be just as good.

The big guns will work on everything, but are of necessity heavier than the "standard" calibers and really do need longer barrels to produce any significant improvement over them. I take no pleasure in lugging my 24-inch-barrel, 7mm magnum around after whitetails—that's ridiculous! If nothing larger will be encountered, I find it sensible, and aesthetically more satisfying, to use a sweet little 7mm Mauser that is exactly right for the job. That, though, is strictly a personal preference, and too much energy is certainly better than too little.

However, neither energy, nor momentum, nor penetration, nor perfect expansion is worth a hoot if the bullet is badly placed. And so we come to the crux of the matter, the "bottom line" if you like: Good shooting is 90 percent of killing power. A good, cool shot who understands his bullet's capacities, and who has a sound knowledge of animal anatomy, can successfully take a cartridge way out of its class—as Bell proved with his use of the 7x57mm on elephant.

Study energy figures and use them to clinch campfire arguments if you will, certainly learn everything you can about bullet performance, and by all means choose a cartridge of adequate power. But if you want clean kills, practice your shooting. Nothing enhances killing power like placing that bullet in the right spot!

The Hornet Still Stings

⊕ **Chapter 16**

Eclipsed by the .222 Remington and other modern high-velocity cartridges, this efficient and versatile little number has a secure future with varmint stalkers and small-game hunters. (American Rifleman *magazine, June 1982*)

The Rio Grande turkey is a singularly stupid bird that will run dementedly up and down a fence looking for a hole to escape through until he at last realizes that he has wings and can fly. But with his exceedingly sharp eyes, alertly suspicious nature, and total lack of curiosity, he is about the most difficult creature to stalk on foot that I have pursued. Before learning to call them, I spent several mornings and evenings still-hunting along a creek, listening for their gobbling and then attempting to sneak up on them. With contemptuous ease they frustrated my best efforts, driving home the humiliating lesson that I was not nearly as good a stalker as I had thought. But now, shortly after sunup on a bright, dew-wet spring morning, a tom had gobbled just over a little brushy ridge whose summit was crowned with granite boulders like the decaying battlements of an ancient castle. This time, just possibly, I had a chance!

Crawling up to the crest with the Savage Model 340 rifle slung under my chest, and taking care that a tree broke my silhouette, I slowly peeked around one of the boulders. Nothing. Then I caught a movement in the brush surrounding the open glade at the foot of the ridge. So I slithered a little farther out into the gap between the rocks, found a rest for my forward hand, loaded the rifle, and waited. Presently two birds appeared and puttered around the glade, scratching here and there like giant chickens. A quick glance through the binocular confirmed that both had beards. Range? About 100 yards or a trifle more; the rifle was sighted for 150 yards. No problem there. But where, exactly, was one supposed to shoot a turkey? Well, his heart and lungs ought to be in the front half of his body, so why not try centering that? Finally one of them stood still for a second, broadside, and at the Hornet's crack collapsed in an explosion of feathers. Immediately reloading, I lay watching him through the scope until I was certain that he would not get up, then hurried down to collect my prize.

With his wings spread, his tail fanned, and the sunlight shimmering on his iridescent plumage, he was magnificent! (He was magnificent eating too; you may keep every domestic turkey ever hatched—I'll take mine wild.) Though I have hunted the lion, the elephant, and the noble kudu, stalking that gobbler on a beautiful spring morning with a .22 Hornet in my hands was as thrilling and as satisfying a hunting experience as any I have enjoyed. The memory will remain with me always.

I was using Remington factory ammunition loaded with the 45-grain pointed-softpoint bullet. Because the rifle was zeroed a little high at 100 yards, and also because I was looking down at the bird, I had hit it high on the right side. The bullet smashed the lower half of a vertebra, lacerated the top of the lungs, and exited just below the left wing root. I was surprised at how little meat damage there was. The exit hole was only little-finger size, and hardly any of the meat was blood-shot.

Coincidently, the first time I ever fired a Hornet (9 November 1952), I also used a borrowed Savage Model 340 (then called the Stevens Model 322) to take a very large bird—not a turkey but the equally great Kori bustard of the East African plains. And later the same morning I also knocked over a 50-pound Thomson gazelle with it. Shortly afterward I obtained a beautiful, trim little Zbrojovka Brno .22 Hornet rifle for myself. The Czechs always made good guns, but this one on a miniature Mauser action—twin front locking lugs, long Mauser extractor, and all—was outstanding and, with a Weaver B4 scope, weighed about 6½ pounds. I thought it would be just the thing to carry around on the ranch to keep baboons and other vermin out of the corn and to bag an occasional guinea fowl or impala for the table. It proved to be just a tad over-destructive for body shots on guinea fowl, unless I used the "solid" full-metal-jacket bullets available from DWM, but it did a fine job on steenbok, duiker, and the smaller gazelles. I quickly discovered, though, that it was no long-range cartridge—the slightest bit of wind would blow it right off a gazelle at 200 yards.

Later, I let a friend who was pioneering a new farm on the high plains bordering the Masai country have it. Charlie lived by that rifle for several years. It kept his stewpot filled with bushbuck meat, slew scores of the zebra and wildebeest that swarmed in from the Masai to devastate his green, new-sprouted wheat, eliminated two sheep-killing leopards, and even accounted for a buffalo cow that was poleaxed with one of the tiny slugs to the base of the skull. I would give a lot to have that rifle back!

Does all this mean that I consider the Hornet to be a fair-enough big-game cartridge? By no means! Nor does the fact that it was popular with the Indian and Eskimo hunters of the far North—Roy Dunlap recorded that the list of kills accompanying a Winchester Model 70 .22 Hornet sent to him for rebarreling stated: "6 polar bears; over 50 moose; 800 seals . . ."—so qualify it. Charlie was a very fine and careful shot who held his fire until certain of placing the bullet exactly where he wanted it, either slipping it in through the ribs just behind the shoulder blade or hitting the spinal column in the neck.

The Hornet is strictly a varmint and small-game cartridge suitable for animals weighing no more than 50 pounds out to a range of 200 yards maximum. It has some merit in a survival situation—the U.S. and Canadian Air Forces still issue survival weapons (either the bolt M5 or the over-under M6 combination gun with .410 bore shotgun underneath) chambered for it. But the Hornet is not a sporting cartridge for big game, as an entry in my journal will illustrate:

"April 10. Impala, young male. Weight c. 140 lbs. on the hoof. .22 Hornet, ICI softpoint ammo. Range 90 paces. Bullet entered middle ribs, angled forward through part of liver, lungs (behind heart), and was found between offside ribs and shoulder blade, in one piece and nicely mushroomed to about ⅓-inch diameter. Buck ran some 100 paces in thornbush. Found no blood, took quite a while to track him, but he was still alive, though down, when found and finished with a neck shot. The 8x60mm (196-grain bullet at 2,560 FPS) would have smashed the off-shoulder and exited, likely dropping him in his tracks, or at least within a couple of seconds . . ." Need one say any more?

(I do not apologize for the above. Let him who never did a foolish or irresponsible thing in his youth cast the first stone. And I learned the lesson.)

Though somewhat clouded in dispute, the story of the development of the Hornet has been told often enough. Suffice it to say that Winchester, taking note of the results Messrs. Wotkyns, Townsend Whelen, and others had obtained while experimenting with the .22 WCF case (vintage 1885, black-powder, 45-grain bullet at 1,540 FPS), started to manufacture .22 Winchester Hornet ammunition in 1930 before it or any other manufacturers had rifles available for it. Things moved at a more leisurely pace in those days. Though Griffin & Howe and R. F. Sedgely were building custom Hornets by modifying .22 rimfire Springfield M1922 rifles (and also, I am told, by using M1922 barrels on altered '03 actions), Winchester did not get around to chambering the Model 54 for its new offspring until 1933, being beaten to the mark by Savage with its Model 23-D by almost a year. The later Winchester Model 70 also was chambered for the Hornet, of course—a touch incongruous putting that tiny 1.710-inch cartridge into a massive action designed to accommodate the long .375 Magnum round, was it not?

In 1949 Winchester came out with the Model 43, a fine though inexpensive little bolt-action more appropriately scaled for the .22 Hornet. It was also available in .218 Bee, .25-20, and .32-20. The USAF M5 survival rifle was a military adaptation of the Winchester Model 43 design, I am told. Production ceased in 1957 with only some 63,000 Model 43s made, and they are no doubt something of a collectors' item now. More's the pity—they were excellent hunting rifles.

Be that as it may, the shooters of the day greeted the Hornet with loud "Hosannas!" and hailed it as a champion long-range varmint cartridge, which, compared to the likes of the .25-20, I suppose it was. Despite competition from the .218 Bee, the .219 Zipper, and the great .220 Swift (not to mention a host of wildcats), the Hornet retained its popularity all through the 1930s and '40s, until the advent of the .222 Remington in 1950 stopped it cold in its tracks. By the mid-'60s—when so far as I know only one domestic rifle, the Savage 219 single-shot, was still chambered for it—its race seemed to have been run in this country. Walther, Krico, Anschutz, Brno, and other European manufacturers continued to chamber beautiful little rifles for it, but they were not readily available here and were in any case too expensive for most of us.

Today, however, there has been a modest revival of interest in the little cartridge, and, apart from the Contender single-shot pistol, it is also available in Ruger's No. 3 single-shot carbine and most recently the new Kimber bolt-action. It's also available in the Harrington & Richardson Model 157 break-open single-shot, the upper barrel of the Savage 24V combination gun, and in the Savage 340 five-shot bolt-action rifle. When I went to the local gun store to borrow a Hornet, this latter is what I got. A few weeks previously, the store had had several Hornets in its rack, including a couple of Ruger No. 3s, which is what I'd had in mind; but now, just before the opening of the spring turkey season, they were all gone except for this solitary Model 340.

The Savage 340 is no gun-fancier's rifle. The action with its split receiver bridge, single-lug bolt with twin extractors, and bent sheet-metal trigger guard and floor plate is reminiscent of a slightly overgrown .22 rimfire, while the trigger on mine had a rather horrible long, grating 6-pound pull. It had a 24-inch barrel, an overlarge stock, and a Tasco 3–9X variable-power scope in the side mount that Savage provides, and it all weighed 8.9 pounds, which is preposterous! But then, it was not designed for effetists. It is an inexpensive but strong, rugged, and very practical gun that is right at home bouncing around in a pickup or on a tractor.

Shooting from the bench at 100 yards, four five-shot groups with Remington ammunition gave an average extreme spread of 1⅝ inches. One group, abnormally large due to two flyers, went 2½ inches. Otherwise, the average group size would have been closer to 1¼ inches. Average velocity was right on at 2,682 FPS, though the extreme spread of 150 FPS might be considered excessive.

Hercules 2400 (which was developed specifically for the Hornet back in the 1930s, to give the 45-grain bullet 2,400 FPS) and IMR 4227 are the traditional powders for reloading this cartridge. But the latest *Hornady Handbook* (third edition) indicates that Winchester 296 Ball powder might be the optimum choice with both 45- and 50-grain bullets, so that is what I used. With Remington cases and Remington 7½-inch BR primers, the following loads gave the best results in my rifle:

1) 45-grain Sierra Hornet, 11-grain W296, 1.757 inches overall cartridge length produced 2,800 FPS muzzle velocity and 1 inch average groups at 100 yards.

2) 50-grain Sierra Spitzer, 10.5-grain W296, 1.780 inches overall cartridge length produced 2,590 FPS muzzle velocity and 1⅞-inch groups at 100 yards.

Because of its slow 1 in 16-inch twist, 40- and 45-grain bullets are the recommended weights in the Hornet, while the 50-grain is said to be the maximum that can be stabilized. Up to at least the late 1940s, Hornet barrels were generally made with a groove diameter of .223 inch rather than the present standard .224 inch. Bullets are available in both diameters. The old rifles with .223 bores are apparently safe enough with factory ammunition, but take care with hot handloads. One should also realize that in this diminutive case small variations in powder can have large effects, and that a variation of $^1/_{10}^{th}$ grain in the Hornet is roughly equivalent to ½-grain variation in the .30-06.

My rifle liked the 45-grain Sierra bullet best. When started at 2,800 FPS and zeroed 1 inch high at 100 yards, it was on at about 150 yards and was 1¾ inches low at 175. But watch the wind! Shooting at 175 yards on a windy day, but taking care to fire only in the lulls, I got a five-shot group measuring 2⅜ inches. When I fired another five shots disregarding the gusts, I got a "group" that spread out over 9 inches!

Wondering whether this load might be too destructive on turkeys, I tried it on a jack rabbit that was sitting quartering-on at about 30 paces. The bullet smashed the humerus just below the shoulder joint, liquidized the lungs, separated several ribs from the backbone on both sides, passed through the stomach, and penetrated the small of the back to exit 1½ inches ahead of the hip joint. On the shoulder there was a gaping 2-inch hole where bone had exploded violently outward, but the exit hole was only ½ inch in diameter. The lack of bullet fragments indicates that the bullet held together surprisingly well. It might chew up too much meat at close range but should be OK out at 100 yards, where it has slowed down. I had planned to use the less explosive 50-grain slugs on turkeys, but because of their superior accuracy, I believe I will stick with 45-grain bullets, loading them down to 2,700 FPS to be on the safe side.

Why bother with the Hornet when the .222 Remington will do everything it will and at half again the range? Good question, but I feel that a more valid comparison is with the .22 Winchester Magnum rimfire. For the handloader the Hornet is a more logical step up from the .22 Long Rifle, in that it will give better performance than the magnum rimfire at less cost.

Here in the backwoods of Texas, a box of 50 .22 Hornet cartridges costs $17.45, compared to $5.35 for 50 .22 WMR. But wait, 50 unprimed Hornet cases cost me $7.79, or 15.6 cents each. To find out how many times they could be reloaded, I took one case and, using the 45-grain Sierra bullet and 11 grains of W296 load, I fired and reloaded it 20 times, at the end of which the primer still seated firmly and the case looked good as new. So, we should safely be able to count on 10 reloadings per case. Bullets cost me $4.47 per 100, and a can of powder costing $10.65 should give at least 630 loads. Thus the cost of one reloaded Hornet cartridge adds up like this:

Bullet	4.75 cents
Powder	1.69 cents
Primer	1.15 cents
Case	1.56 cents (10 firings)
Total	9.15 cents per round

Which makes the cost of a box of 50 a quite reasonable $4.58.

Given the fact that the bullet accounts for more than half the cost, considerable further savings could be achieved by using cast lead bullets. In fact, it should be possible to get the cost down close to that of .22 LR ammunition, which in these parts costs four cents each for the high-velocity hollowpoint stuff. The *Lyman Cast Bullet Handbook* lists various loads with a cast 45-grain gas-check bullet that go from 1,600 FPS to well over 2,200 FPS. This latter surpasses the .22 WMR by a significant margin, while the first is a fine load for squirrel and other small, edible game.

In the main, there are three types of varmint hunters. The first and largest group delights in knocking off woodchucks and such at 400 yards and more. Though an extremely challenging sport, this is more shooting than "hunting," as little stalking is involved. The rifleman's skill and equipment are being tested. Here the Hornet has no place. Then there are the callers. For situations where foxes, bobcats, or even coyotes can be brought within 150 yards, the Hornet would seem to be entirely appropriate. The last and smallest group consists of those big-game hunters who use varmint hunting to sharpen their hunting techniques and stalking skills during the off-season. Rather than snipe at a chuck at a quarter-mile, they will try to sneak up within 100 to 150 yards, and for them the Hornet is perfect, as it is for those who would keep their shooting eye on running jack rabbits.

It has often been suggested that the mild report of the Hornet makes it preferable in populated areas, but I doubt there is much in it—I would bet a chocolate-chip cookie that your average non-shooter would notice the crack of a Hornet about as readily as that of a .222 and would be equally upset by either.

But it is certainly a very useful gun for a farmer or rancher to have around for eliminating such pests as chicken-stealing foxes, raccoons, badgers, or feral dogs and cats, and for putting maimed or sick livestock out of their misery.

And not least, it is a turkey cartridge par excellence! Everything I have read or discussed with dedicated turkey hunters tends to confirm my own very limited experience: The Hornet has exactly the right velocity, bullet weight, and expansion. It is as close to the perfect turkey rifle as you can get. The turkey is among the most demanding of our big game, tougher than moose or caribou and, in the opinion of some, more challenging even than the whitetail (John Wootters once remarked that the man who sets out from camp with the intention of killing a gobbler, and does so regularly, is indeed a hunter). This fact alone would justify the Hornet's continued existence.

But what matters even more, this littlest of our centerfire rifle cartridges is just a heck of a lot of fun, and in the end, that, friends, is what shooting and hunting are all about!

The 7x57mm Mauser

$\bigoplus$ **Chapter 17**

Despite its less-than-stunning ballistics with most factory ammunition, this old workhorse's versatility has won it a faithful international following. (American Rifleman *magazine, November 1986*)

Paul Mauser developed the most successful and long-lived cartridge of his career in 1892 when he adapted the basic rimless case of the 7.9mm M88 Commission cartridge—later known as the 8x57mm or 8mm Mauser, though he had no hand in its design—to produce a 7mm military cartridge for Spain.

Although its body to the shoulder is shorter and its neck is much longer, the case has the same length as its parent and is thus called the 7x57mm Mauser; but in the past it was also quite commonly referred to as the 7mm Spanish Mauser. It was originally issued with a roundnose, metal-jacketed 173-grain bullet that attained 2,296 FPS in a 29-inch barrel.

Americans remember the 7mm Mauser for its record at San Juan Hill in the brief Spanish-American War of 1898, but in Africa and England it achieved fame by its performance in a graver and more testing affair, the South African (or Boer) War of 1899–1902.

The Boers or Afrikaners were white South Africans of Dutch and Huguenot descent who found British rule so vexing that they trekked north across the Orange River and into the wilderness with their herds and covered wagons. They crushed the Zulus at what became known as the Blood River, drove off Mzilikazi and his nascent Matabele, and eventually established the independent republics of the Transvaal and the Orange Free State.

But continual friction between the Afrikaners and the British government eventually led to war, when in October of 1899 the Boer republics invaded the British colony of Natal. The Boers had no standing army to speak of, but in times of war every burgher over eighteen years of age was expected to join his local "commando," equipped with his own horses and rifle. They operated as mounted infantry, using horses for transportation but mostly fighting on foot.

They were superb rifle shots. The majority of them lived on remote homesteads in wild country teeming with game, where skill with firearms was a simple, everyday necessity. In preparation for the war the Transvaal and the Orange Free State had imported quantities of Mauser M95 rifles chambered to the 7x57mm cartridge, and made them available to the burghers.

Deneys Reitz, whose father had been president of the Free State and was secretary of state of the Transvaal under Kruger at the outbreak of war, fought in the ranks throughout the conflict and left a fascinating account of it in his book *Commando*. At first he was refused enrollment in the Pretoria contingent because he was only seventeen years of age. But when he complained to President Kruger, "Oom Paul" took him to General Piet Joubert's office, where the commandant general personally handed young Reitz a new Mauser carbine and a bandolier of 7mm ammunition.

At first the Boers had it all their own way, while the British, as is their custom, bumbled around ineffectually until it dawned on them that the matter was serious. Then the tide was turned, and within a year both the capital cities and most of the towns of the Boer republics were in British hands, and it seemed that the war was over.

But not so. The Boers had little need of towns; they dispersed into the vast land in small units to fight a fast-moving, hard-hitting guerrilla campaign. Their commandos would appear out of nowhere to annihilate an enemy force, overrun a camp, or ambush a convoy and then be gone with their supplies replenished before the lumbering British columns could catch them. In this way the embattled burghers stood off the full might of the British Empire at the height of its power for more than eighteen months, from October 1900 until a peace was signed in May of 1902. And when they finally surrendered, they did not do so unconditionally, but on terms.

That the Boers succeeded in holding out for so long was in no small measure due to their marksmanship. Reitz described one very lethal engagement between British soldiers and a party of Boers on a rock-strewn hill:

"Both sides were maintaining a vigorous short-range rifle contest, in which the soldiers were being badly worsted, for they were up against real old-fashioned Free State Boers for whom they were no match in sharpshooting of this kind. Time after time I saw soldiers looking over their defenses to fire, and time after time I heard the thud of a bullet finding its mark, and could see the unfortunate man fall back out of sight . . ."

This fight cost the British 400 casualties compared to thirty suffered by the victorious Boers. Reitz attributed the disparity entirely to the fact that the English soldiers were no match for the burghers in rifle shooting. Those who would disparage the value of an armed civilian population, and of marksmanship training, would do well to ponder the lessons of the Boer War, in addition to those of Afghanistan and Switzerland.

The 7x57mm made such an impression on the British that in the period before the Great War (WWI) they almost invariably referred to it only as "the Mauser cartridge," or even just "the Mauser." They also meant to adopt a 7mm cartridge and a Mauser-type rifle to replace the .303 Lee-Enfield, but WWI intervened and nothing came of it.

The 7mm Mauser was adopted as a military cartridge by several other nations, including at some time Mexico, Chile, Brazil, Uruguay, Peru, Serbia, Persia, and China, and quickly became a popular big-game cartridge as well. Mauser chambered its M98 sporting rifles for it, and most British and European gunmakers offered it as a standard cartridge, as did both Remington and Winchester at times.

For sporting purposes the 7mm was provided with a 173-grain or 175-grain roundnose, softpoint bullet with plenty of lead showing, and with a full-metal-jacket solid bullet of like weight for use on thick-skinned heavyweights such as elephants and rhinos.

A lot of elephants were killed with it, too. That long 173-grain solid at moderate velocity penetrated deeply—one from a military cartridge that I tested on plywood boards gave about ¼ inch more penetration than a 400-grain FMJ from a .416—and its mild recoil allowed many people to shoot it rather well.

An elephant is so massive that one cannot really expect to be able to bludgeon it down with any legal cartridge that can be fired from a shoulder arm. Penetration and exact bullet placement are the essential requirements; when they are not fulfilled, even the mighty .577 Nitro Express fails.

Which is not to say that I recommend the 7mm for elephant hunting, far from it! I never used anything but a .458 Winchester myself, but I could shoot that gun as quickly and as accurately as any of my other rifles, at short range. The point is that given a proper solid, the 7x57mm has the ability to reach an elephant's brain from almost any angle, and there is no reason to doubt that an exceptionally gifted rifleman who remained cool under pressure and thoroughly understood elephantine anatomy could have used it to bag many hundreds of elephants, as some of the old-timers did.

The original roundnose softpoint was a very reliable bullet that expanded to some degree even on the small stuff but generally retained enough weight in its shank to provide the requisite penetration on the largest thin-skinned animals. A schoolmate of mine once stuck one into an elephant's ear-hole to see what would happen. The jumbo came down like several tons of bricks; but whether it would have got up again is not known, because my pal's companion immediately walloped it with a .470 to make sure it did not do so.

Shortly after my father arrived in Kenya in 1927, he acquired a 7x57mm Waffenfabrik Mauser sporter with a 28-inch barrel and used it for all his hunting until WWII. I believe he took one buffalo with it, and he certainly bagged two lions with just one shot apiece. But mostly he hunted the abundant plains game, all the various antelopes and zebra. How much game he killed with it I do not know, but it was a considerable amount. All through the Depression and the war he was expected to provide meat to help feed the numerous workers on the coffee and sisal plantation he managed. He had shot out the rifle's barrel by 1942—on game, not on targets.

Today's hunters agonize endlessly in trying to decide on exactly the right bullet to use for a particular animal under a certain set of circumstances. This would have amused my old man immensely. He just used the 173-grain RNSP with great success for everything from snap-shooting reedbuck and duiker on the run or drilling two gazelles with one shot to save ammo, to knocking off an eland or a hartebeest at eye-straining long range on the windswept, heat-shimmering plains. He was, of course, in practice, and he did shoot remarkably well.

The only real disadvantage with the 173-grain roundnose bullet was its poor trajectory beyond 200 yards, so lighter and ballistically more efficient projectiles became available quite early on.

John Rigby & Company, which rather specialized in the 7x57mm, brought out a version with a 140-grain spitzer at 2,750 FPS well before the Great War. It was listed as the .275 Rimless (Rigby). Kynoch (I. C. I.) later offered the same bullet weight at 2,900 FPS from a 29-inch barrel in a load that was often referred to as the .275 High Velocity.

In Germany the firms of DWM and RWS made 7x57mm ammunition with a great diversity of bullets that ranged from the light 108-grain flatpoint at modest velocity (probably meant for roe deer) up to the redoubtable Brenneke-designed 177-grain Torpedo-Ideal-Geschoss at a thumping 2,560 FPS (as claimed). Many of these loadings are still available in the RWS brand from Dynamit Nobel of America in Stonehurst Connecticut.

The 7mm Mauser gained enough favor with American hunters in the 1920s and '30s that both Winchester and Remington thought it worthwhile to manufacture the ammunition and to chamber rifles for it. But its popularity gradually faded. For a long time after WWII none of our domestic gun manufacturers offered rifles for it, and the cartridge seemed to be sliding into obsolescence.

Nowadays, however, the 7x57 has been reanimated and is reasonably lively. Although neither Winchester (USRA) nor Remington had rifles for the 7x57mm in their 1986 catalogs, Ruger listed it as being available in both its M77 bolt-action rifle and in the No. 1 Single-Shot. Fine foreign-made sporters such as the Whitworth, the Parker-Hale, and the Steyr-Mannlicher, among others, can be obtained in 7x57mm, and various ex-military rifles in that caliber are presently being imported.

Many of the latter are elderly M93 Mausers that are said to be weaker than the M98 and modern bolt-actions and may well be worn from long service. They are the chief reason our ammunition manufacturers never load the 7x57mm to other than mild pressures, and anyone reloading for one of these old guns should follow their example.

At present Winchester (Olin) lists the 7x57mm only with a 175-grain RNSP at 2,440 FPS, and Remington has it only with a 140-grain spitzer at a nominal 2,660 FPS. Federal Cartridge Corp. offers both weights, and Hornady's Frontier line now includes 7x57 ammunition loaded with its 139-grain BTSP at 2,700 FPS and a 154-grain Spire-Point at 2,600 FPS.

It is all good ammo, but a fellow with a *strong, modern* 7x57 rifle can obtain significantly higher velocities through cautious and careful handloading.

I have two 7x57mm rifles. One is an elegantly slim 35-year-old Brno Mauser sporter that my brother-in-law purchased used in 1958. He slew all manner of middling-size game with it, including a huge 240-pound leopard that killed one of his calves. Twenty years later, after hunting was banned in Kenya, he gave it to me. It now has a new 22-inch E. R. Shaw barrel, wears a Bushnell Banner 4X Compact scope, and shoots delightfully well.

The other 7x57mm, a Ruger M77, really belongs to my younger son, and it was also bought secondhand. I fitted it with a fine Leupold Compact 4X scope, and after I had cleaned its bore thoroughly it would group five shots into 1½ inches to not over 2 inches at 100 yards with loads that suited it. But it seemed to alter its zero with every change in the humidity, which piqued me to the extent that I sent it off to the D. F. S. Corporation to be fitted with a fiberglass stock.

D. F. S. offers synthetic stocks of classical design for Remington 700 ADL, Winchester Model 70 post-'64, and Ruger M77 long-action rifles only. They have a high, straight comb with a drop from the bore-line of ⅝-inch at both nose and heel, 13½-inch length of pull, and come completely finished with a recoil pad, sling swivel studs, and a black wrinkle paint job for $169 plus $7 shipping and handling, at the present time.

The butt of the stock is foam-filled to reduce resonance, and a solid resin fill extending from the pistol grip to halfway along the fore-end is used for strength and to firmly support the action. The bedding areas inside the stock are slightly oversize, so that each individual action can be bedded in precisely with Acraglas or a similar material.

I asked D. F. S. to paint my stock a medium gray instead of black, which it will do for an extra $15, and had the company bed the rifle into it. That costs another $49, but I think it is well worth it—the rifle's accuracy is notably improved, and it will now usually stay well under 1½ inches for five shots at 100 yards with several different loads.

The enhanced accuracy is certainly due more to the D. F. S. Corp.'s perfectly executed bedding job than to the fiberglass stock. But I confidently expect that the synthetic stock will cure the rifle's infuriating propensity for shifting its point of impact and will reliably maintain its zero whatever the weather.

The D. F. S. stock also saved a little weight. Previously the Ruger weighed over 8¼ pounds field-ready. Now, with scope, sling, and five rounds of ammo, it goes 7 pounds 12 ounces.

The Brno, with its very slender walnut stock that is weak in spots from oil-saturation, is rather a delicate rifle that I treat gently. In contrast, the D. F. S.-stocked Ruger, despite its attractively lean lines and light weight, is a rugged piece that is fit for hard usage under rigorous conditions—it is truly a *hunter's* rifle.

There are other marked contrasts between the two rifles. The Ruger has a slightly longer chamber and a decidedly longer throat, so that its bullets can be seated out approximately 0.06 inch farther than with the Brno. (Its throat may be slightly eroded.) The Ruger cannot abide boattail bullets. It scattered 140-grain and 160-grain Sierra boattails out over 2½ inches but grouped the flat-base versions of the same bullets into not much over 1 inch.

On the other hand, the Brno shoots beautifully with 140-grain Sierra boattails, and even better with the 139-grain Hornady boattail Spire Points. But it does well with many flat-base bullets, too. It really is not very fussy.

With factory ammunition, the Ruger gives from 40 to 80 FPS less velocity than the Brno, and with handloads it needs a grain or two more powder to reach equal velocities. The corollary here is that safe maximum loads for the Ruger would produce excessively high pressures in the Brno, sufficiently so to blow primers and lock the bolt, if not worse.

These two 7mm rifles illustrate perfectly why handloading manuals seldom agree on maximum charges and velocities and why it is essential to reduce any listed maximum charge by several grains before trying it in one's own rifle.

As to propellants, IMR 4350 seems to me to be the best all-round powder for the 7x57. It gave good velocities and very acceptable accuracy with all bullet weights from 130 grains and up. However, my lot of 4350 is several years old, and some of the more recent lots seem to produce less velocity for the same charge. Hence, IMR 4320 may be preferable with the 130-grain bullet, and it certainly produced outstanding accuracy with high velocity with the 139-grain BTSP bullet in the Brno.

With 160-grain bullets, the slower-burning IMR 4381 begins to equal IMR 4350, and with 175-grain bullets it is definitely superior in my rifles.

The 130-grain Speer was very accurate indeed in the Ruger, and no doubt it would make fine pronghorn medicine. But I would personally prefer one of the 139- to 145-grain bullets for antelope and open-country deer. For all-round use on medium-size game, and for deer in cover, I like Hornady's 154-grain Spire Point or the Nosler 150-grain Solid-Base spitzer. But if I were taking the little Mauser after elk or moose (which I would not hesitate to do) or any of the larger African antelope, I would opt for the 160-grain Nosler Partition bullet, or for the 175-grain RNSP if I was using factory ammunition. Under some circumstances the 175-grain Nosler Partition bullet handloaded to give near 2,600 FPS might be the best of all.

I am a subsistence hunter at heart. I have lived all my life on ranches or farms where the greater part of the meat on our table has been gathered with the rifle, so I hunt deer for the venison, not for horns. Consequently I hate to blow them apart, or to tear huge, gaping holes in them. I like to kill cleanly but also neatly.

My wife hunts whitetail with a 7mm-08, and one of my sons uses the Ruger. Both have done very well with various 139-grain or 140-grain bullets loaded to the same 2,600 FPS that Remington 7x57 ammunition yields with its 140-grain bullet. I tend to use the 154-grain Hornady in the Brno, but again at about 2,600 FPS. At this speed both weights seem to expand well but not violently (except the 140-grain Nosler Ballistic-Tip, which is too explosive for my liking), and they kill quickly. The animals may run 20 to 40 paces before dropping but seldom require a finishing shot, and there is generally an exit wound to leave a blood trail.

We do not use any type of artificial stand or blind, but still-hunt on foot and shoot from the best field position we can improvise when the opportunity occurs. Although we seldom shoot at over 150 yards, neck shots are rare. Mostly we shoot for the lung-heart area, and will take the deer from any reasonable angle, but not from dead astern. Under these conditions the two 7mm Mausers and the 7mm-08 have now between them given us 20 consecutive one-shot kills on white-tailed deer.

Not only is the 7mm Mauser a superb deer cartridge—the world is full of good deer cartridges—but it is in my opinion the least that can fully qualify as a general purpose big-game cartridge. The reason is this: To be certain of being able to smash through heavy shoulder bones and reach the lungs on moose and elk and like-size African animals such as kudu when the occasion demands it, I want a well-constructed bullet of good sectional density that weighs at least 150 grains and preferably more. The .25 calibers lack sufficient weight of metal to qualify. The 6.5mms can but barely meet my specifications, so I draw the line right under the 7x57mm.

It has been suggested that in designing the .30-06 our military merely enlarged the 7mm Mauser. I do not know that there is any truth in that, but the fact is that the 7x57 performs exactly like a smaller edition of the Springfield cartridge. It propels bullets of the same sectional densities (but 20 to 30 grains lighter) to very similar velocities, and the trajectories are virtually identical.

Like the .30-06, it is a thoroughly dependable round that gets the job done efficiently without any great fuss or furor. The '06 is more powerful, and may be preferable on the biggest beasties. But for 90 percent of all the big-game hunting that most of us do, the 7mm Mauser is ample. It is one of my favorite cartridges.

The .223 Remington

 **Chapter 18**

This epochal cartridge rivals in popularity the famous .30-06, says the author.
(American Rifleman *magazine, December 1985)*

T he most important cartridge to appear during the last 35 years—it may
in fact be the most consequential since the advent of the .30-06 nearly 80
years ago—is not the .300 Winchester Magnum or the .308 Winchester
or even the phenomenally successful 7mm Remington Magnum. It is a cute little
number—some have called it trifling—known as the .223 Remington when in
civilian dress and as the 5.56x45mm NATO when on active duty.

Its popularity already rivals that of the .30-06 and will undoubtedly soon
surpass it. The chief reason for this is that the U.S. adopted it as our military
cartridge for use in the M16 rifle and standardized it in 1964 with a 55-grain
boattail full-metal-jacket (FMJ) bullet at about 3,200 FPS muzzle velocity as the
5.56mm Ball M193.

By the late 1960s the M16 with M193 ammunition was the standard-issue
infantry weapon in the Vietnam War. Mixed reports were heard about the
effectiveness of the cartridge and the reliability of the rifle. Some of the problems
with the latter were traced to a change in the propellant powder and failure to
clean and properly maintain the weapon, while it seems that others were rectified
by minor changes in the design. By all reports, malfunctions with the present
M16A1 are rare indeed.

In 1981 the NATO alliance agreed to standardize on the 5.56mm cartridge,
but with a Belgian FN-designed SS109 68-grain semiarmor-piercing bullet as
standard. (See "How Does NATO's New 5.56mm Round Measure Up?" by C. E.
Harris, *American Rifleman,* May 1982, p. 42.)

J. B. Roberts Jr., the *Rifleman's* research editor, tells me that one reason for
this was to enhance penetration in both hard and soft armor at ranges beyond

500 meters, and that an additional bonus is that sensitivity to wind drift is much diminished.

The U.S. equivalent of the SS109 is the Cartridge, Ball, Cal. 5.56mm M855, which meets the specifications contained in the NATO standardization agreement while utilizing, I believe, a 62-grain bullet at 3,085 FPS. Because these comparatively long and heavy boattail bullets are not adequately stabilized by the 1 turn in 12-inch twist of the M16A1, an improved version with, among other things, a heavier barrel rifled with 1 turn in 7 inches has been adopted as the M16A2.

The new M855 cartridge will replace the M193, but only as the older ammo is used up and M16A1 rifles are phased out in favor of the A2. Colt has begun turning out M16A2 rifles in quantity, and the first of them are being delivered to the Marine Corps. The M193 ball retains enough accuracy with the 1 in 7-inch twist A2 barrel for government work, so there is no ammo supply problem on that score.

The Sporting Arms and Ammunition Manufacturer's Institute (SAAMI) does not recommend using M193 Ball in commercial .223 Remington chambers, because the bullet ogive may impinge on the throat of the civilian chamber and cause excessively high pressures. But Colt and Ruger both chamber their .223 rifles to military 5.56mm specifications, and it seems to me that for safety's sake all manufacturers should do the same.

The original Colt AR-15 civilian version of the M16 had a 1 in 12-inch rifling twist, but the latest AR-15A2 has the same 1 in 7-inch twist as its military counterpart. The Ruger Mini-14 has a 1 in 10-inch twist, and this may or may not work with the new M855 ammo. We are cautioned to crimp ammunition that will be used in the autoloaders, to prevent the bullets from being driven down into the cases during their rather violent slam-bang feed cycle. This is feasible with many 55-grain bullets, but efforts to emulate M855 ammunition are hindered by the fact that it is at the moment almost impossible to find heavier bullets with crimping cannelures.

The Colt AR-15, the Ruger Mini-14, and many other imported military-style semiautos are extremely popular with shooters today. Others deplore them and accuse them of giving the shooting sports a bad image. This should not be so. Used with the same degree of responsibility and regard for safety required with any firearm, they are certainly no more objectionable than other guns and project no worse an image than those much-vilified handguns!

It is not a bad thing for at least the younger civilians to have some familiarity with the type of personal weapon they might be called upon to use if we again become involved in an armed conflict. Besides, they are just one heck of a lot of fun to shoot—but, my goodness, do they get through the ammo!

While I expect that a greater quantity of .223 ammo is still being burned up in the autoloaders, the cartridge is becoming a favorite with varmint shooters when chambered in an accurate bolt-action rifle or the Ruger No. 1, and it is also catching on in the big single-shot pistols such as the Thompson/Center Contender. Its growing popularity has killed off the slightly larger .222 Remington Magnum and has taken a lot of its turf away from the excellent little .222 Remington.

It's possible that we could get by with but two factory-chambered .22-caliber centerfire varmint cartridges: the .22-250 Remington for the serious enthusiast who considers anything less than 300 yards as being unsportingly close range, and the .223 for everyone else.

The .223 Remington, which became available under that name in 1964, utilizes a rimless 1.760-inch-long case with a comparatively short neck of about .203 inch and a head diameter of .378 inch. This compares to the .473 inch of standard cartridges such as the .30-06. Its case is .06 inch longer than that of the .222 but almost $1/10$ inch shorter than that of the .222 Remington Magnum. It would have dangerously excessive headspace if fired in that chamber. Despite its name, it uses .224-inch diameter bullets, as do both the .222s, the modern .22 Hornet, the .225 Winchester, the .218 Bee, the .220 Swift, and the .22-250.

The standard factory load for the .223 Remington consists of a 55-grain softpoint, hollowpoint, or FMJ bullet at a listed muzzle velocity of 3,240 FPS from a 24-inch barrel. In addition, Winchester has a 53-grain hollowpoint for which it claims 3,330 FPS. Federal offers a 40-grain hollowpoint bullet at a sizzling 3,650 FPS.

Actually, a study of the .223 loads and ballistic tables in Sierra's second-edition reloading manual suggests that 55 grains is about the optimum bullet weight in this cartridge, and that the 55-grain Boattail Spitzer will give a flatter trajectory out to 500 yards, and less wind drift, than any other Sierra bullet.

The 63-grain Sierra and the 70-grain Speer are both semi-pointed bullets short enough to stabilize in the 1 in 12-inch twist that's standard in the .223 Remington, but Sierra warns that its 69-grain BTHP MatchKing requires a twist no slower than 1 in 10 inches. This might also apply to Hornady's new 68-grain BTHP match bullet.

In any case, if a scope-sighted .223 rifle is zeroed at 200 yards with a 55-grain spitzer at 3,200 FPS, it should strike about ½ inch high at 100 yards, 2½ inches to 3 inches low at 250 yards, and 7 inches to 8½ inches below point of aim at 300 yards. However, at that distance the remaining velocity is down to around 2,000 to 2,100 FPS and may not expand some bullets violently enough to give instantaneous kills. No doubt this is why most authorities call it a 250-yard varmint cartridge. Within that range I imagine that it will also do an excellent job on coyotes and other animals of up to some 50 pounds live weight.

The .223 has taken a lot of deer and will kill many, many more. Nevertheless, it is not a deer cartridge. In the hands of an experienced shot who does not get excited, and who will hold his fire until he is sure of placing his bullet in the brain or spine, or until he is certain of being able to slip it through the ribs to take the top of the heart or the great blood vessels, it will do well enough.

But the .223 is no good for fast shooting in thick cover, for angling shots, or at anything like long range. And a nimrod who proposed to seriously hunt trophy deer with the cartridge would have to be kidding, or worse. In the hands of those chaps—and they are many—who take their rifles out of the closet once a year to hie off to the woods in search of venison, it is a wounder, plain and simple.

One such hunter told me that he had just popped a doe with his .222, trying for the neck. He heard the bullet hit, he said, but she merely flinched and ran off. Then he asked me to sight in his rifle for him! If he had been using a .30-30, there might at least have been a blood trail we could have followed with some hope of recovering the animal.

For most of its life the .223 has been chambered in bolt-actions that were unbecomingly massive for its dainty size. Now Kimber of Oregon has come to its rescue with its Model 84 rifle designed specifically for the .223 Remington cartridge, and what a beauty it is!

Its general appearance is similar to that of the .22 rimfire Kimber Model 82 (also offered in .22 Hornet and .218 Bee) with identical stock lines. Mine is the severely simple "classic" style that I prefer. It has the same checkered steel buttplate and blued pistol grip cap. The safety, neat bolt release, and integral scope-mounting dovetails are identical, while the contours of the quite decently heavy barrel appear to be the same. The barrel on my rifle is 22 inches long, measured from the bolt face, and is rifled with six grooves, 1 turn in 12 inches.

The action is different from that of the Model 82. The bolt locks into the receiver ring with two lugs in Mauser fashion, but the long, non-rotating extractor, the ejector whose slot is at 5 o'clock on the bolt face rather than bisecting a lug, and the coned barrel breech are all more reminiscent of the famous pre-'64 Model 70 Winchester. The magazine, which has an internal length of 2.325 inches and easily holds five cartridges rather than the listed four, has a hinged floor plate with a catch in the front of the trigger guard that again resembles that of the Model 70.

With a Leupold Compact 3–9X scope mounted in Kimber's Brownell-designed detachable rings, five rounds of ammunition, and a military-type shooting sling with a proper loop, the rifle weighs exactly 7½ pounds. I do not care for variable-power scopes in big-game hunting, but on a rifle of this nature they can be most useful, and this compact Leupold is in harmonious and pleasing proportion to the graceful little rifle. Because it is well-balanced, the Kimber settles down nicely despite its light weight. It is as delightful to handle and shoot as it is easy to carry. And, my word, it does shoot, far better than a light sporter has any right to do, and lots better than I can hold it!

Kimber's Greg Warne sent me three five-shot groups he had shot with it with different handloads. All were under ¾ inch, and one went a tight .495 inch. I have managed to shoot some individual groups that small, but I would say that for me, over the long run, it is a slightly better than one-minute-of-angle (1.047 inches per 100 yards) rifle with loads it likes.

The Kimber likes Nosler's 52-grain HP match bullets, as the four five-shot groups so far fired with them averaged 0.65 inch widest spread at 100 yards from the bench, but of the hunting bullets tested to date, and there are many I have not yet tried, it does best with the Speer 52-grain HP and Sierra's 55-grain BTSP.

Fifteen five-shot groups with the 55-grain Sierra Boattail and various charges of both H4895 and H335 powders averaged 0.95 inch extreme spread, with the largest group measuring 1.195 inches and the smallest 0.72 inch. This is pretty fair consistency.

No special accuracy techniques were used in loading this ammunition. I just did exactly as I do when reloading for any ordinary big-game rifle. The cases were all of one brand, Winchester, and had all been fired approximately the

137

same number of times. CCI 400 primers were used exclusively, and the bullets were seated so as to be about .04 inch short of the lands. The maximum overall cartridge length for the .223 Remington is given as 2.260 inches, but in my rifle I could not seat any of the bullets I have used to that length without jamming them quite firmly into the rifling. Bullet seating depth must be adjusted to suit the individual rifle's throat and magazine.

More precise loading procedures would probably have improved the accuracy to a degree, and so would a better shot. With the scope set at 9X, I could see quite clearly that even with the rifle resting on the sandbags the cross hairs were wobbling around within a circle of at least ½-inch diameter—and that is when I was holding well! Ninety-degree temperatures with some heat-shimmer and variable wind conditions did not help either, so I reckon that given appropriate ammunition, reasonable conditions, and a good benchrest shooter, this rifle would group consistently within ¾ inch at 100 yards.

One thing I really like is that it puts the first shot from a cold, clean barrel into the same group as the rest, and it shows no tendency whatsoever to walk its shots as the barrel warms up. Not that I have ever let it get scorching hot, but the last shot of a quite closely spaced string of ten goes into the same cluster as the previous nine, which indicates that the barrel was made good and straight in the first place.

Because the Kimber is not a benchrest gun, I tried it at 200 and 250 yards, shooting from prone with a tight sling, to check the trajectory. Using the Sierra 55-grain BTSP and a charge of 26 grains of H335 powder that gives it 3,135 FPS and is nice and easy on the gun, I zeroed it 1½ inches high at 100 yards, where it proved to be dead-on at 200 yards and about 2¾ inches low at 250, just as the Sierra handloading manual said it would be.

We have no prairie dogs, chucks, or other varmints of that sort here, only a few scattered jack rabbits. So I put out empty 12-ounce beverage cans at random from 150 to 250 yards and one at 300 yards. After a little practice, I found I could hit them almost every time out to 200 yards. I put three consecutive shots into a 1.6-inch group on one at that distance—and did quite well even at 250 yards. Then I tried the 300-yard can and sent it spinning away at the first attempt.

"*Whoopee!*" I enthused. "This little gun is fun!"

Luckily, I was then out of ammo, so did not have to try to discover how many shots it would take me to do it again.

It would seem that the .223 Kimber is a very adequate varmint rifle out to 250 yards, and it should not be out of the running at 300 if the shooter can dope the wind and the range correctly. Proper bullet expansion is a concern at this range, though. For the longer ranges it might be wise to choose the frangible Super Explosive or Blitz bullets offered by Hornady and Sierra, or Federal's factory load with the 40-grain Blitz bullet.

Apart from varmint shooting, what else is the cartridge good for? Well, I am not an aficionado of the varmint/big-game cartridge concept. I was raised to believe that the wounding of a game animal is a horrible and inexcusable disgrace to be avoided by all means, one of which is to use enough gun. The way I see it, if a fellow wants to hunt big game, including deer, he has a responsibility to acquire and use an arm that is more than sufficiently powerful for the toughest shot he is willing to try. Seldom will any sort of varmint cartridge meet the requirements.

A varmint/small-game combination is a far more viable idea. Here the .223 in a Model 84 Kimber or similar rifle will fill the bill splendidly, as it can be loaded to match any lesser .22, from the .222 Remington to the .218 Bee, the Hornet, the .22 Winchester Rimfire Magnum, and on down to close to .22 Long Rifle velocities with the jacketed 40-grain bullet.

NRA's *Handloading* book by William C. Davis Jr. warns that in high-velocity rifle cartridges jacketed bullets should not be used in low-power loads developing less than about 1,200 FPS because their friction is such that they may lodge in the bore, and in any case their accuracy is generally poor. But with cast lead bullets, there is no reason satisfactory .22 Long Rifle or even .22 Short or BB Cap equivalent loads could not be developed for the .223.

I have not gone that far, but I did try a 40-grain Sierra bullet with 4 grains of Hercules Unique. This combination gave 1,335 FPS on the chronograph and about 1-inch groups at 50 yards. The same bullet pushed to .22 WMR velocity of 1,980 FPS by 10 grains of 2400 grouped better, but one of the most accurate loads of all was the 50-grain Nosler SP with 16.5 grains of Accurate Arms Company's MP5744 magnum pistol powder. It registered a Hornetlike 2,591 FPS while putting five shots into a neat 0.47 inch at 100 yards.

It will make a superb turkey round and should do well on foxes and such out to at least 150 yards without putting excessively large holes in valuable pelts. It will be a good understudy for a big-game rifle, offering much more realistic practice than a .22 rimfire yet at quite reasonable cost, and might even make a decent mid-range target load. I expect that I will be using a lot of it in my Kimber.

The major manufacturers all offer loads for the .223 using nonexpanding FMJ bullets that could be employed by a non-handloader when minimal damage to meat or hides is desirable, but no ready-made reduced loads suitable for squirrels and other such small, edible game are available. In that case, one of the chamber adapters that allow the .22 Long Rifle rimfire round to be used in a .223 might be worth considering.

Besides the Kimber, I was also able to chronograph some of the handloads and factory ammunition in a friend's Ruger Mini-14 with its 18½-inch barrel. Because it has no scope and I can no longer see a front sight as clearly as I used to, I did not try it for accuracy. But I was most favorably impressed with its reliable functioning. If autoloaders are fussy about their ammunition, I certainly could not demonstrate it with this one. It stuttered cheerfully through anything I fed it without the slightest hint of wanting to malfunction, even with reduced loads down to .22 Hornet level and below. I had to go down to .22 WMR power before it would fail to reload itself. In this one very important respect at least, the Ruger Mini-14 seems to be a darned good gun.

With its 3½-inch shorter barrel, the Ruger recorded from 55 to 195 FPS less velocity than the Model 84, depending on the load. With one box of PMC 5.56mm Ball M193, the velocity difference between the two rifles was a hefty 228 FPS. But this stuff, though fine in the Mini-14, gave over 3,400 FPS in the Kimber, accompanied by indicators of excessively high pressure such as sticky extraction and well-cratered primers. I can take that obvious a hint, so I quit testing it in the Model 84 after five rounds. I intend to abide by the SAAMI recommendation by using no more military ammunition in the Kimber.

The capacity of the .223 case is such that in general it does best with the medium-burning-rate powders such as IMR 4064, 4320, 3031, and 4198, Winchester's 760 and 748, Hodgdon's H4895, H335, and BLC(2), and Hercules R7. Accurate Arms Company has a powder meant specifically for the .223 designated MR223 (what did you expect?) that I would like to have tried, but I was unable to get my hands on any out here in the boondocks. The test rifles were not overly fussy about which powder was used. They performed quite acceptably well with a wide variety. But in my Kimber the best results overall, with full-power loads and 55-grain bullets, were obtained with H4895 and H335, with W748 close behind.

I suggested at the beginning of this essay that the .223 Remington may become the most popular centerfire rifle cartridge of all time, surpassing even the .30-06. There are other parallels. Like the '06, the .223 is a well-balanced cartridge that is easy to reload and has a generous, and growing, selection of available bullets. Being neither too large nor too small, it is an exceptionally versatile round that is about the closest thing to an all-round cartridge in its field, just as the .30-06 is in big-game hunting. In fact, a light, accurate .223 such as the Kimber, together with a good .30-06, could well constitute the optimum two-rifle battery for the hunting of all American game, both large and small.

Make Mine Mauser

$\oplus$ **Chapter 19**

Aagaard regards the venerable Model 98 as the most dependable rifle action ever devised. (American Rifleman *magazine, June 1985)*

I n his definitive work, *Bolt Action Rifles,* Frank de Haas declares, "Without question the M98 Mauser is the best, strongest, and most foolproof military turnbolt action ever made." I am not quite sure of the adjective "best" where military rifles are concerned; if I had to fight a war with a turnbolt rifle, I might prefer the Lee-Enfield because of its ten-shot magazine and very fast reloading. But I do believe that in 1898 Paul Mauser perfected—well, almost—the bolt-action for sporting rifle use, and further that most of the alleged improvements made to it by others since that time have in fact been retrograde steps.

Strong words and an extreme position, perhaps. But it seems that I am not entirely alone in holding this opinion.

Every *Gun Digest* devotes two or three pages to illustrations and short descriptions of some of the most desirable custom guns made in this country. Within reason, price is not a major consideration in the building of these masterpieces; they employ whatever action, barrel, stock, etc., the owner and his gunmaker consider to be the best available for their purpose, regardless of cost.

Checking quickly back through the last five editions of *Gun Digest*, I counted 113 centerfire custom rifles (or actions) illustrated. Of these, 38 were on a Mauser-system M98 action and 22 on the Model 70 Winchester—the pre-'64 Model 70, that is. Next came 12 Sakos, followed by 9 Remington Model 700s (several of which were left-hand), 9 Ruger No. Is, 3 Ruger Model 77s, 2 No. 3 Rugers, 2 Model 1917 Enfields, and 1 Weatherby Mark V. There were 15 other miscellaneous or unidentifiable actions in the total.

Why was an action designed nearly nine decades ago chosen for the very heart of fully one-third of this sample of the highest-quality sporting rifles ever built anywhere on earth?

The answer is partly out of tradition and for the image. The great magazine rifles built in England in its heyday by Holland & Holland, Rigby, Purdey, Westley Richards, and the rest employed Mauser actions almost exclusively, as did Griffin & Howe and others in this country when they were not using those quite close Mauser derivatives, the '03 Springfield and the Model 70 Winchester.

But the main reason is dependability. Paul Mauser designed the M98 to function under the most adverse conditions of mud and snow and dust and neglect in battle; consequently, it takes almost anything the game fields can subject it to without a hitch.

It is noticeable that both the Mauser 98 and the old Winchester Model 70, which together accounted for more than 50 percent of the *Gun Digest* custom guns, are what have been called "controlled-feed" actions.

They both have the long, non-rotating, Mauser-type extractor attached to the bolt body by a collar. As the cartridge rises out of the magazine, its rim slides under the hook of the extractor, which holds it against the bolt face. This ensures that it will be extracted even if the bolt has not been fully closed.

With most modern actions, the cartridge is pushed into the chamber ahead of the extractor, which does not snap over the case rim until the bolt handle is turned down. Consequently, if the bolt is withdrawn before it has been fully locked, a round may be left in the chamber. When it is then pushed forward again, the bolt will pick up another round from the magazine and ram it into the rear of the first one. Should a pointed bullet strike the chambered cartridge's primer with sufficient force, the results could be rather shocking! Though unlikely, this has happened at least once, I am told.

One can remove the cartridges from a Mauser's magazine in perfect safety by just pushing the bolt straight back and forth without turning the handle down, because the firing pin has two shoulders that prevent it from going all the way forward until the bolt has been rotated into the fully locked position.

The Mauser extractor has a tongue that, fitting into a groove running part of the way around the bolt ahead of the locking lugs, controls its fore and aft movement, as do the extractors of the pre-'64 Model 70 and the Ruger Model

77. But the Mauser has a refinement the others lack. The groove is undercut at the front, and the extractor has a matching lip that slips into this when it moves forward a little as it starts to pull the case from the chamber. Thus the extractor is locked and positively prevented from letting go of the case, and the greater the resistance the more firmly it is locked. No matter how badly the case is stuck in the chamber, the Mauser will always extract something, even if it's only a segment of the case rim!

The Mauser and old Model 70 extractors in addition are wider and engage a bigger segment of the case rim than most modern ones, including the Ruger, which for some reason has its hook narrowed.

Mausers were designed to be loaded from the magazine, and the extractor will not normally snap over the rim of a cartridge dropped into the chamber ahead of it. Sometimes it can be made to do so by pressing in on it behind the collar while gently forcing the bolt handle down; or the hook's face can be beveled and shortened slightly to snap over the rim just as does that of the old Model 70. It is, however, easy to ruin the extractor if one does not know exactly how to do it—I speak from personal experience!

The Mauser's extractor is unquestionably the most positive ever used on a bolt gun, but how much does that matter? Well, there is a record of the extractor on a .460 Weatherby Mark V failing in the middle of a buffalo affair *(Rifle,* No. 81, p. 52), and I have personally experienced extraction failures with three different post-'64 Model 70 Winchesters, two of them being .458s.

The Model 70 extractors quit due to dust and crud accumulating unseen under them, but a Mauser extractor would have continued functioning despite that.

The modern plunger-type ejectors found on many rifles are quite reliable, but they cannot be used with a controlled-feed action. They will throw the spent case out as soon as its mouth clears the receiver ring, whereas a Mauser will not eject unless the bolt is jerked all the way back. But short-stroking any bolt-action results in a failure to feed a fresh cartridge into the chamber, regardless.

I find it quite interesting that while Paul Mauser did use the "modern" snap-on type of extractor and a plunger ejector on some of his earlier, more primitive designs, he had discarded both by 1892!

Much has been made of the modern recessed bolt heads, which supposedly are stronger because the head of the case is completely surrounded by a ring of steel. But less of the case is then inserted into the chamber; there has to be a tolerance between the bolt and the end of the barrel, and this gap comes a little way up from the head of the case, where the brass is thinner. Canadian gunsmith Ellwood Epps had a photo on p. 32 of the 1977 *Gun Digest* showing a case that let go at exactly that point in a recessed bolt-head action.

In contrast, the M98 encloses the cartridge in the chamber all the way up to its extractor groove, so that only solid brass is unsupported.

It seems that a recessed bolt head should in turn be surrounded by a barrel extension, as in the Remington Model 700 and Weatherby Mark V; otherwise the Mauser breeching is superior.

In the nowadays quite rare event of a case failure, the Mauser handles the escaping gas rather well. Two generous ports in the bolt body vent into the left lug raceway, whence, on the military rifles and most Oberndorf Mauser sporters, an easy escape route is provided by the thumb slot. Any gas that did get back through the receiver bridge would be deflected from the shooter's face by the flange on the bolt sleeve, a feature that is missing from both the Winchester Model 70 and Remington Model 700. Both of these also vent into the left lug raceway, but of course they lack the thumb slot, so some of the escaping gas could be directed back into the shooter's face if a pierced primer allowed it to get inside the bolt.

The Ruger bolt does have a flange covering the left lug raceway, and also has two long slots and a hole that would port gas down into the magazine well, which would seem to be a better idea. The Weatherby Mark V has the three gas-escape holes in its bolt in line with the ejection port, which is better yet.

The thumb slot in the left receiver wall of the Mauser was a necessity for the quick and certain recharging of the magazine from stripper-clips. It is disparaged for "weakening" the action. This is not so from the point of view of safety, thanks to the fact that the action is locked in the receiver ring, and one could chop off everything behind that without affecting its ability to withstand the firing of the cartridge.

The thumb slot does adversely affect potential accuracy by making the action less rigid and more likely to flex irregularly during recoil. This need not concern a big-game hunter, though, because the accuracy loss is a matter merely of fractions of an inch, and a thumb-slot receiver can form the basis of a 1½-MOA (minute of angle) sporting rifle as well as any other action.

Rather than being a liability, the thumb slot is actually an advantage in the field because it does make charging the magazine a little easier even when one is not using stripper-clips. This is particularly so in an "eyes-off" situation such as when one is desperately thumbing fresh cartridges into the magazine while watching some beast he has annoyed and may have to ward off at any moment.

African professional hunter Nicky Blunt once took a file and cut a thumb slot in a Winchester Model 70 for this exact reason. I am not sure that is a good idea, though, because the Model 70 has nothing to prevent the left locking lug from hanging up in such a slot, whereas the Mauser takes care of it with a guide rib that during the critical period is engaged in the groove found at 12 o'clock in the receiver bridge.

The Mauser is sometimes criticized for having a sloppy bolt that rattles around loosely except when locked. The smooth, tightly fitted actions such as the old Mannlicher-Schoenauer are indeed delightful in the sporting-goods store or the gun room, but Paul Mauser meant his rifles to work in the field, where it matters, and I for one am darned glad of it.

Years ago a friend and I finished a stalk on a herd of impala by crawling on hands and knees across sandy ground. When my companion tried to chamber a round in his Mannlicher-Schoenauer, it jammed. Finally, we got the bolt out and found that two little grains of sand—which my Mauser would never even have noticed—had tied that slick action up solidly.

Also held against the Mauser is the slow ignition and consequent inaccuracy due to its firing pin gathering momentum over a full ½ inch of travel as compared to about ¼ inch for most modern actions. While true in theory and possibly of consequence in benchrest matches and the like, it is nothing for a hunter to fret about. If he misses an antelope or gets into trouble with a bear, it will be because he misjudged the range or jerked the trigger, not because the firing pin took a few extra milliseconds to fall. Besides, that long travel seems to ensure that it will give the primer a solid clout. I can remember no ignition problems with a Mauser that could be blamed on the action, but I have experienced a couple with modern speed-lock actions.

The original M98 bolt-sleeve three-position safety that swings through 180 degrees is probably the best ever fitted to a turnbolt rifle. It cams the cocking piece back out of contact with the sear, when fully engaged it locks the bolt, and it can hardly be knocked off accidentally. When fast shooting may be required, it is turned to the upright, 90-degree position. Then the thumb easily sweeps off the safety as the rifle is coming to the shoulder and continues to come to rest in its proper place on the left side of the grip. In this halfway position, it does not lock the bolt, which can then be operated with the safety applied.

The only thing wrong with the safety is that it does not work under a low-mounted telescopic sight, and one can't blame Paul Mauser for that—scopes were not much in vogue when he designed the action.

For use with scopes, modern Mausers such as the last FNs, the Santa Barbaras, and the Mark Xs adopted a slide-operated safety on the right side of the tang that blocks only the trigger and/or sear, not the firing pin itself. I suppose that they are all right, but personally I prefer a low-swing leaf safety such as the Buehler, mounted on an original-type bolt sleeve, which visibly cams the firing pin back when applied. I also want it to lock the bolt, as I have been badly frightened by a rifle refusing to fire when it should have, due to the bolt handle having been knocked upward. In any event, I take care that the muzzle is pointing in a safe direction when I am loading or unloading the piece.

The Winchester Model 70 three-position safety is the best so far devised for use with scope sights on bolt-action rifles. Safeties of this type are available for Mausers from a couple of makers.

Original Mauser sporters often came with double set triggers, for which I have no use at all, but some, and all the military rifles, used the standard two-stage trigger. Though seldom employed nowadays, the two-stage was really a good and inexpensive design that permitted deep-sear engagement for safety when the bolt was slammed back and forth violently. The long and light first pull of the trigger removed most of this engagement, and then came the easily felt heavier resistance of the second stage, when a slight additional movement would fire the piece. The second stage could be adjusted by careful honing to safely give a very clean, crisp pull.

In use, one took up the slack automatically, without conscious thought, as the rifle came onto the target, and then he squeezed off the second stage when the sight picture was right, in the normal fashion. The only disadvantage is that if one is going to use this trigger, he must have it on all his rifles, else he could be frightfully embarrassed by taking up the slack on a trigger that didn't have any!

Consequently, all my Mausers are now fitted with the excellent Timney adjustable triggers, which I set to give a crisp pull of about three pounds.

Several successful bolt-actions that derive little from the Mauser have been developed. They often have multiple lugs and short, 60-degree bolt lifts (compared to the 90-degree rotation in the Mauser). Some lock up toward the rear of the bolt—which necessitates a heavier receiver—while the Colt-Sauer even employs cam-operated pop-out locking lugs. All of which is very well, but it seems to me that they tend to be needlessly complicated while offering no real advantages that would be readily apparent in the field. I suspect that few of them could match the reliability of the Mauser when the going gets rough.

We speak here of the reliability of a good Mauser, that is. While the design is unsurpassed, it has been executed by all sorts of makers all over the world. The Pathans even made M98s by hand in Pakistan. There are shoddily made Mausers, and others are worn out through hard use and neglect.

It is wise to have any surplus military Mauser rifle or action checked by a gunsmith before using it. But generally the genuine German-made articles are sound, as are the ones made at Brno in Czechoslovakia and of course those manufactured by the famous FN concern in Belgium. The modern Spanish-made Santa Barbara and the Yugoslavian Mark X—which is used in the Whitworth rifles—may lack a little finish, but they are strong and safe actions that will give a lifetime of good service.

I am, quite obviously, no engineer, only a simple hunter. But I have used a rifle as a tool of my trade for a number of years and have had the opportunity to see how many different ones performed in the hands of my clients.

Given the choice, for any serious big-game hunting where reliability is imperative, I will unhesitatingly pick a rifle with a Mauser system M98 action. I am not, however, fanatical about it. Included in my battery of "using" guns is a Weatherby Mark V, two Ruger 77s, and two Winchester 70s. One of the last is my .458 stopping rifle, and it is a late-model 70 at that. It is only coincidence that I have no Remington in the collection, a deficiency I intend to correct if I can get my hands on a limited-edition Classic in .350 Remington Magnum.

Nor do I think that the Mauser M98 is quite perfect. My ideal bolt-action for a sporting rifle would have some features from several different designs. The extractor would be able to snap over the rim of a chambered cartridge like the one on the old Model 70. It would also have the Model 70's safety catch, its bolt handle, and quite likely its excellent and simple trigger. The gas-venting system would be copied from the Ruger Model 77, as would the integral scope-sight bases, which both Brno and Sako have also used for years. As a fancy touch it might have the neat little pop-up aperture sight that Brno hides in the receiver bridge of its ZKK models.

But the essence of it—everything else including the bolt and receiver, the one-piece trigger guard and magazine box, the controlled feed, the bolt-stop and ejector, the breeching, and the utter dependability—would be pure M98, just as Paul Mauser designed it 87 years ago.

The 6.5x55mm

 **Chapter 20**

Still searching for the ideal deer cartridge, Aagaard decided to try a turn-of-the-century round renowned for its deep penetration and gentle recoil. (American Rifleman *magazine, April 1985)*

I t seems that there are fashions in cartridges, as with most other things. We had the era of the .270 Winchester, when for almost a whole generation anyone who knew anything did it all with Jack O'Connor's pet. Later the 7mm Remington Magnum became the rage, while in certain select circles a fellow rash enough to admit slaying a mountain nyala, polar bear, Carpathian stag, bharal, or *Ovis ammon ammon* with anything but a .300 Weatherby Magnum probably would have been blackballed and banished forever beyond the Pale.

Eighty years ago, around the turn of the century and for a couple of decades thereafter, was the time of the 6.5mm. The advantages of the smaller calibers and lighter bullets, made possible by the adoption of smokeless nitro powders, had recently become as obvious to sportsmen as to the military, and naturally some of them could not resist taking a good thing too far.

Several nations had adopted various 6.5mms as their service cartridge. Hunters tried them on game and liked them. Consequently, gunmakers such as Jeffery of London were soon turning out sporters based on the 1893 Romanian Mannlicher military rifle and chambered for 6.5x53R (for rimmed) cartridge that the British called the .256 Mannlicher for the bore diameter of the barrel (often enough they referred to it merely as "the Mannlicher").

The rifles normally had 26-inch or longer barrels, which gave the 160-grain (or thereabouts) roundnose bullet a muzzle velocity of some 2,300 FPS. With its great sectional density, this long bullet gave deep penetration and quite reliable killing power when decently placed.

Together with the ballistically similar 6.5x54mm Mannlicher-Schoenauer that appeared in 1903, the .256 quickly achieved popularity, and hardly an English sportsman of the time ventured abroad without a Mannlicher of some sort in his battery. Even Frederick Courteney Selous, who started his career hunting elephant with a pair of muzzleloading, 4-gauge smoothbores, took a .256 Mannlicher on a hunt in the American Rockies.

Though he is perhaps the best known, the famous "Karamojo" Bell was not the only exponent of small-bores on great game. Another was Major C. H. Stigand, a very experienced African hunter-naturalist who was governor of the Mongalla Province of the Sudan when he was killed in a fight with the Dinka in 1919. He apparently preferred his Mannlicher to anything else, even on elephant (with "solid" full-metal-jacket bullets, of course), despite having been severely bashed by a jumbo in 1912.

Bell himself used a 6.5mm Mannlicher-Schoenauer on elephants for a while, before settling on his beloved .275 Rigby (7x57mm). But he also mentions a long-barrel ".256 Gibbs Mannlicher" that he apparently used as a meat gun to down zebras, giraffes, and the larger antelopes—not only to feed his numerous following but also to provide the rawhides that were required to package his ivory for transportation on donkeys.

In his *Karamojo Safari*, Bell says of this weapon that it used ". . . the long parallel-sided roundnose bullet with the lead exposed in the nose—a superb all-round killing bullet good enough for broadside or end-on shots. With its weight and good velocity, it was at that time the deadliest to be had. . . ."

Another extraordinary character who had much experience with the Mannlicher on African game was Captain (later Colonel) Richard Meinertzhagen. Apart from being an ornithologist of international renown, he was probably the most brilliant intelligence officer the British had in the Great War. He served twice in East Africa, first a four-year tour with the King's African Rifles, then as head of General Smuts's intelligence section in 1915-16, during the campaign in East Africa (now Tanzania).

In his fascinating *Kenya Diary 1902–1906* he says, ". . . I am a great advocate of small-bore rifles, as they are more accurate and easier to shoot with. If one shoots straight, all I require a rifle to do is to penetrate. If one's first shot at a dangerous beast is well placed . . . the beast should not be in a position to charge."

Later he added, "I never use anything else now but the Mannlicher and have such success with it against dangerous game (he is referring here mostly to rhino and lion) that I have complete confidence in it. I am sure the essence of killing dangerous game is to get as close as possible and make certain of placing one's first shot in such a manner as to completely knock the beast out. With a cool head and accurate shooting one can rely for the rest on penetration."

This is all very well so long as one is hunting in relatively open country, as he was. At that time rhino lived on the open plains in Kenya. If he had had to go poking around after buffaloes, rhinos, or elephants in the thick stuff, where one might have to ward off some furious beast at arm's length with a very hasty snapshot, I doubt that he would have found his little .256 quite so satisfactory.

Be that as it may, the popularity and success of the .256s were undoubtedly due to their deep penetration combined with a gentle recoil that enables many chaps to shoot better and place their shots more exactly with them than with harder-kicking big-bores.

Nor were the .256s solely an African fad; certain American hunters also fancied the 6.5mm bore. One of them was explorer Vilhjalmur Stefansson, who lived in the Arctic, mostly by his rifle, for 12 years from 1906 to 1918. He usually carried a standard 6.5x54 Mannlicher-Schoenauer, but it seems that he employed a .256 Gibbs Magnum—135-grain bullet at 2,750 FPS—on his last expedition.

Another was Charles Sheldon, who hunted and explored for months at a time in Mexico, Arizona, the Yukon, and Alaska. He spent the whole year 1907-08 hunting and studying the sheep in the vicinity of Denali in what is now Alaska's Mount McKinley National Park, an adventure he described in his engrossing work, *The Wilderness of Denali*.

Col. Townsend Whelen knew Sheldon well. He wrote that Sheldon used but one rifle, a .256 Mannlicher on the Romanian action, built by Jeffery. It had a 26-inch barrel and a Lyman aperture rear sight on its cocking piece. Sheldon said he had killed more than 500 head of American big game, including 70 to 80 grizzly and Alaskan brown bears, with this rifle, using the standard 160-grain roundnose bullet or, when he could get it, the Stigand bullet that had just a pinpoint of lead exposed.

The Colonel remarks that Sheldon's books and journals showed no indications whatever of any failure of the cartridge to kill well and humanely, even up to and beyond 300 yards. He adds, "Sheldon was a most excellent rifle shot."

There were a surprising number of different 6.5mm cartridges. Many were originally military cartridges, including the 6.5x50 Arisaka, the 6.5x52mm Carcano, the 6.5x55mm, the 6.5x58mm Portuguese, and of course the aforementioned 6.5x54mm Mannlicher-Schoenauer and 6.5x53R. Others, such as the 6.5x57mm and 6.5x54mm Mauser—which was different from the Mannlicher-Schoenauer and was chambered in the neat little short-action Type K Mauser rifles and carbines—the 6.5x61mm, and the 6.5x68mm Schuler, were developed purely for hunting, as was the British ".26 Rimless Nitro Express," otherwise known as the .260 BSA.

By the time I was growing up in Kenya, the Mannlicher-action rifles with their pendulous magazines and en-bloc cartridge clips were about extinct, but Mauser sporters for the 6.5x58mm Portuguese cartridge and 6.5x54mm Mannlicher-Schoenauers in both carbine and half-stock rifle form were often seen. In fact, a chap I knew was still using his long-barrel 6.5x54mm to do in cattle-killing lions and crop-destroying hippos as late as the mid-1970s.

Another chum of mine acquired a 6.5 Mannlicher-Schoenauer carbine while he was managing a huge ranch in the Rift Valley. One of his duties was to shoot a score of Grant or Thomson gazelles every week. This was a government-sanctioned harvesting of surplus game, in the true sense of the word—not sport but just an unpleasant and dirty chore to be finished as quickly and efficiently as possible. So Mike took care of it at night, shooting by spotlight from an open Land Rover.

Once, while I was spending a few days with him, a couple of newspaper reporters from Nairobi visited the ranch to see this cropping operation. We took them out that night, and on the first herd we got into, Mike handed one of them the rifle and told him to have at it. His employer had provided Mike with a lot of old ammunition, so the first shot was a hangfire that went bang as the reporter was lowering the butt from his shoulder after the firing pin had clicked. The second shot went likewise, in the general direction of the moon.

Exasperated, Mike grabbed the gun and demonstrated how to do it. The carbine said, *"Click... Boom!"* five times in rapid succession, and each time it was answered by a thump as a granti went down.

"There," Mike explained. "All you have to do is to keep the sights on the animal after you've pulled the trigger, until it finally goes off."

But the poor fellow was so shaken that he simply could not manage it. He flinched wildly every time, leaving Mike to shake his head in disbelief that any grown man, even a city slicker, could be such a sissy as to let a little thing like a hangfire so disconcert him.

The home-grown 6.5mms have never done well. Western Cartridge Company loaded the .256 Newton for some years between the wars, but it is quite dead now, as is the much more recent 6.5mm Remington Magnum. The .264 Winchester Magnum still hangs on, but it is hardly flourishing. I do not know why this should be, but in the case of the 6.5mm Remington Magnum, the Model 600 carbine it was crammed into never let it develop its full potential.

Personally, I feel that the smaller 6.5mms are the best. There does not, in practice, seem to be anything the .264 magnum can do on game that the 7mm Remington Magnum will not handle better, and I can see no use for a 6.5mm on a .30-06-capacity case when we already have the superb old .270 Winchester.

To me the 6.5mms are most useful in their original role as gentle little cartridges that give reliable killing power out of all proportion to their bore diameter by virtue of deep- penetrating bullets of good sectional density, propelled at comparatively modest velocities.

Though I have always had a romantic regard for the 6.5mms, I never owned one until just a few weeks ago, when I had a 22-inch Douglas 6.5mm barrel screwed into a DWM 1909 Mauser action, and Acraglas-bedded it all in a Bishop semi-finished Classic stock.

For reasons more nostalgic than practical, I chose to have it chambered for the 6.5x55mm cartridge. Though I am an East African by birth and a Texan by choice, I am also a full-blooded Norwegian. The 6.5x55mm was Norway's military cartridge from 1894 till after WWII, used, naturally, in the Krag-Jorgensen rifle. It was extremely popular with civilian hunters and target shooters, and Norwegian hunting literature is full of references to "Krag'n." I do hear that the Swedes may have used the cartridge also! (Possibly because of his Norwegian heritage, Aagaard deigns not to refer to the cartridge by its popular name, the 6.5x55mm Swedish Mauser: Editor.)

In any event, it is a highly developed cartridge in Scandinavia, with an international reputation for outstanding accuracy. Its case capacity and ballistics are practically identical to those of the 6.5x57 Mauser, or to those of the wildcat

6.5mm/.257 Roberts to which many a 6.5mm Jap Arisaka was rechambered. It has one drawback in that its base and rim diameters are .480 inch, compared to .470 inch to .474 inch for such standard cases as the .30-06. It cannot ideally be formed from any other case, and only Norma manufactures it, to my knowledge. The 6.5x57mm is therefore a more practical choice.

But actually, considering the cost of imported ammo, both of them are handloading propositions, and if one is going to handload, he might just as well choose a convenient wildcat. Then the best 6.5mm of them all, I believe, would be the 6.5mm/.308 that we can properly refer to as the ".263 Waters Express," for Kenneth L. Waters who proposed it nearly 30 years ago.

While having the same capacity as the older cartridges, it would use a readily available and very strong modern case, and would in addition be well-adapted to the Savage 99 lever rifle and to such short bolt-actions as the Remington Model 7.

Nevertheless, I have a good stock of Norma brass and am well content with my 6.5x55mm, which I do NOT intend as an all-round rifle! I will not be carrying it as a backup gun while guiding clients, nor use it to snipe varmints at a quarter-mile. I will not take it on a serious elk hunt, nor to Africa or Alaska. Instead I will use it to hunt deer—because I doubt there exists a better whitetail cartridge within any reasonable range—and will certainly take it to Wyoming the next time I get to stalk antelope. It is going to be a fun gun, a gentle, strollin'-in-the-woods gun, a pretty little luxury to delight the heart.

A good variety of 6.5mm bullets are available, ranging from a traditional 160-grain roundnose softpoint (RNSP) from Hornady, through 140-grain spitzers from almost everyone, to a 129-grain SP Hornady, 120-grainers by Sierra, Nosler and Speer, several different 100-grain Varmint bullets, and an 85-grain hollowpoint from Sierra. Nosler can also provide Partition bullets weighing 125 and 140 grains.

Although I did work up some loads for 160-grain RN, the 120-grain, and for Speer's now-obsolete 87-grain Spitzer SP, I will use 140-grain bullets almost exclusively in this rifle. The faster, flatter-shooting and more explosive 120-grain might be preferred by some, but it is out of character for a .256, and may tend to shred too much meat for a venison lover. The 140-grain, whose sectional density equals that of a 190-grain .308-inch bullet, retains the traditional 6.5mm virtues of deep penetration and reliable killing power without being overly destructive, while having a significantly better trajectory than the roundnose 160-grain.

Being something of a skeptic, though, I wanted to test this penetration claim for myself. So I soaked bundles of magazines overnight and shot various bullets into them from a distance of 12 yards. I included one 180-grain Pointed Soft Point Core-Lokt Remington .30-06 load is a known quantity; therefore comparing the behavior of other bullets against it in test media should give some indication of what might be expected from them on game.

First, I tested them in a homogeneous medium of wet paper, where they all set up beautifully, retained their cores, and penetrated much as conventional theory would expect. However, animals are not homogeneous, so next I inserted 2 inches of dry paper—which is quite hard on rifle bullets—near the front of each stack of wet magazines. Then bullets started to come apart, including all three of the 180-grain Core-Lokts and lost only one core out of three, but the real surprise were the 140-grain Sierra boattails. They penetrated deeper than any of the other conventional bullets, and all three retained their cores. Based on my experience with similar bullets in other calibers, I had expected them to be more fragile than the flat-based 140-grain Speers, but I was dead wrong there.

Altogether, I think it reasonable to presume that the 140-grain bullets used in a 6.5x55mm will give deeper penetration on game than the 180-grain Remington Core-Lokt in the .30-06, and that ought to suffice.

The handloads listed were safe in my rifle, but it is built on a strong Mauser M98 action, and is rifled with a 9-inch twist. They could well be too much for surplus Swedish M94 Mausers and Norwegian Krags, which have a steep twist of 1 turn in 7½ inches and were designed for working pressures of not more than 45,000 PSI. Furthermore, my barrel has a long throat or leade that allows the bullet a fair amount of free travel before it engages the rifling, and that could moderate chamber pressure. This is said to be a bad thing for accuracy, and there may be something to that. Though the rifle is superbly accurate with Norma 139-grain factory ammunition—it put 18 out of 20 shots into 1½ inches at 100 yards, and you can guess where the blame for the fliers lies—that bluntnose bullet has the least amount of free travel. The 140-grain Sierra and Speer bullets have to make a long jump before contacting the rifling and will not consistently group into better than two minutes of angle with any load I have so far tried. That is all right for anything I am going to do with this rifle, but it irritates me to the extent that I may have the barrel set back and rechambered to reduce the amount of free travel.

Our whitetail here in central Texas are exceedingly plentiful, but very small. Their antlers are unimpressive, but their meat delicious, so I hunt them strictly for venison. For that purpose the full-power load of even the little 6.5mm 140-grain at over 2,700 FPS muzzle velocity is too much, so I took it out in the rain on opening morning with 140-grain Speer bullets loaded to give about 2,400 FPS.

Naturally, I had not got the rifle completed in time; the barrel remained unpolished and in the white, while the stock was still semifinished or worse. Nevertheless, it killed a deer, a skinny little buck that was behaving so strangely that there had to be something wrong with it. The slender Speer went in behind one shoulder and out in front of the other, poking a neat hole and dumping the deer as nicely as one could wish for.

The other evening, there were still 40 minutes of daylight left after I had finished chronographing some ammunition, so I picked up the 6.5mm and stuffed a few cartridges loaded to give the 140-grain Sierra about 2,640 FPS into its magazine, crossed the sandy creek, went about 100 yards beyond my target, and started hunting.

I worked my way slowly up a little ridge and stopped when I could just barely see over the top. After some minutes I saw movement in the bee-brush below, so got down and crawled, and then slithered on my belly over the crest, with a clump of prickly pear for cover. The movement I had seen was a plump young six-point buck, but his antlers were promising enough that in a year or two he might make a trophy that another hunter would value, so I left him be.

Presently a big doe came out into the open beyond him, and stood momentarily broadside at a little over 100 paces. When the .256 spoke to her, she dropped in her tracks. The bullet had gone a little high and completely severed the spine just behind the shoulders. The top halves of both lungs were severely damaged, but the exit hole in the skin would barely admit my thumb, and meat loss was minimal, not more than 2 inches from each backstrap. Perfect performance, and exactly the sort of work I had designed the gun for.

I'll tell you what; I like this little 6.5x55mm, and believe that in it I may at last have found my ideal deer rifle.

Kenya Days

 **Chapter 21**

Aagaard reminisces about guns and ammunition, Kenya sights, and teaching kids about firearms. (American Rifleman *magazine, September 1984*)

It was an idyllic camp under a wide-spreading old thorn tree on the bank of the Athi River. Joe Cheffings and I had set up our cots, each with its mosquito net, under a fly sheet and were reading by the light of a hurricane lamp, while Kimuli, Musyoka, and the two honey-gatherers were already rolled up in their blankets around the dying campfire.

The wild-honey collectors had wandered into our camp just as we arrived with a Land Rover full of buffaloes, so we had traded meat for their dark and aromatic raw honey. They had cut the meat into strips about an inch thick, salted it lightly, and strung it up all around camp to sun-cure into the African equivalent of jerky.

This peaceful and bucolic scene was rudely shattered by a frightful roar followed by a series of snarling grunts as a lioness charged the camp, intent on driving us off so that she could appropriate the meat. Four Africans immediately stampeded through our tent and up a tree, operating purely on their bushman's instinct since they had not had time to awaken.

I made a lightning lunge for my .375 that rested on two forked sticks driven into the ground beside me, but forgot that there was a mosquito net between us. It came down and enfolded me like Saran Wrap while the cot tipped over and deposited me, struggling frantically and shouting loudly, helplessly in the path of the onrushing brute.

She came on past the fire, but then she lost her nerve and, swerving aside, disappeared into the night. Joe decided to fire a shot to urge her on her way, and stepped outside with his rifle to do so.

"Hold it, Joe," I said. "Don't use that Kynoch ammo you have in the gun, else you'll have to clean it right away. Take one of my Winchester rounds instead."

Twenty years ago much of the Kynoch-I. C. I. .375 H&H ammo obtainable in Nairobi was still chlorate-primed. Upon firing, potassium chloride was deposited in the bore, and, having the same affinity for moisture as its twin, sodium chloride (common table salt), it would turn the bore a rich rust-red if left overnight. Oiling the barrel was not sufficient—it would rust anyway. The chloride had to be removed, which was most easily done by dissolving it with water.

Parker-Hale made a special funnel that, when inserted into the chamber, would allow a kettle full of boiling water to be poured through the bore without getting it into the action. That did the trick, but because it was not always convenient to go through the whole rigmarole immediately, we preferred to use Winchester ammo whenever possible.

The trouble was that the Winchester 300-grain FMJ (full-metal-jacket) "solid" bullet was not entirely reliable, especially not on rhino or elephant. Only that morning I'd had one of them misbehave quite badly. Joe had thumped a buffalo and we were approaching it when another one appeared around a bush to our right front, running straight at us.

At a range of about twenty paces I stuck a Winchester solid into the front of its chest, which caused it to turn and go past with two other bulls so close behind it that despite having flicked the bolt with commendable celerity I could not get another shot into it. (My journal of that date comments, ". . . it always surprises me how fast I can work a bolt when I am frightened!"). We caught up with the wounded bull a few hundred yards farther on in a thicket, but luckily I was able to put it away with no more excitement.

We found that the Winchester FMJ had struck about 2 inches to the right of the sternum, had broken a couple of ribs, and had deposited a 2½-inch-long piece of bone in one lung. But the bullet had apparently disintegrated—the only piece of it that we could find was a fingernail-size fragment of the jacket that was lying outside the rib cage, just under the skin.

I believe this particular bullet was faulty—these Winchester FMJs had thin jackets of gilding metal only and would "rivet" or split open quite often. All the same, I liked them for buffalo because I had the impression that on average they put the black bulls down a little faster than other solids.

I wonder whether the truncated cone shape of these bullets, with the small, flat meplat, had anything to do with it? It is claimed that in handgun cartridges a flatnose bullet gives much more shock effect than one with a rounded point, so it could be interesting to try .375 and .458 steel-jacketed solids in semiwadcutter form on buffalo.

Both Joe's rifle and mine were pre-'64 Winchester Model 70s in .375 H&H. Joe's had the standard 25-inch barrel, but I had a few weeks previously chopped mine back to 22 inches, on the theory that this would vastly improve its handiness and speed for fast shots at buffalo in thick bush. Somehow it did not work out that way, and I came to regret the mutilation because I could never shoot the rifle as well afterward. Eventually I got rid of it and replaced it with my present .375, which you may be sure retains its full 25 inches of barrel.

I have slowly come to the conclusion that fast-handling qualities are dependent not so much on light weight and short tubes per se as on the fit and especially the balance of the piece. I have heard English shotgunners claim that the best-handling guns are balanced so that about 50 percent of their weight is supported by the forward hand. I tend to agree: For me that degree of muzzle-heaviness not only permits the piece to settle down on deliberate shots but seems to be a definite help on running and close-range snapshots as well.

I once ran a very limited test, using a stopwatch, to see how fast we could swing various rifles through 90 degrees and place two shots in the chest area of a deer target at 40 yards, and also how long it took to get two hits on a rolling tire at 20 yards. Among the test guns was a Browning Automatic Rifle in 7mm Magnum that weighed 9.6 pounds and placed about 55 percent of that on the forward hand, and a Colt .223 AR-15 that weighed 7.2 pounds and put only 33 percent of its weight on the front hand.

Every single one of the half-dozen chaps I tested was able to achieve two hits on both the deer target and the rolling tire faster with the 9.6-pound, slightly muzzle-heavy BAR than with the light and muzzle-light AR-15. They all made virtually the same comment: The AR-15 bounced around so much that it was difficult to keep it on the target long enough to get the shot off.

Now, one would have to do a great deal more serious testing before he could lay down any dogma, but I find the above results quite interesting. At the very least, they suggest that with the American penchant for going to extremes, we may be starting to overdo the "light is right and short is fast" theme.

Light rifles are recommended for mountain hunting, and I'll go along with that, within reason. But how much difference does the weight of the rifle actually make? The heaviest item the climber has to carry is his own body.

If we figure that the fellow toiling up to the sheep mountain, wearing heavy boots and clothing and laden with rifle, ammo, binocular, camera, and a spotting scope, is moving a total of 200 pounds, then the 2-pound difference between a 10-pound rifle and one of only 8 pounds amounts to a scant 1 percent of his total burden.

To put it another way, how much farther would the hunter who gave up halfway up the mountain have got if he had been carrying no rifle at all? The truth is, maybe another 100 yards at the very most.

A difference of a pound or two is of such trifling significance that there is no sense in reducing the weight of the rifle to the point where it becomes so difficult to hold steady that one's shooting is impaired. That old bromide about carrying a rifle more than one shoots it is a specious fraud that, if taken to its logical conclusion, would have one carrying a walking stick.

I presume that one carries a rifle with the intention of shooting it, and I further presume that one shoots for the purpose of hitting something. The minimum rifle weight he requires to be able to shoot adequately well in the field varies with the individual, but for serious hunting I personally am not comfortable with a rifle weighing much under 8 pounds or having a barrel shorter than 22 inches.

Both Joe Cheffings and I had aperture sights on our .375s. Mine was a Lyman 48 receiver sight with the sighting disc removed, while Joe's home-made creation similarly employed a large aperture surrounded by a thin strip of metal. These "ghost-ring" apertures are the fastest of all iron sights—you do not have to line anything up, but merely look through them while placing the front sight on the target.

However, not all "peep" sights are fast. The one on the standard Ruger Mini-14, for example, is desperately slow because its wide disc and bulky housing obscure one's view and make it difficult to pick up the target, particularly when it is moving. It is no doubt a fair target sight, but it is unsatisfactory for most hunting and, I believe, for war.

One of the best metallic sights for these purposes was the "battle sight" on the No. 4 Lee-Enfield, which again was nothing but a large hole defined by a thin rim of metal. Although a target sight with a tiny peephole through a rectangular slide that could be adjusted for various ranges was also provided, the battle sight was superior for most serious purposes.

Actually, with its rugged reliability, its ten-shot magazine, and its very fast short-throw bolt-action, the old British .303 Lee-Enfield was possibly the best of all the bolt-action battle rifles, and in trained hands it could come surprisingly close to holding its own against the autoloaders.

The British units stationed in Kenya the last few years before that country gained its independence were equipped with the FN "self-loading rifle" L1A1 (known in the British army as the SLR), but with our No. 4 Lee-Enfields we of the Kenya Regiment would give them a hard run for the money at the annual East Africa Command Rifle Meetings.

One of the most fun shoots was the falling-plates competition. Each team of four riflemen was issued five rounds and had a dozen metal plates about a foot square to nock over. Two teams at a time lined up on the 300-yard firing point and, on the whistle, would run down to the 200-yard line, assume the prone, load with five rounds, and endeavor to knock their plates down before the other team could.

Inexperienced SLR squads would start shooting as fast as they could pull the triggers. For a few seconds there would be a horrendous drum-roll of fire interspersed with the clang of falling metal, while billowing dust obscured the targets. Then would come a sudden hush as they ran out of ammo, and the dust clouds would gradually settle to reveal three or four plates still standing.

We had no difficulty beating such teams, and in the year I am thinking of we reached the finals, where we met the Duke of Wellington's Light Infantry. These veterans thoroughly understood that only hits count, and demonstrated the superiority of the self-loader when used properly—one well-aimed shot at a time—trouncing us by all of two seconds.

We also competed with the Bren light machine gun (which was the squad automatic weapon) and with the Sterling 9mm Parabellum machine carbine. Both were capable of full-automatic fire, but no one ever won who fired them in bursts. We established beyond questioning that at any range beyond twenty yards we could obtain more hits in any given time with the change lever set at "repetition" (semiauto) than we could with bursts of full-auto fire.

Typically, a twenty-pound-plus Bren gun fired from prone with a bipod would put the first shot of a burst into the bull at 200 yards, the second shot into the outer ring at 1 o'clock, and all the rest way over the top of the four-foot target. As Col. Melvin Johnson once wrote, "If someone is going to shoot at me, I hope that they will do so on full automatic and without using a bipod!"

The Sterling, which I believe is still in service with the British armed forces as the L2A3, was an excellent submachine gun. Its magazine cartridge follower was in the form of double rollers, which cured the jams to which the Sten gun had been so prone. I cannot now recall that I ever experienced a jam with the Sterling; it functioned with remarkable reliability. I see that a semiauto only version, with a longer barrel, is now offered for sale here.

Some folks deplore the present fad for military-style weapons such as the Uzi, the Sterling, the various Heckler & Kochs, the AKs, AR-15s, and so forth. I do not! Many people who are not interested in hunting, and who find formal target shooting rather a bore, get a tremendous lot of harmless fun and recreation out of them, and anything that will get more voters involved in any form of recreational shooting is certainly to be encouraged!

All the same, I personally have little use for submachine guns. During the Mau-Mau thing, most of us preferred the U.S. M1 carbine, of which we had just a very few available, because the Sterling often seemed to be lacking in penetration. Of course, a lot of the 9mm ammo we were using was World War II-vintage stuff, which may have accounted for it.

Nevertheless, when I rose to the lofty rank of corporal and was entitled as a squad leader to be issued a Sterling, I refused it and chose instead a No. 5 Lee-Enfield—the so-called "jungle carbine." Under almost any circumstances, I would still make the same choice today.

The Kenya Regiment, Territorial Force, was a British equivalent of a reserve unit, and I fear that our unconventional ways often shocked the proper English chaps in the regular army. We knew each other well; in fact, most of us had gone to school together, so we found the outward trappings of military discipline to be both rather ridiculous and also quite unnecessary.

Officers were saluted and addressed as "sir" once a day at muster parade, but for the rest we operated on a first-name basis. Esprit de corps was sky-high. We were the best darned outfit in the country, and anyone who "let the side down" was far more severely punished by the scorn of his comrades than by any official reprimand.

We would disappear into the forests of Mount Kenya or the Aberdares for days at a time, as comfortably and confidently at home there as a sneak of leopards. We could read sign, live off the land, and play his game of hide-and-seek and the sudden ambush as well as any Mau-Mau. And above all, we could shoot.

We had grown up on farms and ranches where firearms were as common and as available as any other tools, and our training in their use had started at an early age. I cannot have been more than four or five years old when my father began to teach me to hold and squeeze with an RWS .177 air rifle, and only a couple of years older when I graduated to a Winchester Model 67 single-shot .22 rimfire.

That was a fine boy's rifle; it put a lot of guineas and dik-dik and a couple of steenbok on our table, and I wish I still had it. Some of my schoolmates had already "controlled" numerous buffaloes in defense of their fathers' crops while in their teens; others had several elephants to their credit before they were out of high school, while all of us were wont to shoot "bucks" for the family larder quite regularly.

My father kept an FN Browning's Patent .32 auto pistol in an unlocked bedside drawer all through my childhood. I was taught that I was not to touch it without permission, and I never did so—mainly, I believe, because my curiosity about it had been assuaged by being allowed to fire it quite often.

Because we live today on a ranch a long way from town, I can raise my kids the same way. There are accessible firearms all over this house, but because the children know they will be permitted to shoot with any of them—under supervision—for the asking, they have never violated the rule about not touching them without permission.

It is regrettable that this excellent system under which our grandfathers, and their fathers before them back to *Homo habilis* and Adam, learned their skill at arms is rarely feasible today. For the vast majority of city dwellers, it is imperative to keep firearms securely locked away.

But even so, I feel that the right time to start training children with firearms and allowing them to shoot (under supervision) is just as early as they want to do so. I want my kids to grow up thoroughly familiar with firearms and having no more fear of them than of chain saws or automobiles, but with the most serious respect for their capabilities and for the safety rules pertaining to them.

There really is no "gun problem" in this country. Considering the enormous quantities of firearms that are in circulation, the number of accidents with them and incidents of their misuse are astoundingly low. All the same, if I had my way, a course in firearms safety and handling would be mandatory in every high school in the land. This would do far more good than all the gun laws ever proposed, and it might even help to make us a nation of riflemen again.

That brings us to the dean of riflemen, Col. Townsend Whelen, who once declared that "Only accurate rifles are interesting." Just as the exact placement of shots is what the rifled tube is all about, the corollary is that in hunting, as in war or on the target range, only the good hits count!

The .458 Winchester Magnum

$\bigoplus$ **Chapter 22**

Generations of British heavy-game cartridges were hastened into retirement in 1956 with the birth of an American pretender. (American Rifleman *magazine, March 1984)*

The phenomenal success the .458 Winchester Magnum has enjoyed is really quite astounding. No other big-game cartridge I can think of has ever come to dominate its field quite so completely. In 1956, when it was introduced, there existed a plethora of cartridges suitable for the hunting, and stopping, of such thick-skinned, heavy-boned, and sometimes truculent African game as buffalo, rhino, and elephant. These ranged from the .404 Jeffery, the .416 Rigby, and the .450/.400 (in two case lengths!) through the original .450 Nitro Express with which John Rigby started it all in 1898, the .450 No 2, the .465, the .470, the .475, the .475 No 2, the .476, the .500, and so on up to the rather stupendous .577 and .600 Nitro Expresses of stunning fame. There were altogether too many of them, and I doubt there was ever any profit in manufacturing this ammunition.

Today they have for all practical purposes been totally supplanted by just one cartridge, the .458. This dominance is so complete that one of our best-known outdoor writers could state that on four African safaris he had not met a single professional hunter who was using anything else as a backup gun. Nevertheless, some controversy swirls around the .458, and the cartridge has its share of detractors.

They recount dismaying stories concerning malfunctions, squib loads that barely propel the bullet out of the barrel, softpoints that break up, and a general lack of penetration. One could get the impression that he would be better off tackling old *nyati* with a BB-gun!

Some of this is emotional, I believe, because it is almost invariably stressed that when Winchester announced the cartridge, it had the appalling effrontery to claim that its upstart equaled or even surpassed the noble and classic .470 Nitro Express. Surprisingly enough, it seems that many of those who are still outraged by this lèse majesté are Americans rather than African resident hunters!

Nor had I heard any such criticism of the cartridge until I arrived in America from my native Kenya. I knew full well that the limited capacity of its sawed-off .375 H&H case resulted in muzzle velocities of around 2,000 FPS rather than the advertised 2,125 FPS, and I could accept that someone had at some time experienced failures due to faulty ammunition—that has happened with every cartridge on the list, though it is luckily quite rare these days. But the suggestion that the .458 was inherently such a poor cartridge that failures were common left me incredulous. It still does. I carried a .458 for a decade of guiding clients in Africa, have fired some thousand rounds of the stuff, and have used or seen it used on a score of elephants, about 100 buffaloes, and on a few lions and smaller game. Though far from overwhelming by African standards, that much use should have revealed any common failings.

I experienced none. Never a misfire, squib load, failure to feed attributable to the cartridge, or any other such horror. It always did exactly what one would expect a 500-grain .458-caliber bullet of .341 sectional density to do when propelled at 2,000 FPS—it put a bloody big hole in anything and penetrated very well, at least as well as the .375 H&H and probably slightly better.

This was with the full-metal-jacket Winchester "solid." The Remington solids seemed to be a trifle more likely to bend or rivet, and while the softpoints of both brands were excellent on lion, they were a touch fragile for anything larger. So I always used solids on buffalo, taking care not to hit a second animal should the bullet exit the intended quarry. My brother-in-law once hit a wounded buffalo in the root of the tail. The bullet was recovered, unmarked except by the rifling, bulging the skin in the left "armpit." I thumped another one, running at seventy paces, just in front of the hip joint. That solid came out through the base of the neck. It is hard to imagine the crying need for more penetration than that, surely!

On elephant, the .458 will of course reach the brain from any angle at which that shot is normally attempted. This is no big deal—almost any cartridge from the 6.5mm Mannlicher-Schoenauer on up will do that given a proper solid. The .458 is capable of immobilizing an elephant from astern with a shot to the spine just above the tail, or by breaking a hip. Likewise it will reliably break the shoulder or upper leg bone. It might not then always get through to the chest cavity, but that does not matter. An elephant goes nowhere very fast on three legs; he is, in effect, anchored and available for the coup de grâce.

The most experienced user of the .458 that I have known was Ken Clark, who during eight years as game-control officer for the Kenya Forest Department shot some 3,000 buffaloes and 500 elephants while protecting nurseries and plantations of young trees from their depredations. He started out using a .318 Westley Richards, but when his superiors insisted on something heavier, he got one of the first .458s to arrive in the country, a Winchester Model 70 with the original barrel length of 25 inch. It served him to his perfect satisfaction both for control work and later as a backup gun while guiding clients. He was something of a gun enthusiast and had a small collection of rifles, including a .375 by Holland & Holland and a beautiful .416 Rigby. But I never knew him to use anything but the .458, or an equally well-worn .300 H&H Magnum, also a Model 70. Nor do I recollect his mentioning any failures that he could blame on the .458 cartridge or the rifle.

A lot of the control work was done at night with a spotlight and entailed fast shooting on running animals to drop several of them before the herd got away. Consequently, there were often cripples to follow-up the next morning, and Ken probably had to stop more buffalo charges than the average guy.

His advice on how to handle that situation was quite interesting: "When you have time for two shots," he said, "put the first one into the center of his chest. If that fails to stop him, or if you will only have time for one shot, then you must let him come really close, within a few feet. He comes with his nose up, pointing at you. But in the last instant before impact he drops it to present his horns. Now is your time; he is so close that you cannot possibly miss, so just drive your bullet down through the middle of the boss of his horns into the brain." Fortunately I always managed to trip them up before they got that intimate and have never had to try Ken's technique.

Though I have not found the .458 to be lacking in penetration, I felt that it might be interesting to have some measurable comparisons with other large-game cartridges. Besides the .458, I had available a .416 Taylor with 400-grain Barnes bullets, a .375 H&H, a .338 Winchester Magnum, and a .30-06. From 12 yards I fired both solid and softpoint bullets over the chronograph screens into stacks of wet magazines interspaced with planks of ¾-inch plywood. I could get five shots on each stack without the "wound channels" interfering with each other, and on each stack one of those five was a 180-grain Pointed Core-Lokt .30-06 Remington factory round, used as a control to check that the resistance offered by the various stacks was reasonably comparable.

The solids were tested on five plywood planks (each separated from its neighbor by 2 inches of wet paper) backed by a long stack of damp magazines, while the softpoint testing employed only two pieces of plywood plus the stacks of damp paper.

I was shooting from a solid sandbag rest on a sturdy table, taking great care to place each shot and to ensure that the stacked magazines were in line. All the same, half of the solids fired veered enough off course to exit through the sides of the magazine stack, and many of them had clearly tumbled. There is a common belief that roundnose solid bullets will invariably penetrate in a dead-straight line unless they are deformed by striking heavy bone. This is not so: They usually deviate to some degree. There would be nothing unusual or surprising in taking a straight-on frontal brain shot at an elephant and subsequently recovering the bullet at the base of his right ear, for example. And in many cases, where the bullet has been bent like a banana or flattened on one side, the damage was caused by the bullet tumbling, rather than vice versa.

The one .416 solid that was recovered demonstrated that a bullet can tumble without having glanced off heavy bone. It had started to tumble about a foot before it came to rest, while traveling through a homogenous medium of damp paper, and was found lying with its nose pointing about 45 degrees from the direction of travel. Yet it was totally undamaged, in such perfect shape that I would not hesitate to use it again.

Taking into account the very limited nature of this test, one can only say that the .458, .416, and .375 H&H all gave very similar penetration—something over 5 feet with solid bullets—and that no significant superiority of one over the others was established. Despite its prodigious sectional density of .409, the 600-grain Barnes solid did not do any better in the .458 than the 500-grain Hornady, likely because it could be given only 1,750 FPS velocity. It would be interesting to see what it could do in a .460 Weatherby.

Among the softpoint bullets, the 500-grain Hornady roundnose softpoint, started at 2,050 FPS in the .458, penetrated deeper than the rest by such a significant margin that its superiority was clearly established. Hornady strengthened this bullet a few years ago, I believe. Actually, it is now probably too tough to open up much on light-bodied animals such as leopard but should be fine on lion and heavier game. I would not mind using it even on buffalo, at least for the first shot, with the magazine full of solids. That should apply to the Winchester factory product as well—I have been told that the company uses Hornady bullets in its .458 ammo.

No matter how amusing tests of this sort may be, they can provide only a very rough approximation of what can be expected on game. And though a bullet which fails in damp paper is unlikely to prove satisfactory on large animals at short range, the results must be interpreted cautiously and with many reservations. I can, however, come to one firm conclusion, which coincides with game-field experience: The .416 Rigby (whose ballistics the .416 Taylor matched exactly), the .375 H&H, and the .338 Magnum are renowned for giving very deep penetration. Yet in every firing, with both solid and softnose bullets, the .458 beat them all. Tales to the effect that the .458 lacks penetration may be dismissed as nonsense.

Nevertheless, the case is short on powder space. Though both IMR 4320 and IMR 3031 have given me excellent results—up to 2,100 FPS muzzle velocity with good accuracy—full-power charges with these rather coarse-grained powders are slightly compressed. So some reloaders may prefer ball or spherical powder. Hodgdon's H335 does well, filling the case only to the base of the bullet and requiring no compression. In my rifle, using Remington cases and Winchester 120 primers, 73 grains of H335 gave 2,050 FPS with the Hornady 500-grain softpoint. There were no signs of undue pressure, despite its having been a hot summer day with the thermometer standing at 95F. The full-metal-jacketed solid is slightly longer than the softpoint, intrudes farther down into the case, and hence requires a grain or two less powder.

It should go without saying that this load is NOT necessarily safe in any other rifle, and that a handloader should start with the lowest load suggested in the reloading manuals.

Handloaders should also be aware that the Model 70 African rifles have a very long leade or forcing cone that permits the bullet about ⅞ inch of free travel before it engages the rifling. Loads that are safe in a Winchester could be excessive in custom barrels or foreign rifles if they lack this feature. My other .458 is a Westley Richards with a custom barrel whose short leade allows the bullet only $^1/_{16}$-inch free travel. With the same lot of Remington factory ammo, it gave 100 FPS higher velocity than the Model 70, though possibly a fourth of this could be attributed to its 1-inch longer barrel.

There is evidence that with straight-walled cases such as those used by most revolver cartridges, the .375 Winchester Big Bore, and the .458, the bullet should be gripped firmly enough so that on firing a certain level of pressure is reached before it starts to move, else the powder may not burn properly. Yet I have encountered .458 ammunition whose bullets were so loose in the cases that they could easily be twirled with the fingers, which might account for those squib loads that have been reported on rare occasions. A reloader should therefore take care that his cases have sufficient neck tension to grip the bullets tightly, in addition to using firm crimps. This will also prevent the bullets from being pounded down into the cases under recoil in the magazine.

It has been suggested that the .458 would be a far more effective cartridge if only its velocity could be increased by a few hundred feet per second. Of this I am somewhat skeptical. The reports I have on the performance of the .460 Weatherby in the field do not indicate any startlingly vast improvement over the .458 despite 650 FPS more velocity. With solid, nonexpanding bullets, I suspect that increasing the diameter of the bullet—or actually its frontal area, which varies as the square of its diameter—is a more effective way of boosting stopping power. But even then one has to go up to .577 before anything very appreciable is accomplished.

However, if someone must have more *oomph*, a good way to get it might be to utilize the full-length .375 Magnum case by rechambering to the old wildcat .450 Watts Magnum. The Winchester Model 70 is basically a magnum-length action, so having it altered by a competent gunsmith to handle a cartridge 3.60 inches long should not be too difficult or expensive (though it would, of course, invalidate any Winchester warranty). I approximated the .450 Watts by seating bullets out to give 3.60-inch overall cartridge length in .458 cases, and single-loaded them in my Model 70 (the bullets still had ½ inch of free travel). Using IMR 4320 powder, I was able to reach 2,250 FPS with apparently safe pressures. An advantage of the Watts chamber over some of the other .458 wildcats, at least for a resident of

Africa, is that factory .458 ammunition could still be fired in it and would likely show minimal velocity loss compared to that obtained in a standard chamber.

The .458 can, of course, be loaded down to the equivalent of any .45-70 load with the 300-, 350-, and 400-grain bullets offered by Hornady, Speer, Sierra, and Barnes, and with a large variety of cast lead bullets or even round balls. Some information on reduced and/or cast bullet loads can be found in the Speer and Lyman reloading manuals, in the *Lyman Cast Bullet Handbook,* and in Ken Waters's *Pet Loads.*

I have not gotten into any of this, because as far as I am concerned the .458 is strictly an African cartridge for dangerous game. And even there I used it mostly as a backup gun, preferring a scope-sighted .375 H&H for my own hunting except on elephant. I also advised my clients to bring a scope-sighted .375 rather than an iron-sighted .458, and for the same reason—they would be more likely to put in a killing shot with it. A scope-sighted .458 is fine, if one can handle it. But the majority of the hunters I guided would not have been able to do so; they had sufficient trouble dominating a .375 or, often enough, a .300 magnum.

The traditional open V back sight is a second-rate choice, fit only to serve as an emergency standby. The "ghost-ring" aperture (Jeff Cooper's apt description) is vastly superior under all conditions, for any purpose whatsoever. To achieve the "ghost-ring" effect with a Lyman or Williams receiver sight, simply screw out the sighting disc and fling it away. Making no conscious effort to center the bead, merely look through the resulting large aperture, seeing it, if at all, as a hazy halo—the ghost ring. Then slap the foresight on the target and shoot. With nothing to line up, and nothing to obscure half the target the way a leaf back sight does, it is lightning-quick.

But best of all, except under exceptional circumstances such as constant driving rain, are low-power scope sights of around 1.5X. It is easier to place the shot accurately with them at any range, and, used properly with both eyes open, they are the fastest of all sights.

Hunters contemplating their first African safari tend to imagine themselves warding off all manner of ferocious beasts at arm's length. It really ain't so. Chief game wardens take a frightfully dim view of professionals who allow their clients to get bashed. Consequently, we would by all means endeavor to put a stop to the play before it got anywhere near that far. I have used my

.458 far more often to stop a sick and angry beast before it got into the thick stuff, where it could cause us grief, than I have to clean up blood-and-thunder charges at zero feet. This can necessitate shooting at well over 100 yards, where the superiority of the scope is quite evident. It is also the reason I like to sight in a .458 to be 2 inches high at 100 yards. Then it will still shoot to point of aim at 25 yards but will allow a vital hit to be made on a buffalo or galloping lion with a dead-on hold out to nearly 200 paces.

The present Model 70 has one shortcoming, and that is its extractor. Dust and other muck can collect under it unseen, until suddenly it quits. That has happened to me two or three times, and can be a mite inconvenient. The remedy is to take the extractor out at regular intervals and give everything a good cleaning (taking care not to lose the plunger or its spring—it might be smart to have spares). Then the African model really is a very fine rifle, with an action that becomes superbly smooth after a little use. With its 22-inch barrel and naked weight of 9 pounds, it is an excellent compromise between portability, recoil effect, balance, and speed of mounting for use as a backup gun.

Recoil effect? Yes, indeed, a .458 kicks. It is a pain to sight it in from the bench, unless one is enough of a sissy to place a sandbag between the butt and one's shoulder, as I always do. Fired offhand, it will not hurt anyone, provided he has a firm grip on it. But I can assure you that in the excitement of using it in its designed role, it has no more apparent recoil than a .22! Come to that, my buddy Wesley Nadeau enjoys shooting his .458 off the bench or even from prone, and claims that its recoil is merely exhilarating.

The .416 Rigby has always been well-respected in Africa. Among its admirers was that thoroughly seasoned Tanganyika elephant-control officer, Commander David Enderby Blunt, RN, who wrote the book *Elephant.* The last time I hunted with his son, who was one of the best hunters of all the professionals I knew, quiet little Nicky Blunt of the raucous laugh was still using his father's old .416. He said that he was perfectly content with it—it had never let him down, and he was unable to tell that the bigger boomer killed any better.

The .416 Taylor, a wildcat on a necked-down .458 case, easily matches the original ballistics of the Rigby. I have seen it used on only one hunt, but it was mighty impressive on the three buffaloes taken with it, and the 400-grain Barnes solids performed to perfection. In my tests the Barnes 400-grain softpoint with the .049-inch-thick jacket expanded well while retaining 79 percent of its weight for deep penetration. It should make super lion medicine. An American hunter going to Africa for any of the Big Five would do well to consider this cartridge, if he is a handloader. It is probably almost as good a stopper as the .458, while having noticeably less recoil and a somewhat flatter trajectory. It should be able to do most of the work of both the .458 and the .375.

But not quite all of it. The .375 does shoot flatter, quite significantly with either the 300-grain Sierra boattail or the 270-grain Hornady spire point, making it a more suitable cartridge for any of the antelope and zebra. Despite some opinions to the contrary, I have always found the .375 to be very reliable on buffaloes and elephants when used with a good solid like the Hornady, and excellent for lions with the Winchester 270-grain Power Point.

I also like the .338, and suspect that it may be equal to, or possibly even better than, the .375 Magnum on any American game and all the thin-skinned stuff in Africa including maybe lion. I have seen it used on only a couple of buffaloes but got the distinct impression that it thumped them less hard than a .375. When it comes to using solid bullets, the .375 H&H is most likely superior.

If I were returning to Africa, what would I take for dangerous game? I am not quite sure. The .416 really appeals to me, and would be most tempting. But it is a wildcat, and ammo could become a problem in an African country where handloading is verboten, whereas every professional hunter has a stock of .458 and .375 rounds that his clients left behind. Nor can the .416 on its own fill all the requirements of an African resident hunter quite as well as a combination of the other two. So I guess I would stick to my original battery, a scope-sighted .375 for all-round use on the larger game, with a .458 as a stopper.

I am a timid fellow who is easily frightened. But when the situation gets bristly and it's time to dive into the bush after something that might resent me, there really is nothing I would rather have in my hands than a good Winchester Model 70 chambered for the .458 Magnum. Because I reckon that Winchester's claim is justified: In the field it will indeed do anything its famous predecessors, the .450, .465, or .470, ever did, and with the superb Hornady bullets available today it quite likely surpasses them. Winchester's .458 is a fine round that has deservedly become a classic African cartridge in its own right, on its own merits.

"...rhino's characteristic response to danger, real or imagined, is to charge in its general direction, making as ...ch noise as possible in the hope of frightening away whatever it may be." (chapter 4)

Finn's brother-in-law Peter Davey used his Brno Mauser 7x57 on this leopard, circa 1960. (chapter 1)

Shortly after arriving in Africa, the author's father acquired a Mauser M98 in 7x57 and was soon puttin to use on troublesome lions, circa 1928. (chapter 1)

nes McAusland took this tusker with a .375 H&H Magnum, a typical example of a rifle used for dangerous me. (chapter 2)

kudu's heavy, ridged horns typically make 2½ complete spirals and may tower four feet above the head. etting two kudus in two days in Kenya is fantastic." (chapter 3)

"The rhino has keen hearing, with large, trumpet-shaped ears, constantly swiveling around independently pick up the faintest whisper of sound." (chapter 4)

"While most lions are shot over bait, some adventurous hunters prefer the challenge of tracking a cat in th cover." (chapter 5)

could well be said that the lion is the 'King of Beasts.' " (chapter 5)

appy clients with a good lion." (chapter 6)

Richard McDaniel's 42-inch buffalo is the kind of trophy any hunter would dream of. (chapter 7)

n once saw a buffalo bull chase away several lions that were harassing another buff. "Encountering small, 't-knit bachelor groups of protective Cape buffaloes adds a degree of excitement to a safari." (chapter 7)

n shooting the .470 from the bench. (chapter 8)

Finn's offhand position with the .470. "A fi[rm] grip is necessary!" (chapter 8)

"The traditional fast reloading technique." (chapter 8)

"The Keneyathlon Challenge—at each firing point there would be a proctor to point out the targets and marked areas where we had to shoot; to inform us of the drill for that stage; and to record our scores." (chapter 9)

"One of 11 competitors prepares to set off in the first running of the Keneyathlon under the watchful eyes of event officials. Speed on foot and accurate shooting were involved." (chapter 9)

Finn fires on a target gong while a proctor scores his shots. "The distances had to be estimated." (chapter 9)

"Some targets were best taken from prone position." (chapter 9)

he Keneyathlon Challenge. Finn reaches for a cartridge with the majestic Sangre de Cristo Mountains lew Mexico) as a backdrop." (chapter 9)

nn culled a whitetail despite concern that he might "mar the costly Rigby finish." (chapter 10)

*The author pronounces Remington's .416 round a worthy claimant as a premier all-round heavy/dangero[us]
cartridge. (chapter 11)*

...od stock design moderated the .416's recoil, but Finn said, "twenty shots from the bench were enough!" ...apter 11)

Aimpoint was used to experiment for the chapter discussing which is faster, scope or irons?" (chapter 12)

While son Harald operates the stopwatch, Finn turns and puts an aimed shot into a stationary target as p[...] of his testing. (chapter 12)

Dunlop Farren with Finn and Kinuno, the tracker, after taking an oryx with his .338. (chapter 13)

…n, who says he personally favors the .338 only where really heavy bullets are used, took this 6x6 elk in …itish Columbia's Muskwa River Region. (chapter 13)

Fitted with a fiberglass stock and used as a loaner, Aagaard's .338 proved very effective on big game. (chapter 1

The .243 bullet from a Ruger Model 77 performed perfectly for the author's son Harald on this whitetail, but he fe
it lacks the bone-smashing penetration needed for game much over 200 pounds. (chapter 15)

and bottom: "Besides being fun, shooting up water-filled, gallon milk jugs does, indeed, provide a dramatic *stration of energy at work. The trouble is that the body of an animal really does not very closely resemble* *ssel full of homogeneous, incompressible liquid."* (chapter 15)

Berit poses with a 300-pound aoudad ram taken by a client using Finn's old Brno Mauser 7x57mm. (chapter 1)

"My wife, Berit, hunts whitetail with a 7mm-08, and yes, she wears a kilt and gets her hands good and bloody!" (chapter 17)

Through the Depression and WW II, Aagaard's father was expected to provide meat to help feed the numerous workers on the coffee and sisal plantations he managed. (chapter 17)

"The Mauser extractor is unquestionably the most positive ever used on a bolt gun." (chapter 19)

Finn tests the new Kimber Model 84. (chapter 18)

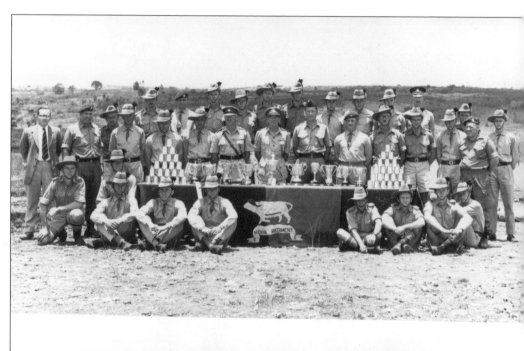

WINNERS EAST AFRICA COMMAND RIFLE MEETING 1960

The Kenya Regiment Team. Finn Aagaard, standing third from left, poses behind the booty at the East Africa Command Rifle Meeting. (chapter 21)

p and bottom: Still searching for the ideal deer cartridge, Aagaard decided to try a turn-of-the-century und renowned for its deep penetration and gentle recoil. (chapter 20)

"Recoil effect? Yes, indeed the .458 kicks. Fired offhand, though, it will not hurt anyone, provided he ha[s] firm grip on it. I can assure you that in the excitement of using it in its designed role, it has no more appar[ent] recoil than a .22!" (chapter 22)

"I used the .375 H&H for most of my own buffalo hunting—because I felt that I could place my shots m[ore] accurately with it than with the iron-sighted .458, and that counts for more than even 200 grains of ex[tra] lead. And I almost invariably carried it when guiding hunters on nondangerous game—the antelope, zeb[ra,] warthog, and such that we illogically lumped together as "plains game," though much of it actually dwel[t in] the bush or on the hill." (chapter 23)

"Matched with the right loads, the .30-06 can handle any game from a turkey to a trophy Alaskan moose like this 66¾-inch bull." (chapter 24)

"I still prefer to hunt on my lonesome; it is by far the most satisfying and rewarding way, except when my wife can accompany me." (chapter 28)

"A stormy day on the Alaska Peninsula produced this big boar for Jim Clifton (left) and Finn. Clifton took

...phy, a ten-footer, with a Whitforth in .375 H&H." (chapter 25)

"Finn's partner Joe Cheffings shot this impressive buffalo bull as they hunted along the Athi River during honey-gathering season." (chapter 26)

"...e staff cut the meat into strips about an inch thick, salted it lightly, and strung it up around camp to sun ...e it into the African equivalent of jerky." (chapter 26)

...gaard's high regard for the .280 Remington (and its ballistic twin, the 7x64) is based on years of field ...erience on game ranging from small gazelles to this 6-point bull elk he shot with a .280 Remington loaded ...h a 160-grain Nosler Partition. (chapter 29)

Sasha's 70-plus-pound elephant was taken with Finn's .375 after a long stalk. Facing are Finn and Kinuno, Fi *loyal tracker. (chapter 27)*

An angry elephant at close quarter. (chapter 27) (Photo by Joe Cheffings)

The author and his longtime tracker and friend Kinuno Mbogo. When Berit visited Kenya after Finn's death, she handed this picture to Kinuno, which was taken when she and Finn visited Kenya in 1990. "The pleasure of being together again showed in their faces." (chapter 36)

...erit Aagaard, the author's wife, with Kinuno the tracker and son Erik holding a Tommy (Thomson gazelle) ...at Berit had shot. (chapter 36)

Kinuno Mbogo and the kongoni *or Coke hartebeest—his first game animal—he shot with a 7x64. "His sm* *reached almost beyond his ears!" (chapter 35)*

The .375 H&H Magnum

$\oplus$ **Chapter 23**

All of us have our pet guns, and Aagaard is no exception. His all-time favorite is a caliber that after seven decades is still unsurpassed as a big *big-game cartridge.* (American Rifleman *magazine, January 1984*)

Though I have owned, used, and loved many sporting rifles, my pet of pets, the last gun of mine that I would ever part with (I might even have it buried with me), is an ancient Winchester Model 70 with all the bluing long since worn off its action and 25-inch barrel.

It is chambered for an even more venerable game-thumper, the .375 Belted Rimless Magnum Nitro Express that Messrs. Holland & Holland came out with way back in 1912, but which is still unsurpassed in its designed role as an all-round *big* big-game cartridge.

It was well worn when I got it in 1969, with its bore darkened from twenty-one years of use with corrosive Kynoch ammo. But the rifling was still sharp, and its accuracy remains good. In fact, I believe that I shoot better at game with this rifle than with any other I have owned, because its ten-pound heft and the "hang" of its substantial barrel allow it to settle down very steadily.

The original stock was split from the recoil shoulder to behind the upper tang, as was quite common with these Model 70s in that caliber, so I replaced it with a very early .458 stock, which also cracked! What appeared to be crossbolts were merely glued-in plastic plugs; the glue failed, the plugs loosened, and the stock split.

The plug holes were too large in diameter for the only suitable bolts I had available, so I filled them with fiberglass before putting the crossbolts in, let everything set, then filed the whole mess down level with the outside of the stock. It looks a bit odd, but has held solidly for fourteen years now.

The Model 70 came with an archaic scope whose cross hairs were way off center when the outfit was zeroed. I immediately replaced that relic with the Weaver K2.5 that I am still using and which is, I am convinced, the ideal sight for this rifle.

A friend of mine insists that a rifle as versatile as the .375 must have a variable-power scope, which seems logical until one has learned better. Though I do not really care for varipower scope sights in any case—finding them to be for the most part an unnecessary complication—I have to admit that there are circumstances under which they can be useful.

But, most emphatically, not on a rifle for dangerous game. There are several reasons for this, but the main one is that sooner or later the darned thing will somehow have got turned up to its highest magnification when decisive, close-range shooting is exigent, and that could be unfortunate.

At close range the 2½X scope is as fast as, if not faster than, any iron sight while still having plenty of resolving power for animals on which one would use a .375 out to all sensible ranges. Whether the work was collecting a bitty little Thomson gazelle for the pot at 250 or 300 yards (which I have done, but rarely—I will make every effort to get closer) or finishing off a wounded buffalo at 25 feet, I have never felt the need for either more or less magnification.

A few weeks after I had acquired the .375, my partner Joe Cheffings and I hied off down to Ray Mayer's huge ranch below Voi, close-by Kenya's Tsavo National Park, where I bashed an elephant. Because the bull was moving, I used a lung shot (with a .458) rather than go for the brain, so he ran a few hundred yards.

But because the bull's tracks were wiped out by stampeding mobs of panic-stricken cows, and because it was during the rains when every wait-a-bit thornbush and twisted-limbed Commiphora tree on the place was enthusiastically engaged in putting on a full year's growth in a few short weeks, we did not find him for three days, and then only because we smelled him.

He was lying propped upright against a tree, and there were lion tracks all around him. As we pulled his tusks, which were loose in their sockets by then, we saw that the lions had been feeding on him behind the ears, where the skin is quite thin.

When Ray heard about them, he became quite agitated.

"I want you to shoot those confounded lions!" he demanded. "They have been killing my cattle, and this is the perfect chance to get rid of them and save me endless grief. Take my 6-volt flashlight and go sit by your elephant tonight; they are bound to come back to it."

So Joe, Kinuno the tracker, and I went back to the elephant that evening, found a suitable spot about 30 yards from it, cleared some intervening brush and put it in a semicircle behind us, and sat down to wait. It was hardly full dark before we heard a strange thumping noise from the direction of the carcass.

I nudged Kinuno, and he turned on the flashlight to reveal a lion on top of the elephant, tearing at the flesh behind the ear so vigorously that the whole head was thumping up and down—which says something about the awesome strength of these cats. Startled by the light, it sprang into the darkness before we could shoot. We turned out the flashlight and awaited developments.

Presently there came a faint pattering that circled round behind us, followed by sniffing and a heavy, exhaling sigh, just a few feet away. The lion had come to discover what that strange light meant. It was a little tense, but with the lion so close that he could have been among us before we had time to turn around, there was nothing for it but to keep absolutely still—the ball was definitely in *simba*'s court.

A few years passed, then the lion moved softly away, and presently there were renewed thumpings and crunchings from the direction of the elephant carcass. This time we let it feed for a good ten minutes before flicking on the light. Now there were two lions, one feeding as before, the other standing on the ground.

The lion on the elephant spun around instantly, but then stood still long enough for me to get the cross hairs onto its shoulders. At the shot it catapulted off the elephant with a roaring cough, there was a crackling of brush, a series of diminishing growls, then silence. "Got him!" I assured Joe with absolute certainty.

We gave it a few minutes, then started toward the elephant with Kinuno swinging the light from side to side. Suddenly there was a movement over to our left, and there was the second lion slipping back toward the elephant. As it passed between two trees the cross hairs were plastered on its chest so nicely that the gun went off, seemingly of its own volition.

A crashing rush was followed by a complete hush, no growls, no groans, nothing. We climbed up on the elephant and shone the dimming flashlight around. No lions.

"You shot awfully fast on that last one," Joe said, accusingly. True, and though the sight-picture had been perfect, some unnoticed limb could have deflected the bullet. . . .

To have gone stumbling around in the dark looking for possibly wounded and angry lions with a fading flashlight would have been more than a little stupid, it might have been terminal. Joe and I voiced the same brilliant thought in unison, "Let's fetch the Land Rover!" Kinuno had to do quite a bit of chopping with his machete to achieve that, but then with the aid of the Rover's spotlight we quickly found both lions, lying within 20 feet of each other.

Two lions with two consecutive shots is not a shabby start to any rifle's career, and from that auspicious beginning it has never looked back.

Various clients, sensible chaps who saw no point in buying a heavy rifle just for the one African hunt that they would ever make, borrowed it to take a few elephant, a couple of leopard, most of the antelope species including both 1,500-pound eland and one 10-pound dik-dik (this last with a full-metal-jacketed 'solid' bullet), and close on 50 buffaloes.

Apart from using it for most of my own buffalo hunting—because I felt that I could place my shots more accurately with it than with the iron-sighted .458, and that counts for more than even 200 grains of extra lead—I almost invariably carried it when guiding hunters on non-dangerous game, the antelope, zebra, warthog and such that we illogically lumped together as "plains game," though much of it actually dwelt in the bush or on the hill.

This was partly because in many areas one could stumble over a lion or disturb a cantankerous old Col. Blimp of a rhino. But it was primarily because such use often enough necessitated shooting at the rear end of a wounded and very frightened animal hightailing it over the horizon, and I do not know of anything that handles that chore better than a .375 H&H.

Under normal conditions, with chest shots from reasonably fair angles and decent ranges, I have never been able to ascertain that the .375 magnum killed game of this class any better than lesser cartridges such as the .30-06.

I well remember shooting a 150-pound impala solidly through the lungs with a 270-grain softpoint, only to have it run 90 paces before dropping. Actually, I believe the .270 Winchester with 130-grain bullets, for one, will give a higher percentage of spectacularly sudden kills on animals of up to about 350 pounds in weight.

But when it is a case of having to break down animals such as zebra, wildebeest, hartebeest, kudu, or oryx—beasts approaching elk in size—that are fleeing from the gun and often at some distance, then I am certain from what I have seen that the heavier bullet of the .375 can make a slight but discernible difference.

While there is pretty general agreement among those qualified to hold an opinion that the .375 is a capital lion gun, some controversy exists about its use on elephant and buffalo. My own experience is that, given suitable bullets, it kills buffalo about as quickly as anything in the .450 to .500 Nitro Express class, particularly as the majority of hunters are apt to place their shots better with it than with a "heavy."

For reasons that are no doubt largely psychological—its massive bullet is quite reassuring—I always carried a .458 when hunting elephant. But my partner Joe took all his jumbos with a .375, and it is certainly "enough gun" for a visiting hunter who will be backed up by a competent professional.

I have heard of some dramatic failures with the .375, and have experienced a couple myself due to bad bullets. Some chaps, of course, will always blame the lousy gun rather than admit that they wobbled, flinched, or got excited and jerked the trigger. But it is a sad fact that some inadequate bullets have been produced for the .375.

One of them, I regret to have to say, was the Winchester 300-grain FMJ with the little flat point. It would bend, rivet, split its jacket, or go to pieces all too readily, and was thus not a proper solid.

It worked OK on buffalo—most of the time—when nothing better was available, but I would not touch it for elephant. The roundnose solids produced by Remington, Kynoch, and Norma were all good, the RWS was even better, and the fine Hornady 300-grain FMJ is as good a solid as has ever been made.

In Kenya the reloading of cartridges was not permitted, so apart from the occasional handloads brought in by clients, I used only factory ammunition. Of all the softnose bullets that I tried, which included those loaded by Kynoch, Norma, DWM, Winchester, and Remington, the 270-grain Winchester Power-Point became my favorite.

I have never had one of these bullets break up or otherwise misbehave; every single one that I have ever recovered has displayed such perfect mushrooming that

Winchester could proudly have used it in its advertising. This excellent bullet is far better for any purpose than the rather erratic 300-grain Silvertip, in my opinion.

I used to hunt buffalo with a softpoint bullet run "up the spout" with a carefully placed first shot, plus a magazine full of solids for follow-up shots, reasoning that if they were required, the creature would either be going or coming straight on. That beautiful theory somehow never quite worked out in practice!

Anyway, after I had three different softpoints blow up in buffalo shoulder joints or on the upper leg bone and fail to penetrate, I quit doing that. Since then I have never used anything but solid bullets on buffalo, which is fine except that one must take care not to wound a second animal, as these bullets will go clean through on broadside shots as often as not.

There is a good selection of bullets available to the handloader. Apart from the "solid," Hornady also offers a traditional roundnose 300-grain softpoint and a 270-grain Spire Point that gives a decently flat trajectory when pushed to 2,700 FPS.

A 30-year-old Holland & Holland brochure recommends ". . . 235-grain Copper Point bullet for thin-skinned game at long range . . ." This load is no longer available, but Speer has a handsome semispitzer softpoint at that weight that can be given 2,900 FPS, when it will shoot as flat as the 150-grain spitzer from a .30-06 out to 300 yards.

Speer also offers the 285-grain Grand Slam, which it claims is ". . . ample for all big game worldwide except for rhino and elephant" (Speer Reloading Manual No. 10). This is a premium bullet with two different hardnesses of lead and a complicated jacket. It is frightfully expensive—I'm reminded of J. P. Morgan's remark to the effect that if you have to ask what it costs, you cannot afford it—but for some purposes it is definitely worth it.

The most beautiful .375 bullet of them all is Sierra's 300-grain Spitzer Boat Tail, with its highly impressive ballistic coefficient of .583. When started out at the 2,600 FPS possible in most .375 rifles, it has practically the same drop at 300 yards as the 235- and 270-grain bullets, and increasingly surpasses them as the range extends beyond that.

This illustrates the often overlooked fact that the .375 is not only a close-range stopper but also a very fine long-range cartridge for the larger game. When employing the 300-grain boattail, it can for this purpose stand to be sighted for 250 yards, when it should give a vital hit on elk and similar-size African antelope out to 325 yards with a center-of-the-chest hold, or to a little over 400 yards with a hold on the top of the shoulder.

If I had to shoot at animals such as elk at very long range—something that I will by all means avoid doing—I would prefer this load in the .375 to any .300 magnum, for instance, because the .375 derives more of its power from bullet weight (and diameter), which remains constant, than from velocity, which diminishes rapidly as the range lengthens.

This bullet does have one failing that is common to all the Sierra boattails I have tried—the lead core tends to separate from the jacket when the bullet meets substantial resistance at high impact velocities. The jacket is thick and does not shatter; rather it looks to me as if the softer lead tries to expand faster than its envelope, causing it to creep forward out of the still-intact shank of the jacket.

I spent a morning slamming various .375 softpoint bullets into several different test media, and every Sierra recovered exhibited core-jacket separation. But in almost every case the core and jacket were lying together, which indicates that the separation did not occur until near the end of the bullet's penetration.

So how much does it matter? One friend tells of smashing both shoulders of a bull elk with it, while another reported that the 300-grain Sierra gave outstandingly good results not only on several of the larger African antelope and on lion but also on Cape buffalo. On the other hand, another friend swears that it failed him by going to pieces on the shoulder of a truly monstrous brown bear.

The Speer 285-grain Grand Slam gave the greatest penetration by a small but consistent margin in all my tests, and never showed a sign of wanting to break up or lose its lead core. Besides a jacket that becomes very heavy behind the cannelure, it also has a partial partition a third of the way up from the base that seems to serve very well to hold the lead in place.

I believe that this is the stoutest softpoint presently available for the .375, and would confidently bet my life on it. Even so, if I were to be granted one wish concerning the .375, it would be that Nosler would once again produce a Partition bullet for it. A 300-grain semispitzer would be ideal, I believe.

Du Pont's IMR 4064 was always a good powder in the .375 H&H, and is still my favorite with all bullet weights up to and including the 285-grain Speer. The reloading manuals seem to agree that IMR 4350 will give the highest velocities with 300-grain bullets, but only with charges that are heavily compressed. So I have settled on from 75 to 77 grains of Winchester's 760 Ball powder with the various 300-grain bullets, which requires no compression of the powder, produces velocities in the 2,500- to 2,550-FPS range, and gives good accuracy in my rifle.

If I were still confined to factory ammo, I would sight my old cannon in so that the Remington or other good 300-grain solid hit point of aim at 100 yards, when the 270-grain Winchester Power-Point would strike 3 inches high at that range, which is perfect. That combination should most adequately serve any purpose to which a .375 H&H can reasonably be put.

In handloads, I think I would use the Sierra boattail for medium game up to elk in size, and for all long-range work. But I would change to the Speer Grand Slam if I expected to have to bash large bears, lions, moose, or big bull elk at close range, while the Hornady 300-grain solid would meet all requirements should buffalo or elephant be on the menu.

Though full-power loads are usually not unduly destructive when used on the smaller big-game animals—presumably because such targets do not offer enough resistance to cause the heavy bullets to set up violently—reduced loads that work well on deer at moderate ranges and are gentle on the shoulder can easily be developed for the .375 magnum.

To get the requisite expansion, the 235-grain Speer—which has worked well for me when loaded to 2,300 FPS with 64 grains of IMR 4064—is probably the heaviest bullet that should be used, while the 220-grain Hornady at not over 2,200 FPS might be better. But because I find little joy in lugging a 10-pound rifle around after whitetails, I have not pursued this theme very far!

And so we come to the question of recoil. A .375 magnum kicks, no question about it, but not unbearably so in a rifle of suitable weight. Several clients, upon trying my 10-pound M70, have remarked in surprise that it really was not much worse than an 8-pound .30-06, and most of them shot quite adequately with it on game.

One does not handle a piece of this power with the same light touch one might employ with a varmint or silhouette rifle. The butt must be solidly against the shoulder, and a firm grasp of the fore-end is essential if one wishes to remain in control. Practice helps, and here reduced loads can be valuable in allowing one to become familiar with the rifle while working up gradually to full-power loads.

The .375 H&H is a classic African cartridge, the most useful all-round big-game rifle for that continent that has ever been produced. But what about North America? I am told that Alaskan guides like it as a backup gun on bear—I'd go along with that—and it would not be too much out of place on a moose or elk hunt. But neither would it be necessary!

Dangerous game aside, we probably do not need anything more powerful than a .30-06, while cartridges such as the .338, 8mm Remington Magnum, or the .300 magnums are undoubtedly ample for anything we have on this side of the pond.

Nevertheless, hundreds of .375s have been sold that will never see Africa or Alaska, and if someone gets a romantic kick out of using this legendary cartridge of famous renown on elk and moose, or even on white-tailed deer, there is nothing wrong in that—and I expect it might possibly get the job done! Because "getting the job done" is what the .375 H&H is all about—it has been doing exactly that for seventy years on elephants, on jack rabbits, and on everything in between.

I am not much of a trophy collector, valuing the few heads I have around the place mostly for the experiences they recall. It follows that that battered and evocative old .375 is by far the most valued hunting trophy I own. I have only to glance at it for the memories to come flooding back.

Then I am reminded of Eric Lindstrom's (Soren Lindstrom's father) tremendous buffalo that he picked off with it from a large herd at 150 yards. (He is a fine shot, and we were not going to get any closer.) The bull staggered into a covert of thornbush and stood facing us with only its head visible, some 200 yards away across a gully.

I sat down with the .375, tightened the loop of its military-type sling around my upper arm, and squeezed off a shot with the cross hairs level with the top of the boss of its horns. The bull disappeared, but when Soren Lindstrom (the PH who was guiding his father on this trip) and I worked our way most carefully into that cover from behind, we found it dead with the bullet hole precisely in the center of its forehead.

I remember the fantastic stalk we made on Lowell Douglas's greater kudu, high up on the shoulder of Donyo Nyiro, the Dark Mountain. And the leopard that came to the lion kill, and the lioness that almost came into the blind with us, which would have made it rather crowded in there. And the elephants that fed on the acacia trees over our tents one night on the Uaso Rongai, treading so delicately that they disturbed not a single guy rope.

I remember standing in bright sunshine in a dew-wet glade up in the Lolgorien forest, contemplating a single drop of blood that gleamed accusingly on a leaf where the dark tunnel led into the somber shadows. And the easy comradeship and slow, relaxed talk by the campfire with Kilimanjaro looming in the moonlight over the flat-topped thorn trees behind the camp on the Lolterish stream.

And then I remember the buffalo, the only one I brought with me out of Africa, that I hunted entirely on my own. No guides, no gunbearers, no trackers. Just me and the old bull . . . and the .375.

The .30-06, the American Standard

 **Chapter 24**

For more than seven decades American sportsmen have made the '06 the yardstick by which other cartridges are measured. The author, long a hunting guide both in this country and in Africa, says its versatility is unmatched. (American Rifleman *magazine, April 1983)*

The .30-06 is the greatest general-purpose, big-game cartridge ever produced. That, at least, seems to be the opinion of American hunters, who keep the ancient round at the top of the sales list year after year.

Fifty years ago this would not have been surprising, because apart from the .270 (whose light bullet was suspect), it really had no competition in its class. It was the serious trophy hunter's cartridge par excellence.

Grancel Fitz used it to bag every available species of North American game, Hosea Sarber and Jay Williams bashed innumerable Alaskan brown bears with it, Stewart Edward White used the '06 on three long African hunts and rather preferred it to the .405 Winchester on lions, while Col. Townsend Whelen, after testing it meticulously, was firm in his praise of the round.

The .30 Government cartridge, Model of 1906, ruled high-power target shooting, regularly won the 1,000-yard Wimbledon Cup event, and, according to Jack O'Connor, was even handloaded with 7.62mm pistol bullets for use on varmints.

Nowadays it is very different, and a lot of the .30-06's ground has been shot away from under it. The .308 has taken over the target shooting role, the magnums dominate the 1,000-yard matches, the long-range varmint poppers do it with hotshot .22s, those who roam the globe seeking record-book trophies and the Weatherby Award use 7mm or .300 magnums almost to a man, while no one in his right mind would dream of jousting with dangerous bears while carrying anything less potent than a .338 Winchester Magnum.

The competition today is fierce indeed, and for a 77-year-old cartridge to remain at the top of the heap, it must have a lot on the ball, no?

That the .30-06 has. It has been described as being exceptionally versatile, as being a "workhorse," and as having all the recoil and power that the mythical average hunter can handle. The fact that these are tired old clichés detracts not one whit from their truth!

What the .30-06 does is provide absolutely reliable killing power on all American game (except perhaps the largest bears), with bearable recoil in a portable rifle that need not weigh more than 8 pounds or have a barrel longer than 22 inches. Such a combination is equally at home in the whitetail woods, on the antelope prairies, or slogging up a sheep mountain; and it works as well on a moose in a Canadian willow patch as it does on javelina in the Texas brush.

More different factory loads are produced for it than for any other cartridge—Accelerator, 110 grains, 125-, 150-, 165-, 180-, 200-, and 220 grains. And the plethora of jacketed .308-caliber bullets available to the handloader is mind-boggling! Actually, though, three big-game loads and a few special-purpose ones will take care of any conceivable situation.

For long-range antelope, deer, and likely caribou, a good 150-grain spitzer boattail (or flat-base) such as the Sierra or Speer at 3,000 FPS cannot be beaten, and will match the trajectory of a similar 130-grain .270 bullet (3,100 FPS) out to 400 yards. Sighted 3 inches high at 100 yards, it should be on at 275 and have a point-blank range (where the bullet does not drop more than 4 inches below line of sight) of about 325 yards. At 400 yards the bullet would strike about 13½ inches low, compared to 12 inches low for the .270.

For the chap who does not reload, Federal offers the 150-grain Sierra boattail bullet at 2,910 FPS in its Premium line. The trajectory should be almost identical, giving one inch more drop at 300 yards, at the most.

These high-velocity loads are quite destructive at close range. We eat a lot of white-tailed deer; they are small and seldom taken at over 100 yards. So for a meat load I use any 150-grain softpoint bullet with 46 or 47 grains of 4895 powder (either brand), which gives about 2,550 FPS velocity, excellent accuracy, and such mild recoil that my small 12-year-old son handles it easily. An even milder load is the 125-grain Sierra with one grain less of the same powder.

Both of these have given perfect results on our 100-pound deer, killing well without messing up too much meat.

Any load that is reliably adequate for the game will occasionally do a lot of damage, especially if it hits heavy bone. But I have the distinct impression that if impact velocities can be kept below 2,400 to 2,500 FPS, the incidence of bruised and bloodshot meat is greatly reduced.

The .30-06 is hardly the ideal varmint cartridge, but some may want to use it on pest species to keep in practice between hunting seasons—not a dumb idea at all! In my rifle the 110-grain Sierra hollowpoint with 54 grains of IMR 3031 gives nice accuracy, and at 3,275 FPS the trajectory should be similar to that of the .223 Remington with 55-grain bullets.

Turkey and whitetail seasons run concurrently here. So I have spent some time trying to find a turkey load that could be used with the rifle sighted for its standard big-game load. Presently I use the Hornady 150-grain full-metal-jacket boattail bullet with 41 grains of IMR 3031. This strikes 1 inch high at 100 yards, and has sufficient accuracy and 2,300 FPS of muzzle velocity. It worked faultlessly on the only gobbler I have so far taken with it.

A good plinking load that is on point of aim at 50 yards in my rifle consists of the 100-grain Hornady "Short Jacket" (or Speer "Plinker") with 25 grains of IMR 4198. I carry a couple of these to administer the coup de grâce when required. At a muzzle velocity of around 1,800 FPS, they do not seem to expand, so they could no doubt be used on small game such as cottontails and squirrels. I would not know—I have a very fine .22 rimfire that I use for that purpose!

The classic .30-06 big-game load is the 180-grain bullet at 2,700 FPS. That is still the best all-round load, for my money, though a handloader with a strong, modern rifle can push it up to around 2,800 FPS (most manuals list one or more maximum loads giving that velocity).

I have seen a tremendous amount of game taken with that bullet weight; in Africa everything from 50-pound gazelles to deer-size impala, leopard, zebra, 1,500-pound eland, and 2,500-pound giraffe. In this country, mouflon sheep, white-tailed deer, Barbary sheep, pronghorn antelope, hogs, Axis deer, fallow deer, and elk have fallen to the loading. So reliable have I found it to be that I have to conclude that if it lives on this continent (those confounded great bears excluded) and one fails to kill it cleanly with a good 180-grain bullet from a .30-06, the fault is entirely the shooter's—he did not point it right!

Both the Winchester and Remington 180-grain ammunition have worked well for me, but in handloads I like the Hornady 180-grain Spire Point "Interlock." Loaded with about 56 grains of IMR 4350 to give 2,750 FPS, it is very accurate in my rifle and has given excellent results on all sorts of game. Those recovered so far have all exhibited textbook mushrooming to about .60-inch diameter while retaining 55 to 65 percent of their original weight.

All the same, for elk and moose I would change to the 180-grain Nosler Partition bullet, and in factory ammo would choose the same bullet, which again is available in the Federal Premium line.

When zeroed 3 inches high at 100 yards, the 180-grain spitzer at 2,750 to 2,800 FPS is on at 250 yards and about 4 inches low at 300 yards. This gives it a point-blank range out to that distance on deer and pronghorns, or perhaps 50 yards farther on bull elk and moose. And 300 yards is as far as I care to shoot at any game.

The 165-grain bullets are described as having almost the flat-shooting ability of the 150-grain spitzers and almost the effectiveness on big game of the 180-grainers. Which also suggests that they do neither job perfectly! A 165-grain bullet can be given not much over 100 FPS more velocity than a 180-grain one, resulting in not quite 1 inch less drop at 400 yards—a difference so meaningless that I will simply stay with the 180-grain bullets. In all honesty, though, their performance on game is not very different to similar 180-grain bullets, and I expect they would give satisfactory performance on animals up to elk size.

When it comes to close quarters on the biggest game, a 220-grain roundnose softpoint at 2,410 FPS (factory figure) or up to 2,550 FPS in handloads has always been the traditional choice. Barnes offers a 250-grain RNSP that has the greatest sectional density—.376—of any commercial bullet under .458 inch of which I am aware. This can be given 2,300 FPS, which ought to perforate anything that walks from stem to stern, and should make the .30-06 fully the equal of the renowned .318 Westley Richards of African fame. Maybe, but I ran a few tests and now have my doubts.

A client of mine happened to clobber a big six-point, ten-year-old bull elk. We cut it up for him, so I had fresh elk leg and shoulder bones to play with.

I clamped them in front of a cardboard box full of wet magazines and shot through them with various loads, comparing two bullets at a time on the identical bones of a pair. I followed that up by shooting them through two 1-inch pine boards into wet paper, arranged this way: ½-inch paper, a pine board, another ½-inch paper, the second plank, then stacked damp magazines. I could get five shots on each target, so I tested most of the heavy bullets three times, once on each of three different stacks. Then I had enough material left over to test some other loads once each. Though far from conclusive, the results were quite interesting.

The performance of the 200-grain and 250-grain RNSP bullets was rather disappointing. They had a tendency to come apart or lose their lead cores, and the 200-grain boattail bettered them, while the 180-grain Hornady came within a hair of matching them. If these bullets have any purpose, it is as stoppers to be slammed into large, heavy-boned game at close range. I have to infer that they are not up to the work.

The 150-grain boattail surprised me. It penetrated less than the others, as anticipated, but it got through a hefty bone and stayed in one piece. It should do a good job on the small- to medium-size game it was designed for.

Two other conclusions can be drawn. The first is that how an expanding bullet is constructed matters much more than its weight or its sectional density. And the second is that when the utmost in bone-smashing penetration is imperative, the 200-grain Nosler Partition bullet is the only way to go. In each test it outperformed every other bullet by a wide and significant margin—except for the 180-grain Nosler, which came very close. It is interesting to note that both the Noslers penetrated a shade more than the 300-grain Sierra boattail fired from a .375 H&H!

If for some strange reason I could have only one load for the .30-06, the 180-grain Nosler Partition would be it. Despite its exceptional penetrative qualities, the front end of this bullet is quite soft and expands readily enough to give good results on even the smaller animals.

I can recollect only two men who are definitely "agin'" the .30-06—Col. Charles Askins and Elmer Keith. The Colonel's aversion, apparently, has little to do with the cartridge's effectiveness but stems mainly from the fact that it bores him!

Guns and Hunting

I have the very greatest respect for Elmer Keith's knowledge and experience—he has indeed "been there"—but in the matter of the .30-06 his testimony is so diametrically opposed to that of every other experienced user of the caliber that I have to discount it. It should be remembered that many .308 bullets of 50 years ago were rather sorry, and I can find no evidence that Keith has used a .30-06 on any sort of game since the early 1930s!

A year or two before they closed the shop on hunting in Kenya, the manager of Nairobi's main gun store told me that they sold more .30-06 ammunition than any other centerfire by a large margin (the .375 H&H held second place). Throughout the length and breadth of Africa thousands of resident and visiting hunters used the cartridge (mostly with 180-grain bullets) with perfect satisfaction on every one of that great continent's fabulous variety of nondangerous game—and, in truth, on an astounding number of elephants, lions, and buffalo as well.

The only client I ever had out who took all his trophies with just one shot apiece used a battered old Model 70 .30-06 with factory 180-grain ammo. Eland, zebra, *kongoni,* impala, little "Tommy," Grant gazelle, warthog, what-have-you, he dropped them with a single shot at ranges from 50 to 300 yards. That is a record awfully hard to improve on!

Among the Masai of Kenya, it is a paternal duty to send one's sons out into the world properly outfitted with buffalo-hide shield, short sword, and long, heavy, narrow-bladed spear. The custom appeals to me, and as a native-born African I intended to abide by it.

Consequently my first-born, Erik, 12½ years of age, found a big-game rifle under the Christmas tree this year. It has a commercial FN Mauser '98 action, a 20-inch barrel, and a shortened stock (which I'll replace when he is bigger). He is not yet permitted to use it without supervision, but it is his, he keeps it in his room, and he is responsible for it.

The caliber, of course, is .30-06. Way too much gun for a boy? Nonsense! With the mild 150-grain load, he shoots it very well indeed, accounting for two deer with two shots during the last week of the season, one a perfect heart shot at 150 yards.

The point is that with that single gift I have effectively and economically discharged that part of my obligation—he is "properly outfitted" to cope with any likely game-field adventure that calls for a centerfire rifle!

The .30-06 is about the most powerful cartridge that can reasonably be chambered in a short and handy 8-pound rifle. It has a flat enough trajectory for 300-yard shooting; it is an easy cartridge to reload, one in which a great variety of powders and bullets will give acceptable results. It can be loaded down to match the performance and recoil of any milder cartridge while giving away no advantage in rifle weight or bulk, at least where factory-made sporters are concerned (a .243 by Ruger, Winchester, or Remington is much the same size and weight as a .30-06 in the same model). And it works beautifully on nearly anything!

Colonel Whelen summed it up perfectly many years ago in the 1961 *Gun Digest:* "No, for all American big game," he wrote, "the .30-06 Springfield rifle, or a good .30-06 of another brand, is never a mistake." There is no other cartridge about which one can say that with quite the same degree of confidence.

King of the North Country

The author discovers that the brown bear along the coast of Alaska is as awesome as the wet, rugged wilderness it rules. (American Rifleman *magazine, May 1992*)

A s the Peninsula Air turboprop made a wide sweep preparatory to landing, the bare, brown barrens seemed to stretch away forever beyond the little town. With its numerous winding, translucent green rivers and creeks as well as myriad gleaming lakes and ponds, the land appeared to be half water and I was struck by an incongruous thought: *Why, this reminds me of Maun and the Okavango Delta in Botswana.*

Now King Salmon, Alaska, and Maun, Botswana, are half a world apart in distance, geography, and climate, but both are frontier towns on the edge of the wilderness that engender a sense of adventure and freedom. Both are inhabited by the same self-reliant breed of humans who cope matter-of-factly with a mamba in the shower tent or a bear in the pantry. And both are abuzz with the comings and goings of bush planes, King Salmon even more so than Maun. From King Salmon a highway runs seventeen miles to Naknek on Kvichak Bay, and that is it. Anywhere else one wishes to go, he flies.

A Peninsula Air Cessna took Jim Clifton and me to Phil Shoemaker's camp in a national wildlife refuge. Here Shoemaker, a registered guide, has a snug plywood cabin on forty acres where he lives most of the year with his wife, Rockie, and their two children. The cabin also serves as headquarters for his guiding operation. Seven hours of walking upriver, he has another stout plywood cabin on a five-acre homestead, in addition to which, during hunting season, he puts out three or four spike camps in suitable locations.

Waiting to leave on the plane that brought us in was Steve Hittinger, who had scored on a 9-foot, 7-inch brown bear while hunting with guide Frank Nissen.

They had come on it in some alders while stalking a different bear, but when Nissen saw how wide this one was between the ears, he decided they ought to take it. Hittinger hit it through the center of the chest with a 250-grain Nosler Partition bullet from his .338 Winchester Magnum. The bear swung toward them, so Hittinger shot it again, this time in the neck. It cartwheeled down the steep slope and ended up in a gully right at their feet.

Another client, Ron Moody, took a 9-foot, 8-inch bear with a 27¼-inch skull. Moody used 220-grain Nosler Partition bullets in a Browning BAR chambered to .300 Winchester Magnum. After falling to the first shot, the bear started to get up, whereupon Moody settled matters by breaking its neck. This bear wore an ear tag, and fish and game department records showed that it had been tagged 60 air miles away in the spring of 1990, when it was 10 years old and weighed 950 pounds.

Hittinger and Moody reported having seen up to 25 bears a day, so Shoemaker decided that we would hunt from the same camp and that he would do the guiding. He ferried us out to it forthwith in the Super Cub, which we tied down to anchors sunk deep into the ancient gravel bar that served as a landing strip.

Fierce winds can do amazing things to light aircraft. Once, when Shoemaker was barely airborne with a client who was an aggressive lawyer, an eddy took all the lift from the right wing. Despite his best efforts, the plane veered sharply and landed in the alders, upright but with both wings broken and partially torn off. Phil scrambled out in a hurry and turned to find the lawyer just sitting there despite the fuel that was dripping down all around him from the ruptured wing tanks.

Red-faced and arms akimbo, he demanded, "Are all your clients subjected to this sort of thing, Shoemaker?"

After that incident, Shoemaker no longer uses a battery in his plane (to lessen the fire hazard) and must start it by swinging the propeller.

The camp lay several miles back and up from the river, and a couple of nearby hills commanded good views over the country. Our shelter was a Quonset-shaped hut of strong canvas over a tubular metal framework. It was made by the Weatherport Company in Gunnison, Colorado, which offers them in many sizes. They are apparently much used by the oil companies on the North Slope, where they are said to have withstood winds of 125 MPH. Ours measured about 12 feet by 12 feet and had ample room for three cots, a kerosene stove, a table, and a Coleman gas range.

The fish and game department has counted up to 350 brown bears in Shoemaker's valley in summer, but in late fall most of them travel beyond it to hibernate around the headwaters of the river. About forty are true residents that remain to hibernate in the scree slopes above the valley. All summer the bears gorge on the salmon in the river, but by the time bear season opens in October, the runs are over and the bears start drifting toward their denning areas.

Apart from stunted cottonwoods and willow thickets along the river and scattered alder patches, the broad valley appears to be open grassland, rather like a Wyoming antelope prairie. This is an illusion. In fact it is soggy, waterlogged tundra where one can sink in thigh-deep at any step. Consequently, hunters wear what Shoemaker calls "Alaskan hushpuppies" (hip boots) all the time. It is heavy going, and when one does find drier ground on the slopes and hills, it is apt to be full of depressions scooped out by the ice, like small shell craters.

The best way to hunt these bears is to get up on the hills and glass for a trophy-size boar. They are generally moving, and because they can cover soggy ground appreciably faster than a man can, we saw many that we had no hope of catching. One gets hot crossing the tundra and climbing the hill; then pretty soon he is freezing, sitting still glassing in the chill wind. Extra clothing carried in a daypack is a necessity, as is a three-quarter-length raincoat to go with the hip boots. It rains a lot in that country. Synthetic riflestocks make sense, as do scope covers and a piece of tape over the muzzle of the barrel, and stainless steel would be nice.

The cold had come unusually early this year, and the bears were already on their way out. We saw ten the first day, two the next, then the tally dropped to zero. Phil decided that we would walk down to the cabin on the five-acre tract to see if there was more traffic along the river, hunting as we went. Shoemaker used the radio in the cabin to arrange for guide Tim Stelzer to walk up from headquarters the next day. The weather was not kind, and we saw nothing much except several huge bull moose, their palmated headgear gleaming in the willows. Phil swore that one of them was a candidate for the Boone & Crockett book.

Tim, a tall, dark, competent young man, came in that evening. We would hunt with him while Phil walked back to collect the Super Cub and go check on his other hunters.

It was a decidedly brisk morning with strong winds and intermittent showers or driving rain when we set out to wade the river and climb a hill a mile upstream. Once up the hill, Jim headed for the shelter of an alder patch while Tim and I were digging extra clothes out of our packs. Almost immediately he called that he had seen something big and dark go into a willow thicket. I joined him, and presently we saw a bear emerge and amble off across the tundra. Tim identified it as a mature boar that would likely square about nine feet. Under the circumstances, Jim opted to try for it. Actually, a nine-footer is a lot of bear under any circumstances. The question was, could we catch it? The bear was traveling at an angle away from us, going toward a creekbed. If it went up the creek, we would likely never see it again, but if it turned downstream, we had a chance.

We had to hurry. Tim and Jim left their packs, but I decided that I would not be separated from the warm, dry clothes in mine for any reason. We reached the creekbed. Nothing. Had the bear turned upstream, or perhaps crossed the creek and continued across the tundra? We were about to move on when the bear appeared, walking along under the opposite bank about 100 yards away.

"Yes, he'll go nine foot!" Tim said.

Jim was using handloads with the superb Trophy Bonded solid-shank 300-grain bullets in his Ramline-stock Whitworth .375 H&H. He dropped into the kneeling position and fired. The bullet clapped, but the bear merely turned and started up the bank. Jim shot twice more, and then started fumbling under his jacket for the ammo pouch on his belt. The bear was still going. It was over 150 yards away and would soon be out of sight, so I tried for the root of its tail with my .35 Whelen. I failed to allow for the strong wind, and the 250-grain Nosler Partition broke a hip joint and put the animal's back end down, effectively anchoring it so that Jim could finish it off.

His first shot at the moving bear had been too far back. It had landed in the ribs about a foot behind the shoulder and had exited just in front of the opposite hip. (Jim now thinks a slip-on buttstock cartridge holder is preferable to a belt pouch when wearing heavy clothing or raingear.)

As we walked up to it, the bear seemed to shrink, and Tim cautiously appraised it at perhaps just under nine feet—a wise guide always tells his client that the trophy is a little smaller than he actually judges it to be. The boar was wearing an ear tag, Number 236, and, hidden by its long hair, a radio collar. There was pus in the hair all around the collar, and a fist-size cyst of raw flesh had grown out from under it. When we cut the collar off, we found that it had worn through the hide in several places, exposing the muscles. Later on, a state wildlife biologist in King Salmon was able to tell us that the bear had been tagged and collared by the U.S. Fish & Wildlife Service in 1986 when it was 3½ years old. In the intervening five years, it had obviously put on considerable girth. He also showed us the type of collar that the state uses nowadays. It has a canvas panel designed to rot and allow the collar to drop off within a year, whereas the old type used on our bear was of solid leather.

Normally a bear is skinned out completely where it falls, and most of the fat is scraped from the hide to reduce the weight. But conditions were so miserable that Tim elected to leave the head in the hide and carry it all back to the cabin, where he could work on it in relative comfort. When we had got it onto his big packframe and lashed down so that it would not ooze out, Jim was unable to lift the pack off the ground. Our conservative estimate is that it must have weighed at least 150 pounds. Tim got the pack on, we both helped him to his feet and pointed him in the right direction, and off he went. Tim said he had inveigled macho types into carrying out their own bear hides by telling them that only the toughest could do it, but Jim and I merely laughed at him. While Tim was working on the hide the next day, a mama bear and her three cubs came strolling along the river within 150 yards of the cabin—what marvelous country!

Though "The Book" records only the skull of a bear, every hunter and guide I have ever met discuss bear size solely in terms of how much the skin "squares." When laid flat on the ground without any stretching, the hide from Jim's bear measured 9 feet, 10 inches from nose to tail and 10 feet, 2 inches claw to claw across the front legs; thus it "squared" 10 feet. A 10-foot bear is the equivalent of a 40-inch ram or, in the old days, a 100-pound elephant. Anything over 9 feet is very fine indeed, and many a hunter has been extremely happy to go home with a decent 8½-footer.

Among them, the five grizzly hunters Shoemaker guided that fall season collected three boars that went over 9½ feet and one 8½-footer. The chap who did not score had seen many bears, but none of those he could have reached was quite what he wanted. In contrast, when flying out of King Salmon I met an acquaintance who had been hunting elsewhere on the Alaska Peninsula. He had not even seen a bear, not one.

The big bears are fascinating beasts. I find them as awesomely impressive as anything in my native Africa, excepting only the elephant. Before the coming of modern firearms, bears were the lords of this country. They feared nothing except bigger bears and were accustomed to taking whatever they wanted. Sometimes they still act that way. I personally have not the slightest desire to kill a bear, though I would like to go back in the summer to fish—Phil says you can catch 200 salmon a day in the river if you want to, and if your arm holds out—and to watch the bears. But if I had not hunted other dangerous game, I would feel differently about that. The bear population seems to be holding up well, and I think a keen hunter should by any means endeavor to experience Alaska many times and a brown bear hunt once in his life.

Buffalo and
Wild Honey

 **Chapter 26**

A charging bull and a camp-raiding lioness add spice to a buffalo hunt in the time of the honey harvest. (American Hunter *magazine, November 1990*)

T he entire adult male population of Thabu and its environs, numbering perhaps twenty all told, were happily and gloriously drunk when Joe Cheffings and I pulled in there after half a day's drive over the rough, dusty, and often hardly discernible track from Emali on the Mombasa road. It was the equivalent of winter here just south of the equator, with overcast skies and cool days. The long rains had dried up only a few weeks ago, and it was the season to harvest the wild honey.

Honey is a valuable and sought-after commodity out in the thornbrush country where the people live much as they always have. The women till parched patches of corn, millet, and beans in little *shamba*s scratched out of the scrub; the boys and youths herd goats and a few small, humped cattle; chickens scratch in the yards of homesteads where several grass-thatched mud-and-wattle huts (always delightfully cool inside) and storage bins are surrounded by a thorn fence; and the men—well, the men do that which is proper for men to do. They order and supervise, they clear the brush for a new *shamba* when necessary, and they burn charcoal for sale in the cities, where firewood is unobtainable. They go off to the cities and farms and plantations to seek wages when they have to, they "poach" an impala or a duiker or an eland from time to time with their poisoned arrows, they get together to talk and trade and settle disputes and arrange marriages, they collect the wild honey, and they drink the beer that the women brew.

The beer may be brewed from the home-grown grains or from store-bought sugar. It is thick and evil-smelling and, if drunk fresh enough, is said to continue to ferment inside the imbiber and to keep him lit up for hours or days. The best beer of all, though, is brewed from honey. The African honeybees usually nest in hollow trees, like most of their kin. The tribesmen do not domesticate them, but they do provide them with hives by suspending three-foot-long sections of hollowed-out logs from branches of suitable trees out in the woods. At the proper time they stultify the bees with smoke, lower the hive to the ground, and remove the combs, honey, grubs, and all. Bees crawl all over them, but as long as they remain calm and move slowly they sustain remarkably few stings. Natural nests are tackled similarly, except that the gatherers normally have to chop a hole to reach the honey. It is, by the way, a heinous crime to rob another chap's hive. That is regarded in the same light as horse stealing was in the Old West, and may bring similar retribution—it is simply not done. Natural nests are free to whoever finds them, of course.

We were looking for a man named Musyoka, who had been with us when we had hunted rhino in this district several years previously, and who had impressed us with his knowledge of the country and the movements of the local game populations. When we finally got it through to him that we wanted him to come with us and help us find buffalo, he mumbled his assent, and, since he already had his blanket wrapped around him, he saw no need for any further preparation and forthwith climbed into the back of the old short-wheelbase Land Rover. We drove the dozen miles down to the Athi River and camped under a large, shady tree on its bank. Joe and I put up a fly-sheet to ward off the dew, set up our cots and mosquito nets under it, and placed a folding table and two chairs outside while Musyoka built a fire and camp was made. For our supper I shot three grouselike yellow-throated francolins with a Brno .22 rifle.

The first morning, we explored upstream on foot. The land, which at that time was unpopulated below Thabu, ran down to the river in a series of big, rounded ridges and consisted of fairly open woodland interspersed with areas of tight, thorny brush. The coarse grass had largely been burned off, leaving the ground carpeted with the bright green new shoots only a few inches high. Visibility was quite good, except in the thick patches. There were herds of impala, numerous waterbuck along the river, hundreds of guinea fowl and francolins everywhere, many buffalo, some elephants, and only a few rhinos, for which we were thankful. Altogether it was a delightful country to hunt.

We saw no big herds of buffaloes, but tracked two bulls up from the river until we eventually lost the spoor about midday. Musyoka complained that an ugly sore on his ankle hurt too much for this sort of hunting. He suggested that we enlist Kimuli, a cohort of his, to help with the tracking while he stayed to look after camp. Besides, he was out of snuff, and we had failed to provide him with any, as was proper and expected. We spun a coin, with the result that Joe drove to Thabu to collect snuff and Kimuli while I took a bath on a sandbar in the river and got supper ready. (The few crocs left in the Athi after the hammering they had received from hide hunters in the late 1940s did not eat people, much.)

Shortly after dawn the next morning we found where a herd of buffalo had drunk during the night, and followed them up. After about a mile we spotted them moving slowly up along the next ridge. Through binoculars we caught a glimpse of a very large beast whose horns looked promising indeed. We initiated a fast approach to intercept them, but as we worked our way through the brush in the valley between the ridges, a gray form stirred in a thicket to our left and two stout horns stabbed skyward as their owner raised its head to wrap its pointed upper lip around a particularly succulent thorny twig. Rhino! We backed off and made a detour downwind, but had not gone fifty yards before we came upon another rhino. As we stood momentarily nonplussed, Joe suddenly brought his Winchester .375 H&H up into the aim. There between the two rhinos, and not thirty steps from us, was a big buffalo bull.

Collaboration having been previously agreed upon, I raised my .375, another M70 fitted with a Lyman aperture sight and with its barrel chopped off to 22 inches. Joe fired, and as the buffalo lurched forward I swung and shot immediately after him and the bull went down. Three shocked rhinos went off in various directions, snorting their choleric dismay—where the third popped up from I do not know, but there it was—and a long rumble of hoofs and a drifting cloud of dust up the ridge announced that the buffalo herd had stampeded as well.

Joe shot the buffalo once more for safety's sake, but it was already done for. His first bullet, a 300-grain Kynoch softpoint, had broken the upper leg bone and penetrated forward through the lungs and just under the spine at the front of the chest cavity, where we found the remnants of its jacket. My bullet had gone a bit far forward and by chance had broken the animal's neck. It was a big, mature bull, and as fat as I can ever remember a buffalo being, with layers of lard around its kidneys and encasing its entrails. But its head was not much. We were able to get the Land Rover right up to it, and left little but guts and bones for the vultures.

Musyoka and Kimuli spent the afternoon cutting the meat into strips about an inch thick, which they hung up on bushes and bark ropes until the whole camp was festooned with drying flesh. Joe and I took the tenderloins and hung a backstrap in the big tree. There the cool, dry breeze soon formed a crust on it, and it kept perfectly for several days. The steaks we cut from it were more delicious every day, but became smaller and smaller as the crust thickened.

That evening the two Africans were already wrapped in their blankets by the fire while Joe and I were still reading in our beds by the light of a kerosene lamp, when a lioness charged camp with a frightful, hair-raising crescendo of snarling grunts. Obviously she meant to run us off so that she could appropriate the meat. With their bush-honed instincts Musyoka and Kimuli were on their feet and running for the tree before they were awake, while Joe and I made urgent grabs for the rifles lying beside our cots. I forgot about the mosquito net that was between me and the rifle, pulled it down, and became thoroughly enmeshed in it as the cot tipped and decanted me, struggling helplessly, onto the ground on top of the .375. The lioness came on until we could see her in the firelight, but by then everyone was shouting so loudly that she lost her nerve and swerved aside. Joe stepped outside and fired a shot to send her on her way. The rest of the night was peaceful, but I noticed that Musyoka and Kimuli kept the fire well stoked.

The next couple of days we hunted hard without getting a shot. We saw a lot of buffalo, but either we found no shootable bulls or the wind swirled and gave us away. Then, as I got up one morning at first light, I saw the black silhouettes of three buffalo bulls standing in the silvery ribbon of the river a quarter-mile below camp. Joe and I took our rifles and hurried down there to try to ambush them, but they were gone ahead of us. With Kimuli we followed their tracks, and found that they had joined up with a herd.

Some while later we heard a metallic tapping sound and came upon a father-and-son team of honey gatherers who were rapping on likely trees with their pangas (machetes) to learn whether the trees contained bees. Eventually we caught up with the buffalo where they were bedded down in thick brush, but before we could get a clear shot at a bull, some of the cows spotted us and away they went.

Guns and Hunting

When we got back to camp we found the honey gatherers there, visiting with Musyoka and roasting buffalo meat over the fire. They said they had come upon, but had not disturbed, another bunch of buffalo, and the son, a cheerful and willing youth, offered to lead us to them.

The buffalo were not where the honey hunters had left them. As we began to try to unravel the spoor, Kimuli stopped and pointed to a flock of tickbirds (red-billed oxpeckers, members of the starling family) that were flying past. As we watched, they wheeled and descended into a patch of brush.

"That is where the buffalo are," he declared confidently.

We sneaked into the thicket, and presently Kimuli whispered that he could see them. About twenty-five yards away across a little clearing we could make out a bull lying down. It had wide, heavy bosses and what appeared to be a good length of horn, and Joe decided to take it. A bush obscured its shoulder and neck, so Joe moved in closer, until the animal suddenly stood up. Joe fired, the buffalo lunged out of sight, and then a second later it reappeared, coming back the other way. Joe thumped it again, and it fell.

He was running up to it when another bull appeared slightly to our right, coming fast straight toward us with its head high. Joe's attention was all on the downed beast and he did not notice it. A deadly collision seemed imminent, so I shot the oncoming bull in the center of the chest at about twenty paces, whereupon it turned aside and went away with two other bulls so close behind it that I could not shoot it again.

We made sure of Joe's bull and spent a few minutes admiring its horns, which really were very pretty. Then we set about the nasty business of sorting out the wounded one. We were following up one set of running tracks, looking for blood, when we heard a peculiar noise in the thick stuff close ahead. The young honey gatherer scrambled up a tree and reported that he could see the bull. I went up and, through a small opening, was able to see the head of the bull, which was lying down, apparently very sick. I put a bullet where I thought its neck ought to be. It got up and staggered out a few steps, allowing Joe and me to fire together and finish it.

I found that my first bullet, one of the notorious flat-pointed solids that Winchester used to provide, had entered two inches to the right of the sternum and had begun to break up almost at once, leaving a piece of its jacket the size of a fingernail outside the rib cage. (This bullet is no longer made, and the present Winchester solid is excellent.) It had put a big hole in one lung and scattered fragments of bone all through it, but with the other lung more or less intact the bull was still alive, if barely, fifteen minutes later. It was a young animal with soft bosses, and I had shot it only because it charged.

It was dark by the time we got back to camp, so we had to leave most of the meat out until we were able to work the Land Rover in to the kills the next morning. We found that a lioness with cubs (almost certainly our camp visitor) had fed on a haunch of one of the bulls, and that hyenas had visited the other but had taken very little. We took a Land Rover load of meat to Thabu, where Musyoka and Kimuli grandly distributed it among the populace, and another load back to camp. We traded meat for honey with our guests, warmed it in a saucepan, and strained it through a piece of burlap to remove most of the dead bees and pieces of wax. Supper was buffalo steaks, baked beans, and bread dripping with aromatic, full-bodied wild honey, and we envied no one in the whole world his dinner that night.

The Toughness of Game

⊕ **Chapter 27**

Are African animals tougher than North American game? The author examines the theory and offers his opinions. (American Hunter *magazine, August 1990*)

E veryone knows that African game is much tougher and more tenacious of life than our American species. Every American—almost—who has hunted in Africa is convinced of the truth of this dogma, and so are a great number of African hunters who have no experience whatsoever with any American game animal.

The reason for this phenomenon, it is postulated, is that African herbivorous animals are on the run from the teeth and talons of hordes of grim and ravenous predators from the very moment they are dropped in the African dust. In contrast, it is claimed, predators have been removed from much of the habitat of the American game species, so they can peacefully grow fat, lazy, and soft throughout most of the year, except for short and tightly controlled hunting seasons. The corollary, of course, is that the African animals require the employment of heavier artillery than do their feeble American counterparts.

Phooey! It is an attractive theory, especially to sportsmen who did not perform quite as well as they might have on an African hunt, but any examination of it reveals that it will hold no more water than a colander. If it were true, caribou, which over much of their range are harried by wolves and other predators (including the native human population), ought to be exceedingly tenacious, whereas in fact they are not so and are often easily killed by native hunters with such underpowered rounds as the .222 Remington and the .22 Hornet. Pronghorns are kept quick and alert by thriving coyote populations that in some areas, together with bobcats and eagles, will have accounted for half the fawn crop by fall. Nevertheless, they succumb readily to the mild little .243 Winchester and the like. I twice hunted elk in a part of British Columbia where the wolves and bears were so thick that for several years hardly a moose calf survived its first season. Supposing the predation theory is valid, these Muskwa elk should be much more difficult to bring down than their kin in Colorado, but if that is so, neither I nor anyone else seems to have observed it.

There are other factors besides predation that sort through the species, weeding out the weak and unworthy. Africa has its occasional droughts, when the dust devils dance under a brazen sky and the animals have to plod ever-increasing distances from the receding water holes in a desperate search for dwindling browse. But American game animals are subjected to that sort of stress every winter. If anything puts a premium on a strong and thoroughly ingrained will to live, it would have to be a hard winter when the shortage of feed is compounded by blizzards, deep snow, and numbing cold. The notion that the beasts of Africa must endure far harsher conditions than those imposed on North American game is by and large a fallacy.

Jack O'Connor could claim a considerable acquaintance with African game and a very wide and deep knowledge of American hunting. I have undoubtedly been in on the taking of many more African animals than he had, but although I have been privileged to hunt more than my fair share of American game during the last decade, my experience with it does not begin to approach his. It is therefore interesting that from our almost opposite points of view we should have come to the same conclusion: African game is no more difficult to put down than its American counterparts, and what will work on whitetails or caribou or elk will be equally effective on the African antelopes of similar size.

The fact is that while some African species do seem more difficult to stop than some American animals, the reverse is also true. By all accounts, the Rocky Mountain goat can go off carrying as much lead as anything its size in Africa. The moose is notorious for soaking up repeated hits while showing little sign of distress—O'Connor said he had never seen one killed stone-dead in its tracks with one shot. And the reputation the great brown and grizzly bears of Alaska have for shrugging off wounds that would immediately immobilize other beasts is unsurpassed by anything in Africa except the buffalo.

I have been in on the taking of only one brown bear. It was wading toward a gravel bar in a river, angling a little toward us, when shot with a .338 Winchester

Magnum. The bear dropped in its tracks, then raised its head. The hunter shot it again, and that was that. Full dark was coming on and we had no time for an autopsy, but apparently the 210-grain Nosler Partition bullet had broken the shoulder blade and smashed through the center of the chest cavity.

Two other bears were taken while I was in camp. A 9½-footer was turning away when Dean Deshon tried for its far shoulder with his .300 Weatherby. The boar fell down, then bounced back up, as they quite often do. Deshon hammered it down decisively with his second shot and then gave it another for safety's sake. The third hunter thumped a small boar twice behind the shoulder with his .338 Winchester Magnum and was somewhat startled to see the bear run 100 yards into an alder patch. (The lesson is that "behind the shoulder" is not the ideal place to shoot anything.) Phil Shoemaker, the outfitter, wrote to me that later in the season one of his guides was charged by a bear that his client had hit too far back, behind the lungs, with a .458 Winchester Magnum. It took a couple more shots from both the .458 and the guide's .375 to put a stop to the nonsense.

African buffalo can indeed be very tough. Mike Drury, the honorary game warden in the district where we ranched in Kenya, once sent a couple of game scouts out to deal with a cantankerous old bachelor bull that was harassing the locals. He loaned one of them his double .500 Nitro Express (570-grain bullet at 2,125 FPS) while the other chap carried a department-issue .303 Lee-Enfield. When they found the beast, they had quite a party and managed to expend 11 rounds of Mike's precious, irreplaceable .500 ammo and about 20 rounds of .303.

"Every time I hit it with the .500," Musyoki, one of the scouts, told me, "the bull fell down, but it would always get up and come for us again. By the time we finally killed it, there was hardly any meat left on it. We had shot it all off!"

On the other hand, Bob Bajan and I crept right into a bedded-down herd of buffalo one noonday, found a decent bull, and then waited 15 minutes for it to stand up to stretch and turn around. When it was broadside, Bob belted it precisely in the center of the shoulder with a 300-grain Silvertip from my .375 H&H. There was an immediate spray of blood from the buffalo's nostrils as it lurched into a run. It went perhaps 50 or 60 yards and fell down. I had Bob give it the customary safety shot, but the bull was already entirely defunct. The bullet had passed through the muscles behind the shoulder joint in the angle between the blade and the upper leg bone, had chopped through the lungs, and had torn up some important plumbing close above the heart. We found it lodged in the far-side ribs, perfectly mushroomed. (It did the trick in this case, but a bullet that will not give complete penetration on a broadside shot when no shoulder bones are struck is not adequate for that size game, in my opinion.)

The rule when dealing with dangerous game is to keep shooting until it is down, and then, when one is sure it is dead, to shoot it one more time. Consequently, very few buffalo receive only one bullet, but if I exclude unnecessary safety shots, I find from my field notes that of the 48 buffaloes my present .375 has accounted for, 21 were one-shot kills while 10 received two shots each. One bull took 12 hits (including some with a .458) before it was convinced, and another took eight bullets. Five received five hits each, and the others were shot three or four times before they went down. Several of these were staggering around, essentially dead on their feet from the first hit, but we kept pouring in lead until they fell.

In addition, a very few were wounded and lost, two of them by the same client, who shot quite competently on everything else but seemed to go all to pieces when we encountered buffalo. Another was lost when a DWM 300-grain softpoint TUG blew up in its shoulder joint as it stood quartering on to us. We saw a big red flower blossom against the black hide as the joint exploded, and we found pieces of bone. We tracked the diminishing blood spoor until late afternoon, when the sign was wiped out by a large herd of elephants. Two weeks later the same thing happened again, only this time I was able to get a .458 solid into the beast and stop it. We found the remnants of the jacket of the TUG bullet and powdered lead lying between the smashed joint and the rib cage. After that I permitted nothing but solid (full-metal-jacket) bullets to be used on buffalo.

As a comment on the legendary vindictiveness of the great black bulls, I might note that of these half-a-hundred buffaloes, only one came for us. A couple of others might have done so if we had not turned out their lights before they could get started, but there was only one genuine, do-or-die charge. My client and I hammered the bull simultaneously in the shoulder, knocking it down at ten feet as it rushed by hard on the heels of my tracker.

Another African animal with a reputation for being bulletproof is the goofy wildebeest. These creatures often seem to be impervious to "shock," and even with a good, solid hit they will typically gallop off switching their tails as if nothing had happened until they suddenly collapse in midstride. With poorly placed shots they will go forever, soaking up additional nonvital hits as if they were merely fly bites. Nonetheless, on the very last day that I hunted in Africa, I dropped two wildebeests with one shot from my 7x64mm rifle (the equivalent of a .280 Remington). The 173-grain RWS H-jacket bullet passed through the lungs of the first and smacked the second in the shoulder. The latter went down right there, and I found the first one dead about fifty yards away.

I had a suitably bizarre experience with another wildebeest (which we urgently needed for lion bait) that I plinked with the .375 at 250 paces. It dropped out of sight in the tall grass, but as I hurried up, I noticed dust arising from where it had fallen. When I got close, I saw that it was thrashing around with all four legs in the air and quickly put in a finisher. I found that my first shot had merely broken a front leg close below the body at the elbow. Why had it dropped? A demonstration of the awesome shocking power of the .375 magnum, perhaps? Not at all. I believe I had just tickled its "funny bone."

The oryxes and some of the hartebeest family, including particularly the East African *kongoni* (Coke hartebeest), are notorious for their hardiness as well. They also appear to be little impressed by bullet-induced "shock" and tend to keep traveling when the shot is poorly placed rather than standing around hunched up waiting for the coup de grâce. But they readily succumb to solid lung-heart hits with the likes of the 7x64mm, the .270 Winchester, the .308, the .30-06, or, for that matter, the old 7x57 Mauser.

Zebras are chunky, well-muscled animals with solid bones that may require the use of fairly stout bullets to reach their vitals from angles other than broadside, but any load that is suitable for a spike elk will do perfectly on them and will serve nicely for the larger antelopes like roan, sable, and kudu as well. Eland, especially the old bulls, are very large animals with weights of over 2,000 pounds on record. They seem less phlegmatic than moose, however, and in my experience are not particularly difficult to kill provided one uses a bullet that has sufficient penetration and places it reasonably well.

Lions and leopards are cats with all the fierce vitality of their kind. They are immensely powerful and unbelievably fast, but they are not hard to kill. I have the impression that brown and grizzly bears may be somewhat harder to stop than lions when shots are not quite perfectly placed.

As for the smaller stuff, I have now been in on the taking of a significant number of white-tailed deer because the bag limits are quite generous here in Texas and deer are the mainstay of our freezer, just as impala were in Kenya. Mostly I use a 6.5x55mm or a 7mm Mauser, while my wife uses her 7mm-08 exclusively. We are careful, rarely needing more than one shot per deer, but then I seldom needed more on impala, either.

Impalas and the other small antelopes and gazelles may not be quite so nervously alert as whitetails, nor as high strung, perhaps. Sometimes they may react less obviously to a bullet strike, though I am not entirely convinced of that because I have seen deer raise their flags and run off as if untouched despite a mortal wound that would cause them to drop within fifty yards. Some of the African species may tend to run a little farther with similar hits than do whitetails, but if that is so, I certainly cannot prove it by the field notes and diaries I have kept for many years. On the contrary, they suggest that with similar shot placement using comparable cartridges, the smaller African antelope are no more or less difficult to kill than our deer.

How do we account, then, for this fable concerning the toughness of African game? I believe it arises from wistful self-delusion and bad shooting. A visiting sportsman in Africa tends to be excited and a little nervous about strutting his stuff in front of an audience consisting of the professional hunter and his trackers, who have likely been in on the bagging of more game than the dude has ever seen. On safari he cannot hide his mistakes, whereas at home there are often no witnesses, so he can gloss over his bad shots and soon forgets them. He hits a zebra or a wildebeest a touch too far back, through the rear fringes of one lung and the paunch, let's say, and when the beast runs half a mile he exclaims, "My gosh, these African animals are tough!" He forgets that with similar placement an elk might have traveled just as far. Soon he is claiming to have hit it "in the boiler room."

The fact is that all too many hunters are rather vague about animal anatomy and do not know exactly where to place their shots, nor do they understand what causes an animal to die. From a hunter's point of view, an animal is killed, or at least reduced to his possession, when its muscles cease receiving conscious, coherent orders from its brain. This can be achieved by severing the lines of communication via the spinal cord, or by putting the brain out of action, either directly or by depriving it of oxygen by cutting its blood supply. (The brain is affected by a lack of oxygen before the muscles are.)

A brain shot is instantly effective, and so is a shot to the spine in front of the shoulders. When placed farther back, a spine shot paralyzes the hindquarters, anchoring the animal for a finishing shot. Many believe that a neck or brain shot must result in either a clean miss or a clean kill, but that is far from being the case. Both offer small targets surrounded by tissue not immediately vital to life. Miscued attempts at them can result in an animal escaping with a torn gullet or smashed jaw to die a lingering death. At any but close range, the heart-lung area offers a more certain target.

The idea when shooting for the vital areas apart from the central nervous system is to cause such profuse bleeding that the blood pressure quickly drops to zero, thus depriving the brain of its essential oxygen supply. The blood supply to the whole body (except the lungs) is pumped out of the heart through the aorta. When this great artery is cut close to the heart before it has branched, the blood pressure is gone almost instantly. The vena cava vein, carrying the venous blood from most of the body, enters at the top of the heart, and the pulmonary arteries and veins arise there also. Thus, above the heart is a thick rope of major blood vessels, the severing of any of which will cause copious bleeding and will bring the animal down through loss of blood in short order. The same is true of the thin-walled upper part of the heart, but the lower portions of it consist of the muscular ventricles, which do the actual pumping. A penetrating wound here that does not tear them wide open will bleed slower and sometimes permit the animal to travel an astonishing distance. The lungs are well supplied with blood, and a good lung shot kills quickly. The closer the shot is placed to where the pulmonary vessels enter them close above the heart, the more severe the bleeding will be and the faster the beast will succumb. Altogether, then, the shot should be directed toward the upper part of the heart.

The heart is quite a large organ that occupies the center of the chest cavity, with the lungs enveloping it on either side. Its lower apex comes down almost to the breastbone, but its vital upper parts, the great blood vessels, and the center of the lungs all lie much higher. Imagine that the animal has a grapefruit suspended in the center of its chest cavity, directly above its forelegs and a good third of the depth of its chest up from the brisket. From any angle, hit that grapefruit. With such placement (given a bullet commensurate with the work), the beast—African, American, or of any other continent—will seldom go as much as one hundred paces and will usually be down within fifty. The truth of the matter is that when a good bullet is properly placed, no game animal on earth is very tough.

Hunting Solo

 **Chapter 28**

Doing it all yourself—from negotiating wild country to finding, stalking, and packing out game—is an exhilarating and satisfying experience. (American Hunter magazine, May 1991)

I have never been a hero worshipper, or much of a disciple of any specific dogma or teacher—I'm just too bull-headed and independent for that, I suppose. Nevertheless I have had tremendous admiration and respect for certain men, and have learned a lot from them.

I started hunting in the era when Jack O'Connor wrote for *Outdoor Life,* Warren Page for *Field & Stream,* and (though I was unaware of his work then) Pete Brown for *Sports Afield.* They were giants in their field, though they did not have the competition that exists today, and I do not think we will see their likes again. I learned much of value from them, but even more from the writings of their senior, Col. Townsend Whelen, whose philosophy regarding hunting struck a chord with me.

Whelen was a career army officer who specialized first in infantry training and marksmanship instruction (about which he wrote a prize-winning and still valid paper in 1903), and then transferred to the ordnance department, where he served as sometime commanding officer of the Frankford Arsenal and later as the head of research and development at Springfield Armory. He was a benchrest and National Match competitor, a varmint shooter, a big-game hunter, and an avid experimenter whose best-known dictum is, "Only accurate rifles are interesting." He was the consummate rifleman, but perhaps above all he was an outdoorsman who reveled in "winning his way alone through the wilderness."

He wrote that although 113 heads of big game had fallen to his rifle, and though he had a few nice trophies on the walls of his hearth-room, he disliked being classed as a "big-game hunter." He rather decried big-game hunting as it was usually done.

"I can see no achievement whatever in a sportsman following a guide, being led by him through a country, the game found for him, and finally being taken to it and told when to shoot . . . But the winning of one's way by one's own effort through a wild country, the overcoming of all obstacles, the trail finding, the discovery of the game locality, the stalk or the still-hunt, the well-placed shot that kills instantly, the butchering, and finally the bringing of the trophy and meat to camp; always alone and unaided, or as the real leader of an expedition—that is a red-blooded achievement, distinctly worthwhile . . . such hunting is the most manly of all sports . . ."

And this: "The young hunter needs a great deal of experience, and that he can best gain by having a teacher—a guide. I think he should regard such experience as his apprenticeship. Until he can go alone, he should not count his coups." *(The Best of Col. Townsend Whelen, The Amwell Press, New Jersey, 1983).*

In short, Townsend Whelen, who delighted in wandering alone for days through the woods with his rifle and a light pack, subsisting on small game taken with the reduced loads he developed for all his big-game rifles, felt that hunting ought to be a do-it-yourself sport, and that no one was fully qualified as a hunter until he could do it by himself. Although I made my living for nigh on twenty years as an outfitter and guide, both in Kenya and in this country, I have to agree with him, at least in principle. No trophy taken with the aid of a guide or companion is entirely one's own, but is shared with them to some degree.

That does not necessarily make the trophy, or the experience it commemorates, less valuable, however; often quite the contrary. The pronghorn on my mantelpiece was taken in company with Dan Dirscherl, who had already filled his tag. I do not remember which of us found the bunch, but we planned and executed the stalk together. I saw the animals first as we eased over the rim of the basin in which they were bedded down, and chose the spot from which to shoot.

As I lay waiting for the buck to get up, I asked Dan for his estimation of the range, which agreed with mine—200 yards or a trifle more. When the buck finally stood up, I made my allowance for wind drift and pressed the trigger. After I had field-dressed the animal, Dirscherl, a big, strong man, insisted on carrying it out by himself the mile down to the nearest spot we could reach with the truck. Dan thus has quite a share in those horns, which is fine and, if anything, causes me to value them the more. They are souvenirs not only of a glorious, sparkling day on the Wyoming prairie but also of a long and enduring friendship.

It is likewise with the lion skull that resides on the other end of the mantelpiece. It is from one of the two lions that I shot off a dead elephant at night by spotlight on Ray Mayers's ranch near Voi. Because I could get onto them faster with my scope sight than Joe Cheffings could with his iron sights, I happened to do the shooting. But the whole experience belongs just as much to Kinuno Mbogo, who operated the light, and to Joe as it does to me. We shared equally in the planning and preparation, in holding our breath when one of the cats sniffed loudly a few paces behind us in the dark, and in the appalling stillness after the echoes of the shot and the crashing rush of the lion through the brush had ceased. I cannot look at that skull without recalling that momentous evening and the special bond forged between friends who have faced danger together and found each other worthy. (I should mention that Mayers had asked us to shoot the lions for him before they started on his cattle, as they would inevitably have done. Shooting them at night would have been both illegal and unethical in sport, but this was "control" work.)

Among my most memorable experiences is a guided mule deer hunt my wife, Berit, and I made in the Gray's River country of Wyoming quite some years ago now. Every morning we started up the mountains on horseback well before dawn so as to be at tree line by first light. The full moon sinking in the west silvered the stands of yellow-leaved aspens as we rode through them, and then a little later the first rays of the sun gilded their other side as well. The high country with its grand vistas of surrounding peaks, with the Wind River Range gleaming in the distance in one direction and Grand Teton peeping over the horizon in another, engendered an intense and indescribable awareness of being alive.

Berit and I shared that day in a stalk that resulted in another hunter taking a huge old trophy buck with close to a 30-inch spread. And we led the horses down into the basin through timber (so that if one of them fell a tree would likely stop it before it rolled all the way off the mountain) while the hunter and guide slid the deer down the sheer scree slope. On the way out, by a route the guide had never traveled before, we had to drag the horses through a narrow chute in the rimrock, glissading them down on their haunches in a shower of pebbles and dust and then cutting sharply to the left so that the animals would not run over us.

On the last day I took a pretty but small four-point that the outfitter considered no trophy but merely a meat buck. Furthermore I shot atrociously, and the guide helped me finish it off. Nonetheless Berit caped it out and insisted on having it mounted, and she was right. As a trophy it is nothing, but as a memento of a wonderful adventure we experienced together, it is priceless.

In addition, and from the other side of the fence, I cherish the memories of many, many hunts shared with the clients I guided, and the lasting friendships formed on not a few of them.

Nevertheless, for the most part I love to hunt alone. It is far more satisfying to have done it all by one's own efforts and skill (and maybe luck)—from the finding and evaluating to the successful approach and the shot.

When I was in a bear-hunting camp in Alaska we noticed white specks in the far distance—caribou. I had a caribou tag and requested that I be allowed to go after them on my own. I ended up crawling on hands and knees for what turned out to be 380 hip-boot paces across the waterlogged tundra to get within 200 yards of a pair of bulls. They were the first caribou I had seen close up. I really did not know how to judge them, but I finally decided to take the one with the double shovels. I skinned and cut it up where it fell, put the backstraps in my daypack, tied my sweaty undershirt to an upraised leg, marked my territory around the meat pile in an attempt to keep the wolves and bears off, and slogged home with the head and antlers across my shoulders. Despite the double shovels, the antlers were mediocre, but they mean much more to me than would even a record-book head taken with the aid of a guide. They are all mine.

I have camped out alone often enough to know that I can handle it, but unlike Whelen, I prefer to have the companionship of a few congenial friends in a hunting camp. Every year three or four of us go to hunt pronghorns on a ranch in Wyoming. We camp by a very convenient artesian well, Jim does the cooking, and the rest take care of the other chores. The talk ranges over every conceivable topic, often far into the night, as antelope hunting is not necessarily a crack-of-dawn affair. But in the morning we go our separate ways. I usually just walk out from camp, carrying a sandwich and a couple of candy bars in my daypack so that I can stay out all day if I like. On my own I can hunt exactly as the mood moves me, without having to take anyone else into consideration. I can go as fast or slow as I choose; I can hunt hard and seriously, or spend an hour on my back in the warming sun, watching an eagle wheel against the sky.

It is the same when Ron and Marcia Murdock, Jim Clifton, and I make our annual elk foray. We hunt some high country near the Continental Divide that is rugged enough that no wheeled vehicles seem able to penetrate it. Reaching the elk range may entail a steep, 2,000-foot climb; consequently it is not overcrowded. Actually it is the thought of having to pack an elk down out of there that puts most people off. It is indeed a pain without horses, but we think the price worthwhile.

We all hunt alone—even Ron and Marcia split up then. Being alone in truly wild country that looks much the same as when the mountain men first saw it, and realizing that one feels perfectly at home in it and is confident of his ability to move through it, find game in it, spend the night in it if he must, and cope with normal eventuality, is a thoroughly exhilarating and satisfying experience.

Of course, going alone is not without risks. If one sprains an ankle or breaks a leg, is bitten by a poisonous snake, or suffers some other disabling accident, or simply gets lost, he could be in real jeopardy. One needs to think about what could happen and be prepared to deal with it.

One evening in elk country Ron, Jim, and I met back at the truck, but Marcia did not come in. Night fell, still no Marcia, and by a couple of hours later it was obvious that something untoward had happened. We knew which general area Marcia had intended to hunt but had heard no signal shots and could thus have accomplished little on that mountain in the dark except perhaps to break our necks. There was nothing to be done before morning other than to wait.

One comfort was that Marcia is as competent a woodsman as anyone I know. She would not panic, and she was prepared. Besides a topographical map and two compasses, she had in her pack two flashlights with extra batteries, a first-aid kit, waterproofed matches, candle stubs, an extra down vest, socks and mittens, a space blanket, cord, raingear, drinking water, and some emergency candy bars. On her belt were a sharp knife and spare ammunition. If anyone could survive a freezing night on the mountain, she would.

After a long while we saw headlights coming up the track toward us. A strange truck pulled up, and an undismayed Marcia jumped out. It turned out that she had become temporarily lost. Coming off the mountain, she had missed the point where her route turned to the right down a subsidiary ridge and had instead continued down the main feature. By the time she discovered her mistake, it was already dusk and she realized she must not try to go back up through the rough country in the dark. Studying her map, she saw that if she continued down the ridge she was on she would come out on a road that would eventually lead her back to where we were waiting with the truck. It would be an awful long walk, but there was no alternative. Luckily she came upon another camp, whose inhabitants were a little startled to have a lady walk in on them in the middle of the night, but who kindly gave her a ride back to our truck.

How much gear one carries depends on the circumstances, but normally the lone hunter should have at least a compass, enough clothing to cope with any likely weather, matches, and extra ammunition or some other means of signaling. Usually when I walk out of the house to still-hunt deer on foot here on the ranch, I do not take even that much, just extra ammo and perhaps an extra sweater tied around my waist. But I do make sure that one or more people know where I am going so that they know in which pasture to look for me if I am not back by an hour after dark. In that case they would stop the truck often, sound the horn, and then listen for my signal shots.

Stand-hunting for whitetails is not quite the same thing as going alone into wild country on foot, but even then accidents can happen. It is wise to arrange for someone to come and investigate if a hunter is not in by a certain time.

Mental preparation is requisite—he who panics is lost—and so is some common sense and the ability to use the equipment one is carrying. A map is of no use to a person who cannot read it and has never practiced finding his way with one, and a compass is unlikely to help much if he has not kept track of the direction in which camp or the truck lies. And regardless of all precautions, there is no question that it is safer to hunt with a companion. But is there anything worthwhile in this life that is without risk?

During the past forty years I must have spent enough time alone in the bush or the woods to add up to many months, and I have never been in serious trouble. If one goes about it sensibly, I think there is less risk in hunting alone than in downhill skiing, rock climbing, playing high-school football, boating, and a lot of other recreational pastimes, and far less risk than in driving a few blocks to the food mart for a quart of milk. So, while exercising all reasonable prudence, I still prefer to hunt on my lonesome; it is by far the most satisfying and rewarding way, except when my wife can accompany me.

The .280 Remington

⊕ **Chapter 29**

Aagaard examines the technical virtues of this fine all-round hunting cartridge.
(American Hunter *magazine, July 1989*)

L et's imagine that a committee of experienced hunters was assigned the task of designing an ideal cartridge for U.S. big game—specifying that it would be used mostly on deer, antelope, and black bears; occasionally to hunt elk, moose, and caribou; most rarely sheep and mountain goats; and the largest bears not at all. The end result would undoubtedly closely resemble the cartridge that Col. Townsend Whelen described as having the virtues of both the .270 Winchester and the .30-06 while being a little better than either of them.

He was referring, of course, to the .280 Remington, also known for a short time as the 7mm Express Remington. And at least theoretically, he had a good argument for his opinion.

The .280 Remington uses what is essentially the .30-06 case with its shoulder moved sufficiently far forward to prevent it from being inadvertently fired in a .270 Winchester rifle. It can shove a 140-grain bullet along to about the same velocity the .270 achieves with its 130-grain bullet, while with the heavier 160- and 175-grain bullets it should match the performance of the .30-06 on the larger species of game. Well, almost. I have to admit that on the biggest stuff I would personally prefer a 200-grain bullet handloaded to 2,650 FPS in the '06 over a 175-grain 7mm bullet at about 2,700 FPS in the .280 Remington. But that is pure prejudice, since my journals reveal no discernible difference between the two cartridges on game in the field.

I have been in on the taking of a lot of animals with a 7mm Express. It was not the .280 Remington but a ballistically identical 7x64mm Brenneke that was my "light" rifle for 15 years in Kenya, and which has now accounted for over 300 head of game, including a few Texas whitetails.

It was used mostly with RWS ammo loaded with the 173-grain H-Mantel bullet at a nominal 2,750 FPS. This was a partition-type projectile with a very frangible front end that almost invariably fragmented during penetration, leaving the cylindrical rear half to plow on like a little solid. It was a very reliable, killing cartridge that performed excellently for me and many clients on all sizes of non-dangerous game (and a couple of leopards) from 50-pound gazelles to 800-pound Grevy zebras. One or two of my acquaintances took eland with their 7x64 rifles, and I would not hesitate to use it on moose, which are of comparable size. I have also taken several deer and an elk with an actual .280.

My experience suggests that the 7mm Express/.280 Remington ought to be an outstanding big-game cartridge. It can indeed have a slight advantage in bullet weight over the .270 Winchester, and in trajectory and recoil over the .30-06, but only when it is loaded up to its potential. And there is the rub. For most of its existence the .280 has been underloaded by Remington, and factory ammo has never come close to reaching the velocities claimed for it. The reason for this, it is said, was to hold pressures down to ensure reliable functioning in the Remington M740 autoloader in which it was introduced in 1957.

Whatever the explanation, the result was that with factory loads the .280 Remington did not match, let alone surpass, the performance of the tried-and-true .270 Winchester. It never achieved any notable popularity, and for a while it seemed likely that it would soon be discontinued.

Remington made an effort to resuscitate it by renaming it the 7mm Express Remington and giving it an improved load that the company claimed drove a 150-grain bullet to 2,970 FPS muzzle velocity from a 24-inch barrel. That would have been more like it, but unfortunately there was a good proportion of hot air in that figure also. Then it became apparent that the term "Express" confused some of the less knowledgeable shooters, a few of whom blew up perfectly good 7mm magnum rifles by firing 7mm Express Remington ammo in them. (Lacking proper support in the larger 7mm magnum chamber, the 7mm Express/.280 Remington case splits open, releasing high-pressure gas that tends to wreck the rifle and blow all sorts of junk back into the shooter's face. It is an extremely dangerous situation, and the greatest care should be taken to ensure that there is no .280 ammo anywhere within reach when one is shooting a 7mm magnum.)

The original .280 Remington designation was therefore reinstated, to the regret of many of us who rather preferred the more romantic 7mm Express appellation. Nevertheless, the cartridge at last seems to be gaining a measure of the acceptance it deserves, and several new loads have recently been introduced for it.

In addition to a 165-grain roundnose Core-Lokt bullet at a claimed 2,820 FPS, and a 150-grain pointed softpoint (PSP) Core-Lokt at 2,890 FPS, Remington has within the last couple of years introduced a 140-grain PSP at 3,000 FPS and a 120-grain hollowpoint at 3,150 FPS. Federal recently announced that .280 ammo with the 150-grain Nosler Partition bullet at 2,890 FPS would be available in its Premium line. It would be my first choice among the factory loads for use on elk and larger game. The listed velocities are derived from 24-inch pressure barrels. In 22-inch-barrel hunting rifles, I obtained not quite 2,600 FPS with the only lot of the 165-grain load that I have chronographed, while a recently tested box of Remington ammo with the 140-grain PSP bullet averaged right at 2,850 FPS.

A decade ago the .280 Remington was available in only one mass-produced rifle, the Remington M742 autoloader. Nowadays Browning offers it in its A-Bolt rifles, and Ruger lists it as available in both its M77 bolt-action and in the No. 1 single-shot. Remington still chambers it in its autoloader, now the M7400, and also in the M7600 pump-action gun. Remington's delightfully lightweight, walnut-stocked, bolt-action Mountain Rifle is available in .280 Remington—a fine combination—and so is the rugged M700 RS.

That last is a quality, utterly practical hunting rifle that is meant for hard use, not display. The metal has a dull gray-black finish that resembles Parkerizing, while the stock is of a synthetic called "Rynite," which Remington describes as a tough, thermoplastic resin. It has a textured, non-slip finish (except on the cheekpiece), a solid-rubber butt pad, and is available either in camo or in a solid black color.

My test rifle bears both the 7mm Express Remington and the .280 Remington designations on its 22-inch barrel. It is fitted with open sights, has a hinged magazine floor plate, and weighs a solid 7 pounds, 11 ounces bare, which means it will go about 9 pounds with a scope sight and a full magazine. I was surprised to discover that there was no pressure point bearing on the barrel near the tip of the fore-end, as is the normal Remington practice, but that instead the barrel was left completely free-floating.

Despite that, the rifle is very accurate; in fact, I cannot remember ever having achieved more consistent accuracy from a standard-production big-game rifle straight out of the box. After mounting a scope, cleaning the bore, and tightening the guard screws, I got it more or less sighted-in with Remington 140-grain PSP ammo. Then, at 100 yards and shot from a sandbag rest, the remaining 15 rounds went into a group measuring 1.6-inch extreme spread, while the three five-shot groups averaged 1.26 inches. In working up handloads with various bullets, I achieved no groups of under 1 inch for five shots. But none went over 2 inches either, and few spread much beyond 1½ inches. It puts bullets of different weights usefully close to the same point of impact at 100 yards as well. Three shots each at 100 yards with bullets weighing 140, 150, 162, and 175 grains formed a 12-shot group that measured just 2.6 inches vertically and 1.5 inches wide. This sort of consistent accuracy with a variety of different loads is a valuable trait in a big-game rifle.

I fitted the Remington with a Burris 3–9X RAC scope, using Weaver mounts. RAC stands for "Rangefinder with Automatic Compensator reticle." Its field of view is somewhat cluttered. There is a fixed horizontal cross hair and a movable one that shifts as the power-change ring is turned. Near the bottom of the field are the two horizontal stadia wires of the rangefinder, which is calibrated for deer measuring 18 inches deep from back to brisket. The instructions are to zero the scope at 200 yards (or so that the point of impact is 1.8 inches high at 100 yards). Then, in use, the power ring is turned until the stadia wires exactly bracket the deer, when the movable (lower) cross hair should be dead-on for that particular range. The range compensator is designed to be used with cartridges having trajectories similar to the 150-grain Winchester Power Point bullet in the .270, the 150- and 180-grain Silvertip bullets in the .30-06, the 200-grain Power Point in the .338 Winchester Magnum, and so on.

I tried the scope on 18-inch-deep, plain, buff-colored cardboard boxes set out at 300, 350, and 400 yards, shooting from prone with the aid of a Harris bipod and using the Sierra 150-grain boattail (BT) bullet handloaded to 2,865 FPS. Even from that steady a position and in good light, I found it difficult to determine when the stadia wires were exactly bracketing the target; consequently, it was easy to get a reading that was 25 yards out either way at 300 yards, and more as the range increased. Practice did help, though.

Then I shot at the 300-yard target with the wrong cross hair and got a beautiful, minute-of-angle three-shot group at the bottom edge of the target. Using the correct cross hair, I managed to make "vital area" hits at 300 and 350 yards, but the shots at 400 yards landed too high, with two out of six going over the top of the target. I checked the trajectory data for the 150-grain Sierra BT and found that at the velocity I was using, it would drop 20.4 inches below line of sight at 400 yards from a 200-yard zero, whereas the scope's range compensator was adjusted for a 25.2-inch drop at that range.

Burris scopes are of excellent quality in all respects, and this one worked exactly as advertised. But, like all scopes of this type that I have ever tried, it is overly complicated for big-game hunting. I pulled it off the gun and replaced it with a Burris Fullfield 2–7X variable.

I am not a great fan of variable-power scopes. The 4X Lyman I had on my 7x64mm served me perfectly well whether I was after bushbuck in thick forest or gazelles and hartebeest on the wide-open plains at Juja, where they had been well-educated ever since Theodore Roosevelt hunted there as the guest of his friend William Northrup McMillan in 1909. All the same, I believe that a good-quality 2–7X variable-power scope is likely the best choice for an all-round big-game rifle.

Rather than adjust my sights for elevation in the field, the system I prefer is to sight-in for the longest distance that will not put the bullet more than 3½ inches high at midrange, and then to consider the point at which the bullet has dropped 4 inches below the line of sight as being my maximum range. This is the distance out to which vital-area hits should be obtained on deer-size game with a center-of-the-chest hold, and it is conveniently referred to as the load's point-blank range. If the animal is farther off than that, I exercise what skills I have as a hunter in an endeavor to stalk closer.

Most .280 Remington loads with spitzer bullets up to 162 grains can be sighted-in to give a 300-yard point-blank range on deer and similar-size game. Then they will strike from 2½ to 3 inches high at 100 yards, will be dead-on at 250 yards, and will land 4 inches or less below the point of aim at 300 yards. For use on elk and moose with their larger vital chest areas, even the 175-grain spitzer bullet can be zeroed for 250 yards, when it will have a 300-yard-plus point-blank range on the big beasts.

Thus, 300 yards is usually the critical range with this cartridge. If the quarry is within that distance, the shooter just holds for the center of the chest, but if it is outside it, he must either make allowances for bullet drop or start sneaking. Some aid to estimating 300 yards can be quite helpful. I use the gap between the horizontal cross wire and the point where the vertical wire thickens as a gauge by comparing it to the apparent depth of the animal's chest, from the top of the back to the brisket, close behind the foreleg. I have found, by empirical means, that with this particular scope, a large deer measuring 18 inches deep through the chest is exactly bracketed by this gap at 300 yards when the power is set at 6X, and that a big pronghorn buck should likewise be bracketed with the scope at 7X. Of course, individual animals do vary in size, and it may be impossible to bracket them precisely in poor visibility, or from the relatively unsteady positions one must often adopt in the field. So none of these range-finding schemes can give other than very approximate results, but they may save a hunter from the grossest errors in range estimation.

Of the factory-loaded .280 Remington ammo, I expect that the Remington load with the 140-grain PSP bullet is the most generally useful. It has as flat a trajectory as the 130-grain PSP in the .270 while delivering a trifle more energy. It should be excellent for antelope and any deer, and would probably do well on caribou also. For larger game the 150-grain bullets might give more reliable penetration, especially the 150-grain Nosler Partition bullet in the Federal Premium load. Some hunters may believe that the roundnose 165-grain Core-Lokt bullet with its very modest (chronographed) velocity will get through brush better than the others, and it might be a good midrange deer load when one does not want to destroy too much meat. But frankly I do not have much use for it.

The handloader has a plenitude of good 7mm bullets to choose from. The 130-grain Speer BT can be pushed to about 3,100 FPS, which should make a dandy pronghorn load, and a variety of 137-, 140-, and 145-grain bullets are available for deer and such. I like a 140-grain bullet at about 2,550 FPS as a "meat load" for deer and have had good success with it in various 7mms.

I have killed one fair-size six-point elk with the 160-grain Nosler Partition bullet in the .280. It was standing in timber a little over 200 yards down the ridge from me, and I had a clear target about two hands' breadth in size on its shoulder to shoot for. Despite clipping a wrist-thick limb on the way, the bullet flew true.

It perforated the lungs and tore up the top of the heart. The bull turned slowly around, took two steps, fell, and slid down the slope. I think that the ammunition manufacturers should offer a similar load, though the 175-grain Nosler might be better yet for moose.

The capacity of the .280 Remington case is such that the slower-burning powders usually give the best results. IMR 4831 works quite well with all bullet weights from 139 grains and up, but I got better accuracy with the 130- to 140-grain bullets by using IMR 4350. Hodgdon's H4831 seems to be a good choice with the 175-grain bullets, and might be worth trying with those of 160 grains as well. Very generally, in a strong .280 Remington rifle with a 22-inch barrel, it is possible to achieve about 3,100 FPS muzzle velocity with 130-grain bullets, well over 2,900 FPS with 140 grains, close to that figure with those of 150 grains, 2,800 FPS with 160-grain bullets, and 2,700 FPS for deep penetration with the elongated 175-grain bullets of great sectional density.

All in all, taking into account its thorough suitability for almost any of the world's nondangerous game, combined with its flat trajectory and mild recoil, one has to conclude that Col. Whelen was quite right—the .280 Remington is about the finest, most practical all-round, big-game hunting cartridge that we have.

Cutting the Kick

$\oplus$ **Chapter 30**

Preparing mentally and physically—then shooting a lot—is the key to taming recoil. (American Hunter *magazine, November 1985*)

"Use enough gun" is certainly sound advice. Because it is a hunter's responsibility to kill his game as quickly and cleanly as possible, the more power he can bring to bear the better—within certain limits.

The chief limit in this context is that imposed by Newton's Third Law of Motion, which maintains that for every action there is an equal and opposite reaction. We call the opposite reaction "recoil," and we dislike it. Too much of it tends to make us close our eyes, grit our teeth, tense our muscles, and get the unpleasant business done with a horrendous jerk at the trigger, none of which does much for our ability to place the shot where it ought to go.

If the gun and the bullet weighed the same, at the moment of firing they would part company, traveling at the same velocity in opposite directions, which could be unfortunate for the shooter. Luckily, firearms usually weigh from 50 to 300 times more than their projectiles, which slows them down somewhat.

The Free Recoil Energy (FRE) of a gun, in foot-pounds, can be calculated by using a formula given in the *Lyman Reloading Handbook:*

$$\text{FRE} = \frac{(\text{weight of bullet in pounds} \times \text{muzzle velocity} + 4{,}700 \times \underline{\text{weight of powder in pounds}})^2}{64.348 \times \text{weight of gun in pounds.}}$$

(To convert grains to pounds, divide by 7,000, the number of grains in a pound.)

It is evident that increasing the bullet weight, powder charge, or velocity tends to boost recoil, while adding to the weight of the gun decreases it. Using the Lyman formula, the FRE of an 8-pound .30-06 with a 180-grain bullet propelled to 2,750 FPS muzzle velocity by 57 grains of powder comes to 23 foot-pounds, while the 150-grain bullet at 2,950 FPS would produce 21 foot-pounds—not a very appreciable reduction. However, a 9½-pound .375 H&H Magnum with a 300-grain bullet at 2,500 FPS could have 41 foot-pounds of FRE, compared with 48½ foot-pounds for one weighing 7½ pounds, which is enough of a difference to be quite perceptible.

The FRE of my 9-pound .458 Winchester Magnum with a 500-grain bullet at 2,050 FPS works out to 69 foot-pounds. That of a similar-weight .300 Winchester Magnum with a 200-grain bullet at 2,850 FPS comes to 29 foot-pounds, while my 7½-pound .243 Winchester comes back with all of 10 foot-pounds of FRE.

The recoil energy of a heavily loaded 12-gauge shotgun is said to approach that of a .375 H&H Magnum, and if it were fired from a benchrest, it would no doubt be quite obnoxious. But when shooting offhand at birds, the body can normally "roll with the punch" so that the felt recoil is reduced to bearable proportions.

Autoloaders, especially the gas-operated ones, usually decrease recoil by an appreciable amount, most likely because they spread the recoil out over a longer period of time, which, of course, is all a recoil pad does.

It is the felt recoil, or "kick," that really matters, and that is not necessarily the same as the calculated FRE because it can be influenced by many other factors. These include how the firearm is used, how it is held, the shape of the stock, the area of the buttplate, and whether or not a recoil pad is fitted.

A Savage Model 99 lever-action chambered for the .308 Winchester cartridge that belonged to a client of mine was the most painful rifle I can remember firing. It had been fitted with a thin rubber butt pad, attached with cup-head screws that came almost level with the surface of the pad. During recoil, the upper screw head would punch into my shoulder like an ice pick, and, my gosh, that really hurt, far worse than any .458! If one is careless, the sharp heel of the curved buttplate of a muzzleloader can do the same thing.

Though they are unnecessary on rifles with less recoil than a .30-06, I have rubber butt pads on all my rifles, even the .22 rimfire. I once spooked a deer when a horn buttplate rang on a stone as I put the rifle down to use my binocular. Rubber is quieter and generally less slippery than most hard buttplates.

It is often said that big bores such as the .375 H&H Magnum and .458 Winchester Magnum should be fitted with solid rubber recoil pads rather than the ventilated variety. This is pretty much a myth—I have used both kinds on my .458s and can discern no difference whatsoever. Actually, most of the pads that appear to be solid, such as the Pachmayr Old English, are in fact much honeycombed inside. Pachmayr, by the way, still offers a profuse variety of recoil pads to suit almost any application.

A promising newcomer is the Sorbocoil pad made by Mylomar Technologies in Rhinelander, Wisconsin. It is made of a polyurethane that Mylomar claims is the finest cushioning material available. The firm says it will remain flexible at temperatures as low as minus 40 F (when I'll be sitting beside the stove, thank you kindly) and that it absorbs up to 90 percent of impact shock.

I am not sure what that means, precisely, nor do I have any way of measuring it. But I did obtain a Sorbocoil Magnum pad and installed it on my .458 to discover what my shoulder could tell me about its effectiveness. I could not feel much difference between the Sorbocoil and the issue Winchester ventilated pad when shooting offhand or from the sitting position, but there was a decided difference from the bench.

When I sight-in a .458 from the bench, I usually place a sandbag between the butt and my shoulder to make sure I do not start flinching. With the Sorbocoil installed, this would not be necessary—it reduced the sting to the point where I could easily fire ten or twelve shots without any discomfort.

I then tried it on a .300 Winchester Magnum with 200-grain bullets at 2,850 FPS. There was a small but obvious reduction in felt recoil, both in the sitting position and from the benchrest. Because this is a long-range rifle that will be fired deliberately and quite often from the prone position, the reduction in perceived recoil was significant enough to make it worthwhile installing the Sorbocoil pad on the big rifle permanently.

It is sometimes claimed that synthetic stocks are so resilient that ultra-lightweight rifles with fiberglass stocks kick no harder than standard-weight ones with walnut stocks. I have not found this to be altogether true. When several of us fired an 8-pound walnut-stocked Ruger M77 and a 6-pound fiberglass-stocked Ultra Light Arms Model 20 using the same 7mm-08 load, everyone declared that the Ultra Light kicked decidedly more than the heavier Ruger. The FRE of the two rifles came to 15 foot-pounds for the Ruger and 20 for the Ultra Light, and I would say that their perceived recoil effects were in about that proportion.

Weight really can tame kick. Many years ago we had a family that included a slightly built thirteen-year-old boy out on safari in Kenya. It was decided that the kid could take a couple of antelope with his big brother's rifle, a beautiful pre-'64 Winchester Model 70 Featherweight in .30-06 with an aluminum buttplate. But after he had touched off one round at a target, he said, "Nothing doing—that thing hurt!"

So Ken Clark, the outfitter, brought out his old Model 70 in 300 H&H Magnum, which had a recoil pad and, with its 26-inch barrel and scope, weighed something over 9 pounds. Despite its more powerful cartridge, the boy found the rifle quite comfortable, and he shot it well enough to collect his game easily, using a pair of crossed sticks to support it.

Ron Freshour of Texas Gun and Machine Company of Texas City, Texas, has built a fascinating two-shot bolt-action rifle for the .50-caliber machine gun cartridge that his buddy, John Hayslip (a school teacher of the sort one wishes there were more of), brought out here together with a box of LC 81 ball ammo.

This rather impressive cartridge, which is almost 5½ inches long and makes both the .460 Weatherby Magnum and the .577 Nitro Express appear trifling, is loaded with a 710-grain boattail bullet and 225 grains of a slightly flattened ball powder in the M2 version. It attained an instrumental velocity of 2,500 FPS in the 24-inch barrel of Freshour's rifle, which means that the 15-pound firearm produced the rather frightening FRE of 168.6 foot-pounds. This is almost 2½ times the recoil energy of a .458 and nearly 60 percent more than that of a .460 Weatherby Magnum. Nevertheless, we spent a pleasant afternoon shooting the monster, not only offhand but also from the bench.

I would not describe the recoil as being mild, exactly, but it was less than that of my .458, and half-a-dozen shots from the bench caused no great anguish or bruised shoulders. In fact, the recoil would still be bearable if the rifle were made a couple of pounds lighter, which would put it within the weight range of the heavier big-game rifles such as the .500 and .577 Nitro Express. Nonetheless, I doubt that a really practical hunting rifle can be built around the cartridge because its size necessitates such a massive receiver and so long a bolt throw that the whole thing becomes rather unwieldy. Besides, I believe I will take great care to avoid any beast that I cannot handle with a .458! So the big gun remains a novelty, a huge plinker with its chief interest lying in the fact that it can be fired from the shoulder at all.

It was fitted with a thick Sorbocoil recoil pad, which no doubt helped, but the greatest recoil reduction was achieved by a muzzle brake adapted from one used on an obsolete shoulder-fired antitank gun. It was 3¾ inches long, flattened on top and bottom, and had a row of ports on each side. Though the ports were angled backward only a few degrees, the brake was evidently very effective. It quite literally laid the tall grass and weeds down for several yards on either side, and was an absolute necessity on this powerful brute.

Muzzle brakes come and go. Though most of them did work to some degree, none but the Cutts Compensator, which was used mostly on shotguns, ever achieved lasting popularity until Larry Kelly appeared on the scene with his Mag-Na-Porting some fifteen years ago. He uses electric discharge machining to cut various slots in the barrel near the muzzle, placed so the vented gases will dampen muzzle lift and to some extent counter the recoil. Nothing is added to the gun; its appearance is not significantly altered, nor, it is claimed, is its accuracy or velocity affected.

Many shooters do evidently derive much benefit from Mag-Na-Porting or other brakes. I do not, at least not with rifles of less recoil than the .460 Weatherby Magnum. I have compared ported and unported .338 Winchester Magnum and .416 Taylor rifles, and have fired a .375 H&H Magnum with and without its removable muzzle brake of another brand. In the end I had to conclude that under field conditions I could stay in control, recover from recoil, and get another shot into the target just as well and as quickly with the unported rifles as with the ported ones. The reason for this, I think, is that I have learned to grip the fore-ends of heavy rifles so tenaciously that they do not get away from me, and I am able to simply hold them down.

Allowing a big gun to pick up velocity before it slams into the shoulder can really hurt. It should be held firmly into the shoulder so the rifle and upper torso move as one. This, combined with a firm grip on the fore-end, will help prevent the scope from being driven into one's forehead (better mount it as far forward as is practical, all the same) and will deter the comb from rising to thump one in the cheekbone.

The other day a friend showed me bruises on his chest caused by the toe and heel of the plastic buttplate on his pre-'64 Model 70 Featherweight in .243 Winchester. Then my wife, who has fired my .375 at game without complaining, remarked that a few shots with a very mild little rifle had hurt her collarbone!

In both cases the rifles had just been held badly, with the butts placed too far in toward the chest. The buttplate or pad should rest against the muscles that wrap around the shoulder joint itself, with the heel well outboard of the collarbone and the toe directly above the armpit, not over the chest. Placing the butt too far out, on the upper arm, can also be painful; the shoulder joint is the proper place.

The shape of the stock may be of some importance. A wide buttplate is more comfortable than an extremely narrow one, while too short a buttstock may allow one's thumb to mash his nose—something the old Lee-Enfield always did to me. It is said that a comb that slopes down toward the front will slide away from under the cheek during recoil. I would not know, because I have never in my life been banged on the cheekbone by any firearm.

If I am careless, the Winchester M70 .458 will sometimes bruise my middle finger against the trigger guard because its pistol grip is just a little too tightly curved. Actually, all hard-kicking rifles should probably have a shotgun-style trigger guard that slopes at the rear so the middle finger would tend to slide over it rather than bang against it.

We are often cautioned that the front sling swivel on a powerful rifle such as a .375 H&H Magnum should be mounted on the barrel rather than the fore-end so it cannot injure the hand during recoil. Because I sometimes use a shooting sling, I have always had the front swivels on my .375s on the fore-end, and in a quarter-century I have yet to hurt my hand on one. Still, if one does not use a sling in shooting, there is no harm in putting the swivel on the barrel, and in the case of the .458, it might be advisable to do so.

Nevertheless, I must insist that if the front swivel gouges a big-game hunter's hand, it is entirely his own fault because he should have been gripping the fore-end so firmly that it could not possibly slip through his hand even in the slightest.

Given a gun of reasonable weight, half the secret in being able to handle heavy rifle recoil is having a decently fitting stock with a suitable pad and a firm grip with the butt correctly placed in the shoulder.

The other half is mental. One has to convince his subconscious that despite all the noise and tumult, any normal adult can fire a .375, or most likely even a "ferocious" .460 Weatherby Magnum, for half-a-dozen shots from offhand without being hurt in the slightest, provided he holds it properly and firmly.

The only way to overcome this natural but pernicious subconscious fear of recoil is to do enough shooting. I do not mean that one should rush out and blast off 100 rounds with his new .458 at one go—far from it. He should work up to it, at first firing only three or four shots—and by no means should they be from the bench—each trip to the range, and gradually increasing the number as he becomes accustomed to the gun. (Youngsters or complete novices should start with very mild or reduced loads.) When one can assume any position he may have to use in the field and calmly get off ten shots while concentrating on his sight picture and trigger squeeze, rather than on kick, he has arrived.

The shooter will then have learned that with big-game rifles, recoil is but a chimera, a paper tiger that he need never fear again. And that, friends, is one very valuable lesson!

Scopes: The Big Element

 **Chapter 31**

Some may argue that things like synthetics and stainless steel are the big equipment improvements for the hunter, but the author says hands down it's the optical sight. (American Rifleman *magazine, August 1993*)

The most significant improvement in the big-game rifle since World War II lies not in the use of synthetics and stainless steel, nor in the exciting new cartridges developed in the interim, but rather in the almost universal adoption of the telescopic sight.

Forty-five years ago a glass-sighted hunting rifle was, if not a rarity, at least somewhat unusual. Today it is one lacking a scope that invites comment, and even the Model 94 Winchester carbine has been altered to better adapt it to scope sights. Back in the immediate postwar era, there was not a great choice.

The second edition of *Gun Digest* (copyright 1946) lists the now-discontinued Weaver models 330, 440, 29S, and 1X, together with the new Weaver K2.5 on a 1-inch tube, and the Lyman Alaskan, and that was about it for big-game hunting scopes.

In the same book, Elmer Keith mentions also the Noske Type A and recommends: "For general offhand shooting, select a scope of 2½ to 3 power, not more; for long-range stalking rifles . . . select a 4X scope." Nowadays, the plethora of scope brands, designs, and magnifications available in both fixed- and variable-power instruments is quite mind-boggling.

The purpose of a scope sight is to allow one to see the target clearly enough to place his shots with the precision required to obtain quick, clean kills. Magnification helps, but too much can be a hindrance by limiting the field of view (there are always trade-offs), and the old rule of optics that cautions against using any more power than is necessary to adequately see still applies.

In addition to magnification, telescopic sights generally provide a brighter image of the target. The human eye has an entrance pupil that varies from about 2.5mm in bright sunlight to 5mm at dusk and 7mm in pitch-darkness, whereas the objective lens of even a straight-tube, 1-inch scope has a usable diameter of close to 20mm. In essence, the scope takes most of the light that enters its objective (there is always some loss) and gathers it into a narrower bundle (the exit pupil), much or all of which can enter the eye (at the optimum eye-relief distance).

The diameter of the exit pupil can be calculated by dividing the unobstructed diameter of the objective lens by the instrument's magnification: A 4X scope with a 28mm objective will have a 7mm exit pupil. Most low-power scopes (or variables at their lower settings) have wide exit pupils, around 8mm for a typical 2.5X, for example. While this means that not all the light in the bundle can enter the eye, it does allow more latitude in the eye placement, both side to side and fore and aft, which is a great advantage for fast shooting.

The Europeans, who hunt a lot in the gloaming, quote what they call the "twilight factor." It is defined as the square root (Z) of magnification (M) times effective lens diameter (D) in millimeters: Z=square root of (MxD). Obviously, this formula gives equal weight to magnification and objective-lens diameter while disregarding the exit-pupil diameter. It is in fact easily demonstrable that one can see the target better as the light fades by turning a big-game variable scope up to a higher power, or by using a larger objective, when all else is comparable.

What it all boils down to, it seems, is that when one needs good "light-gathering" ability, he should choose high magnification combined with an objective-lens diameter that will provide an exit pupil of at least 5 to 7mm. The 8x56mm scope popular in Europe is an example. Best-quality lenses and coatings to ensure good light transmission are also important, naturally.

Another advantage that scopes hold over iron sights is that they place the target and the aiming device—the reticle or "cross hairs"—in the same focal plane so that the eye does not have to shift focus from the rear sight to the front sight to the target and back. Good young eyes manage this readily, but as one ages, it becomes increasingly difficult. Aperture rear sights help; scopes are the solution.

All these virtues have their price. Glass sights are said to be more fragile than irons. That may be so, but the fact is that in the field I have personally broken more iron sights than I have had scopes go out of commission. Bead front sight stems are quite delicate, and a fall once smashed the aperture of the Lyman 48 receiver sight mounted on my .458 Winchester Magnum.

Scopes limit one's field of view to a greater or lesser degree, the more so the higher the magnification. This can cause problems at close quarters, as a client of mine found when he tried to shoot an oncoming elephant between the eyes with his scope negligently set at 9X.

My client commented afterward that he had been able to see only one eye at a time. The answer is to use low power for close-range work. Scopes of low power up to 2.5 or perhaps 3X can furthermore be used with both eyes open and functioning, so that one sees around the scope as well as through it.

Scopes are not particularly useful when their lenses are wet or plastered with snow or with damp leaves. If I had to hunt in areas of constant, heavy precipitation, I would probably use aperture metallic sights. Under the more normal conditions that most of us encounter, quickly removable scope lens covers obviate the problem.

For scope covers I like wide bands cut from an inner tube, or the Butler Creek "Bikini" scope cover. With either, a hard pull back and up on the rear cover lets the thing fly clear, though there is a limit to the size of objective lens that the supposedly "one size fits all" Bikini will work with.

A lot of scope accuracy problems can be traced to the mounts, and in particular to loose screws. A drop of Loctite applied to every scope-mounting screw is cheap insurance.

The Redfield Jr.-type one-piece (or "bridge") base (now made by other manufacturers as well) is not as strong as it looks. It usually has only three attaching screws versus the four common to two-piece bases. As is true also of the Redfield SR-type two-piece bases, most of the recoil is taken by the one ring that has the dovetail foot. The shanks of the windage screws are easily bent if over-tightened. And if the scope is removed and replaced too often, the dovetail foot can wear enough to become loose in the base, which is not helpful.

The one-piece base does have a couple of useful features. The rear ring comes far enough forward to allow mounting some short-bodied compact scopes on standard-length actions without having to resort to extension rings. In addition, the windage adjustment in the base allows the scope to be lined up with the bore without having to crank the reticle way over near the limit of its travel, which can induce focusing and other problems.

Scopes: The Big Element

The new Warne mounts—improved versions of the former Kimber mounts—are excellent, especially when one wants to be able to remove and replace the scope quickly and without affecting its zero, as should be true also of the latest Leupold double-lever "Quick Release" system.

I think the integral receiver scope-mounting dovetails as provided by Ruger, Sako, and Brno are the best solution of all. But, truthfully, I find that the ordinary, simple Weaver bases and rings work as well as anything—except for looks, they are awfully hard to beat and available with mount bases for virtually any common rifle.

The first essential requirement in a big-game scope is ruggedness, the ability to survive the knocks and abuse it will inevitably receive in real hunting without breaking, fogging up, or altering its zero. These requirements are more important than having the finest possible optical quality.

Good definition and light transmission are requisite, but a touch of optical distortion out at the edges matters little as one aims through the center of the field. The Duplex-type reticle introduced by Leupold with four posts that step down to fine cross hairs at their intersection is the best design for all-round use.

As for magnification, I agree with half of Elmer Keith's long-ago advice, and until recently I would have agreed with all of it. For fast, comparatively close-range work in cover, or with dangerous game, a low-power scope is the right choice. I put my first big-game scope, a Weaver K2.5, on a .375 H&H Magnum in 1963. My present .375 still wears a K2.5 Weaver.

Those rifles of my professional hunting days in Africa saw a fair amount of exhilarating close-range action, and the scopes proved to be very fast indeed, even on buffalo at three paces. I would still choose something similar today, such as the Leupold 2.5X Compact I have on my .416 Remington, or perhaps a variable with a 1X or 1.5X bottom end.

I wonder how an Aimpoint-type sight would work on a stopping rifle? With no magnification, unlimited field of view, no parallax, and nothing to line up, you just dab the red dot on the sticking place and press the trigger. It ought to be wonderfully fast. But of course it does rely on a battery, and one does have to remember to switch it on. . . .

The first variable-power scopes were not always entirely reliable, and for a long time I would have nothing to do with them. I used 3X and 4X sights on my general hunting rifles with good satisfaction for years, both in Africa and later in this country. But then one overcast, gloomy afternoon during the Texas deer season a few years ago, I peered through a 3X scope at a doe I had spotted with the binocular in a stand of trees 150 yards away and was shocked to find difficulty in telling which end was which.

On a sunny day last season I had a deer standing in deep shadow in a motte of live oaks, with a little light brush in front of it. With the 8x30mm Swarovski binocular I could see it perfectly and noted that its shoulder was clear. Through the 3X scope, though, I could hardly make it out at all. The range was 120 paces.

Then I ran into the same problem this season, with a 4X compact on my favorite 7x57mm. That doe eventually stepped out where I could nail it, but I was convinced: There are indeed situations where 3X and 4X will not do.

Nowadays, good-quality varipower scopes are practically as stout and as reliable as the fixed powers. The 3–9X variables are still the best sellers and do very well, though the top power is seldom required for big game except when shooting across huge bean fields, clear-cuts, and such.

Actually, the "bean field" shooters sometimes want even more power than the 9X available in many variables, and may opt for something like the Bausch & Lomb 6–24X or Leupold 6.5–20X, which would be quite useful on varmints also. But for most hunting, the biggest scopes are overdoing it, adding unneeded weight and bulk.

I think the 2–7X range is close to ideal, and because I often hunt in the thick stuff, I really like the 1.75–6X scopes with enlarged objectives that both Burris and Leupold now offer. On a very accurate Jarrett-built .280 Ackley Improved, I have a Leupold 2.5–8X, the combination making a superb open-country rig still useful in the brush, though some might prefer a 3.5–10X glass. Actually, a fixed-power 6X serves excellently, except at really close quarters or perhaps for fast shots on moving game, while the long-popular 4X is still a very viable all-round sight.

Many of today's high-power scopes have adjustable objective lenses that can be focused to eliminate parallax at the indicated ranges. Parallax is the apparent shift of the reticle in relation to the target when the eye is moved off-center.

Big-game scopes are generally set to be parallax-free at 150 yards. They will show some parallax at other distances, but of such a trifling order as to be of little consequence. An adjustable objective could be of value, however, in varmint shooting or for very short-range work as is likely to be done with .22 rimfires and airguns.

I cannot make recommendations about specific brands—there are simply too many with which I have had no experience, or no recent experience. It is generally held that the scopes created by such central European makers as Schmidt & Bender, Zeiss, Kahles, Swarovski, et al., are the finest obtainable. They are indeed superb, and also very expensive.

But I do find that for all practical purposes the best American and Far Eastern makes seem to do just as well in the field. Most of my rifles have Leupold or Burris scopes, which have given outstanding service, and I have a few original Weaver scopes still in use. But I am confident that I would be very satisfied with the premier products of any of the other well-known scope brands also.

Decisions, decisions! Perhaps we have too many choices. Picking a telescopic sight was surely easier back in 1946. But today's scopes are incomparably better, and if a hunter makes a little effort to analyze the demands of his hunting circumstances, he can find a scope to suit them exactly, and one that will give him years of reliable and useful service into the bargain.

Arizona Cougar Chase

⊕ **Chapter 32**

Mountain lions are fascinating animals, and there is far more to hunting them than I had ever imagined. (American Hunter *magazine, August 1987*)

The misconceptions entertained about things one has never tried can be utterly amazing. When on rare occasions I gave any thought at all to hunting mountain lions with dogs, I always imagined a troop of horsemen loping easily along after a pack of hounds in full bay until the panting quarry took refuge in a tree and one of the hunters leisurely dismounted to dispatch it with a revolver. Hah! How wrong can you get?

Thus it was with somewhat restrained enthusiasm that I accepted an invitation to join Harlon Carter on a lion hunt in southern Arizona. For one thing, I have long since taken all the big cats I am in any way entitled to, and have not the slightest desire ever to kill another one.

Still, I thought it would be interesting to have a look at some new country and to experience a different style of hunting, and I did very much desire to see a mountain lion. And of course I wanted to meet Harlon Carter, the former chief of the border patrol who took a relatively ineffectual National Rifle Association of a million or so members and built it up to a politically potent and very powerful organization of nearly three million. Of course he did not accomplish that all by himself—it required the joint efforts of many good people. But Harlon's leadership and determination were major factors in making it happen.

I met him at his home in Green Valley, a little way to the south of Tucson, Arizona. A short, stocky, and friendly man, Harlon's drive and vigor remain unimpaired by his seventy-three years. His home, incidentally, is one of the very few I have been into in this country whose walls are lined with more books than my own. I discovered that Harlon is as great an admirer of both Winston Churchill and Theodore Roosevelt as I am, and noted with some envy his quite complete collection of TR's books.

He had his truck packed and ready to go, so as soon as I had thrown my kit aboard we drove over to Rio Rico, Arizona, to meet the outfitter, Ollie Barney, a longtime friend of Harlon's. Ollie is a big, craggy, white-haired Westerner only a few years younger than Harlon, but is still as enduring as rawhide. In addition to his involvement in the construction business and in ranching (from both of which he is now retired), Ollie has for many years held an outfitter's license and has guided hunters to all the game animals available in Arizona, including desert bighorn sheep.

But his first love is chasing mountain lions with hounds that he has trained himself, and that is about the only hunting he does anymore. Over the years he has caught eighty-three lions for his hunters and taken another baker's dozen himself, most of which were stock killers. He has no count of how many he has treed and let go, but it is not a few.

After Ollie had loaded six hounds, two horses, and Pete the mule into his trailer, we set off for Bear Valley Ranch, below Atascosa Mountain in the Coronado National Forest, only a few miles north of the border. The ranch owns but about forty deeded acres and grazes its cattle on its allotment in the national forest. Ranch hand Tom Barkley and his son Mark live on the property, but there is also an unoccupied ranch house that Ollie uses, so we had a very comfortable "camp" with gas stove, lights, refrigerator, hot and cold running water, and even a bathroom with a shower and indoor plumbing.

That evening Ollie tried to teach us something about our quarry. *Felis concolor*, the "unicolored cat," has gone by many names in different times and places—panther, puma, cougar, catamount—but is generally known as the mountain lion in the Southwest, or more commonly just as the lion. Mexicans call it *el leon*, which means the same thing.

It is the second largest cat of the Western Hemisphere, surpassed only by the jaguar, and is quite comparable to the leopard in size, with toms weighing 120 pounds and females 80 pounds on average, though there is considerable individual variation. Various sources list a maximum weight of 275 pounds and suggest that the Rocky Mountain lion of Utah, Colorado, Wyoming, and Idaho is larger than the Sierra Madre race we would be hunting.

The mountain lion is a lithe, muscular predator with a long, heavy tail and a remarkably small head. It is generally a uniform reddish-brown to dull gray in color, although the young are spotted. The pelt of a very large male that Tom Barkley has on his living room wall shows faint but quite definite spots.

At one time lions inhabited practically all of the Americas from the Strait of Magellan to southern Canada. Nowadays they are found in this country mostly in the western states, with small populations in Florida, Louisiana, and, I believe, Tennessee. Every now and again lion sightings are reported from places like Maine, New York State, the Ozarks, and the Hill Country of central Texas.

There are records of mountain lions eating everything from field mice to moose, including grass, berries, insects, sheep, cattle, horses, a peacock, armadillos, skunks, elk, and porcupines. Deer form the bulk of their diet under normal conditions, however. They are usually dramatically pictured in the act of leaping down on a deer from an overhanging branch or crag. But in fact it seems that a slow, belly-to-the-ground stalk to bring them within fifty feet of their prey, followed by a sudden violent rush, is the standard technique, just as it is with African lions and with house cats. It is said that they kill prey mostly by a bite to the back of the neck or to the throat.

Ollie believes that when there is a good deer population, lions generally leave livestock alone. But as with most predators, they are opportunists and occasionally cannot resist the temptation presented by an innocent, unwary calf or, more especially, a foal. A few lions become confirmed livestock killers and naturally pass on the same bad habits to their young. Consequently, mountain lions were for years bountied as vermin, but now most western states list them as game animals. Arizona has no closed season on them, but requires a license and imposes a bag limit of one per year.

Unlike leopards, mountain lions very rarely attack men and cannot be reckoned as truly dangerous game. Hunters have climbed up into the same tree with bayed-up lions to rope them or to prod them with sticks to make them snarl for the camera. Usually no one gets hurt, but it is still a foolhardy stunt that I certainly do not recommend.

Lions may mate at any time of year, but Ollie says his observations suggest that most of the young are born in June and July, when there are a lot of deer fawns. Litters of up to six kittens have been recorded, but three or four is normal. Generally, only two are raised.

Although males and females obviously do get together at the appropriate time, mountain lions are for the most part solitary animals, occupying territories of about ten square miles up to possibly one hundred square miles. When several lions are seen together, it is usually a female with her young. They often stay with their mother until they are nearly two years old, presumably to learn how to hunt.

Lions routinely travel five to fifteen miles in a night, and are shy and stealthy animals that are rarely seen even where they are comparatively plentiful. They do occasionally respond to predator calls, I am told, but the only practical way to hunt them is to course them with dogs.

Lion hounds can be of several different breeds—Ollie's pack includes Walker, Blue Tick, Redbone, and other bloodlines, both mixed and purebred—but are distinguished from the rest by their recognition that lions are their only proper quarry. Aficionados of the sport naturally use their best dogs for breeding, but a lion hound still must be schooled and broken of its instinctive propensity for chasing deer, raccoons, javelinas, foxes, and such. Ollie remarked that the other dogs show a young hound what to hunt, while he teaches it what it must not hunt, either by voice commands or, more rarely, with a shock collar. All the same, many young dogs never develop the requisite interest in running lions, so a good, proven lion hound is valued from $3,000 to $4,000. A houndsman buddy of mine from Colorado tells me that lion hounds that have learned to hold a trail under the poor scenting conditions that prevail in the hot, arid Southwest are in great demand in his part of the country.

In the North, when there is snow on the ground, the dogs are often not loosed until fresh tracks have been found, and then they may be followed on foot. Farther south, on the other hand, tracks are not easily spotted on the dry and rocky ground. In Arizona the dogs have to cover a lot of territory before they find a hot trail, so they are generally followed on horseback. The country is typically pretty rugged, which tends to lead one into some frighteningly desperate riding—at least by my standards! I gathered from Ollie and Mark that mules are better than horses in some of this terrain, as they are more surefooted.

Lions, it seems, are so deathly afraid of dogs that they have been run up a tree by a single, yapping little cur. Normally they can be approached quite closely and are often dispatched with a handgun. Ollie, however, prefers that his clients use a rifle. He pointed out that occasionally a lion will leap out of the tree when a hunter gets too near, and that at other times they will come to bay on ledges and pinnacles where they are beyond sure pistol shot.

Another consideration is that the lion should be dead when it hits the ground, else it may kill or severely maul several valuable dogs before it expires. It seems that at the moment of truth, not all of Ollie's handgun hunters have shot quite as well as they thought they could! I gathered that his vehement feelings on this subject pertained more to conventional pistols and revolvers than to the newfangled, scope-sighted, single-shot pistols that are chambered for what are, in effect, rifle cartridges.

Nevertheless, he advises his clients to bring a short, light, scope-sighted rifle that will ride easily in a saddle scabbard. His own ideal lion gun, which he often lends to clients, is a battered Marlin lever-action for the .44 Magnum revolver cartridge. Its barrel has been shortened to 16½ inches, and 1 inch has been lopped off its buttstock. It carries a 2¾X scope and is sighted to hit dead-on at 100 yards. It has been used on numerous lions and has performed flawlessly, Ollie claims.

Harlon brought an old Remington Model 660 carbine with a 20-inch barrel, chambered to .308 Winchester. It is fitted with an ancient and rusty Lyman Alaskan 2½X scope, and its stock has been lengthened by gluing on an extra slice of wood and a recoil pad. It looks like hell! I was quite amused to note that both Ollie and Harlon apparently regard hunting rifles strictly as tools, and care as little about their appearance as I do. "Handsome is as handsome does!"

The first day, accompanied by both the Barkleys, we spent almost eight hours in the saddle, making a wide circle down to the Mexican border through a grand but rough landscape of live oaks, mesquite, tall ridges, wind-sculptured rocky peaks, cliffs, and deep canyons. About midmorning there was a flurry of dogs and excited barking just ahead, but when we arrived on the scene we found only a freshly killed coyote. The hounds must have been right on top of it before it became aware of them, which is rather unusual. There was no other action that day.

I had done no riding at all for a couple of years, and Harlon had been on a horse for only one day in the last fifty years, so we both got a little saddle-sore. What mattered more was that Harlon's legs were so affected that when he dismounted to lead Pete up a dangerously precipitous stretch of the trail, he was disconcerted to find that he could not stand up. Obviously, this was not good if he should have to leap off his gallant steed and blast a lion in a hurry. Ollie studied the matter and decided that the rifle in its scabbard was riding so high that it forced Harlon's knee outward, and that his stirrup leathers were too short. A little readjustment pretty well cured the problem.

Actually, I find stirrup length to be quite important. If they are too short my knees soon start hurting; if they are too long my butt becomes sorer than necessary. The best system for an inexpert horseman like myself is probably to adjust the stirrups so that when one stands up in them, a clenched fist will just pass between the saddle and the seat of his pants.

On the second day we were joined by Brett Glover, a young lion hunting enthusiast and protégé of Ollie's, who brought along three of his own hounds. We trailered the horses and dogs a way up the road, then rode a few miles in to an old corral, where Ollie left Harlon and me to wait while he and the others took the dogs through some rough canyons.

He had warned us that they might be gone most of the day, but in fact he and Mark were back within an hour. Ollie announced that they had a lion treed, but he did not know how long it would stay. He urged us to hurry. He said that Blackie, a six-year-old hound who had been in on forty-five lion kills, found the scent first and took out on it immediately. While checking to make sure they were going the right way—hounds are quite capable of running a trail in the wrong direction, away from the quarry—Ollie found a lion scrape and the spoor of a tom.

After only a short run, the lion was bayed in a jumble of rock, but as the horsemen reached the spot, it broke and went running down the canyon with the hounds flowing after it. Finally it took refuge in a large oak tree. Ollie had then left Brett to watch it while he and Mark came back to fetch us.

As we went scrambling up the ridge, Ollie's walkie-talkie radio squawked and Brett came on to report, with some despair in his voice, that most of the hounds had gone down to the stream in the bottom of the canyon for a drink. On the way back they had come across the lion's trail again and had taken off along it in great excitement, going away from the tree. Only one dog, named Trash, which he assuredly is not, was left to hold the cat. Ollie told him to do what he could to get the fool hounds back, but not to lose sight of the lion.

We kicked the horses along as fast as we dared through the rocks and brush. As we came over the crest and started down into the canyon, we saw a big oak on the opposite slope with a lone dog under it. The rest of the pack was yowling and carrying on about a quarter-mile up the valley around the rocks where the lion had made its first stand. Eventually, as Brett came up to meet us, we were able to make out the tawny-red rear half and long tail of the cat high up in the tree, but its forequarters were hidden behind the trunk.

Brett took Harlon, on foot, down and around to a spot from which the head and shoulders of the cat were visible, and placed his rolled-up jacket on a rock as a rest for the rifle. The range was about 100 yards or a trifle more across the canyon. But with only one dog baying it, the lion might leave at any moment, and they could not risk trying to get any closer. Harlon was perfectly content to have a rifle rather than a handgun under the circumstances. The target was not large, and he had to hold within an inch of the tree trunk to get his bullet into the right spot on the lion's shoulder.

At the shot, nothing appeared to happen. Ollie was astounded. Surely Harlon couldn't have missed! But watching through my binocular I saw the cat stiffen as the bullet struck; then the end of its tail started whirling in a circle. After perhaps five seconds, the lion relaxed and plummeted out of the tree, stone-dead.

It turned out that it was not the tom whose sign Ollie had seen but instead was a big, dry female. However, Harlon said that because it was a mature, adult lion taken by fair means, and was the end result of an exciting and strenuous hunt, he was well satisfied with it.

We found that his 150-grain Hornady Spire Point bullet had smashed the spine, severed the aorta, and lacerated the top of both lungs. The cat's stomach was full of big chunks of meat and pieces of deer hide with the hair still attached. It had no doubt fed well the previous night.

We had been lucky to get a lion so quickly—on average it has taken Ollie's clients about five or six days of hard hunting to find one. He normally books lion hunters for ten-day hunts and charges $2,000. However, he says he wants to stop guiding hunters as a business; in the future he wants to hunt just for his own enjoyment with his friends, and perhaps with a few regular old clients. But I believe he can refer would-be lion hunters to other good guides.

Apart from being his eighty-fourth successful client, Harlon was also the oldest hunter Ollie had ever guided to a lion. The next oldest had been a young fellow of only sixty-nine summers!

As for me, I thoroughly enjoyed the experience, the beautiful country, the fine companionship, and the chance to learn a little about lions, hounds, and lion hunting. Lions are fascinating animals, and there is far more to hunting them than I had ever imagined.

One thing that strikes me about it is this: I do not see that an ordinary sportsman can justify taking more than one or two mountain lions in his lifetime. But he does not have to quit hunting them; all the thrill lies in the working of the dogs and in the chase, while the kill is rather anticlimactic. If he will be satisfied to photograph them and let them go after they have been successfully treed, a man can enjoy the excitement of running lions with a clear conscience all his life, so long as he can sit on a horse. It is a great sport!

A Professional's Rifle, Thirteen Years Later

 Chapter 33

Simple, rugged, and practical are essential characteristics for the professional hunter's rifle. (American Rifleman *magazine, April 1996)*

In a 1983 essay for *American Rifleman,* I described a "professional's model" rifle I had put together for my own use. Its mission, apart from acting as a backup rifle for those rare occasions when it was imperative that I shoot to prevent a client's crippled animal from escaping, was to serve as an all-round rifle suitable for any big-game hunting in the contiguous forty-eight states.

Such a piece would also do very nicely as an African professional (or resident) hunter's "light" rifle. I suggested that above all else it had to be utterly reliable, both in functioning and in terminal effect.

I still have that rifle. There have been many developments in the interim, and it may be of interest to note which ones have proved worth incorporating. In its original form this rifle had a military Mauser M98 action with a 22-inch barrel in .30-06, a Garrett Accur-Lite fiberglass stock, a Weaver K3 3X scope in Weaver top mounts, standby iron sights, and a modified military-style loop shooting sling. It weighed about 8 pounds field-ready with five rounds in its magazine.

At the time of the article, it was so new that I had used it only on a Wyoming antelope hunt and to take a few deer here in Texas. Since then it has accounted for moose and elk, a turkey, a passel of deer, feral hogs, and a variety of exotic game ranging from 60-pound mouflon sheep to 600-pound nilgai. The rifle has also been used extensively to test handloads, factory ammo, bullet performance, and the like.

In the fall of 1983 a fellow hunter jumped off his horse in the middle of the packstring and shot at a moose with his .300 Weatherby. The packhorse I was leading went wild, looped the lead rope around the butt of my rifle where it protruded from the saddle scabbard, and snapped it in two through the small of the grip. Luckily the outfitter had a spare rifle.

Later I glued the stock back together, with a couple of long screws bridging the break. It is still in service and is probably stronger than before, especially as I also cross-bolted it behind the recoil lug.

Synthetic stocks have really come into their own over the last decade; every major domestic rifle manufacturer now offers them. Properly made, they are stronger and more stable than wooden ones, and can be lighter. Much has been learned about how they should be constructed since that old Garrett was made, and the rifle's younger brother wears the Clifton Arms synthetic stock that is fitted with a neat little bipod that retracts into the fore-end. The Clifton stock is not a lightweight, but it is immensely strong and absolutely stable.

The original rifle is still chambered to .30-06, and so is its brother. Several fine cartridges have been introduced (or legitimized) since 1983, including the .35 Whelen. But, leaving out large, dangerous game, there is still nothing that can quite equal the '06 as an all-round, use-it-on-everything cartridge, at least within 300 yards, when a reasonably light, short, handy, portable rifle is desired.

The rifle was zeroed for a handload that drove the 180-grain Nosler Partition bullet to about 2,750 FPS at the muzzle. That bullet performed perfectly on a Wyoming pronghorn at 230 paces, penetrated completely through a Canadian moose's chest close behind the shoulders, leaving a fist-size hole through the lungs, and did the job on a good number of deer and other game besides. The rifle still remains sighted for 180-grain bullets, but there are so many superb premium bullets available nowadays—Trophy Bonded, Swift, Barnes X-bullet, Jensen, and others—that it is difficult to choose.

The Nosler Partition is just as good as it ever was, of course, and it is never a mistake. (Nosler Partitions tend to leave small exit holes because the front cores disintegrate and the strips of jacket fold tight in against the shanks, which leads some hunters to believe that they do not expand much. Actually, the front half of a 180-grain Nosler Partition is quite soft and always expands.) In my experience, the 180-grain Barnes X-bullet will give deeper penetration than most 200- and 220-grain bullets. One went completely through both shoulder areas of a young bull elk and put it down within thirteen paces.

Premium bullets are now available in factory ammo. Federal offers Nosler Partition and Trophy Bonded in some loads, PMC has the Barnes X-Bullet, and Winchester loads its own premium Fail Safe 180 grains for the '06. When a 180-grain spitzer like the Nosler Partition at 2,750 FPS is sighted to land 2.9 inches high at 100 yards, it will be on point of aim at about 240 yards and 3 inches low at 280 yards, according to the Sierra ballistics program.

Thus, out to the latter distance, 280 yards, one should be able to obtain a killing hit on almost any big-game animal with a center-of-the-chest hold. At 300 yards it should strike 5 inches low. I can't remember when I last thought it necessary to shoot at an unwounded game animal at anything approaching that range.

Originally, the rifle was provided with a steel-tube Weaver K3 scope and auxiliary open iron sights. I wrote that variable-power scopes were not trustworthy, and that if the target appeared too small at 3X, I was not justified in shooting. I have changed my mind. Today's best-quality variable-power scopes are very reliable, they are no longer prone to fogging, and they show no significant change in point of impact as the power is varied. Furthermore, there have been a couple of occasions the last few years when low power has proved inadequate, as on a bright, sunny afternoon when a deer standing in black shade 150 yards away proved to be invisible through the 3X glass. Magnification is undeniably an aid to good shot placement, especially in less-than-optimum light conditions.

The rifle now wears a Burris Signature 2–8X variable fitted with Burris's "Posi-Lock" that replaces the spring that is supposed to hold the erector lens tube against the adjustment screws with a screw-adjustable steel post. This eliminates the whiplash movement of the erector tube under recoil, ensures positive response to sight adjustments, locks the adjustments, and altogether seems like a good idea.

The original Weaver mounts are still employed. They are simple and stout, and allow the scope to be removed and replaced with as little loss of zero as any I have tried. They will not, however, work with all short-tube compact scopes, such as the Leupold 1.75–6X that probably offers the optimum power versus bulk and weight compromise for an all-round rifle.

The rifle's younger brother, the Clifton-stocked FN Mauser, carries a Leupold Vari-X 2.5–8X—an outstanding glass—in a Redfield Jr. bridge mount, with one of the windage screws replaced with a Pilkington lever to allow convenient scope removal.

Attached to the back of the base is the nifty "Little Blue Peep" fold-up auxiliary aperture sight that Redfield no longer makes. It allows the front sight to be a strong post rather than a vulnerable bead set on a slender stem. Iron sights are strictly backup, to get me back to camp, where I always have a spare scope in its own rings already sighted in, in the unlikely event of the primary scope failing.

Both rifles have bead-blasted blued finishes. For use in Alaska and other damp climes, I give all the metalwork a couple of coats of paste wax, which suffices to protect it against rust for up to two weeks. Nevertheless, the stainless steel now offered by all our major manufacturers is the way to go, though some of the electroless nickel and other modern finishes are said to be even more corrosion resistant and are extremely durable.

If I were building my "professional's rifle" today, what features would I want? First, it would still be chambered for the .30-06, and it would be sighted in for a load using a premium 180-grain bullet. If a fellow fails to kill anything except perhaps Alaskan bears and the largest African beasts quite expeditiously with that combination, it is purely his own fault—he did not place it right. Consistent accuracy of around 1.5 minutes of angle is entirely satisfactory for big-game hunting.

The action would be stainless steel, either the latest Winchester Model 70 or the Ruger Model 77, with Mauser-type extractors and the "controlled feed" that I subjectively prefer from having been raised with M98 bolt-actions. For someone not suffering from my prejudices in this respect, the stainless Remington Model 700, Browning A-Bolt, Weatherby Mark V, or Savage 116 would serve just as well. The barrel would also be of stainless steel and 22 inches in length.

The sighting system would consist of a high-quality variable-power scope in the 1.75–6X or 2.5–8X range, with the most simple and rugged easily detachable mounting system available. Integral scope-mount bases such as are provided on the Ruger M77 are my first choice—backed up by a post front and folding "ghost-ring" aperture rear sight if possible. The more unstable a position one has to adopt in the field, the more important a good trigger pull becomes. Clean, crisp, and 2½ pounds is about ideal.

A loop shooting sling, which improves my holding ability close to 30 percent in the prone, sitting, and kneeling positions, would be fitted, and the barrel would be free-floated so that use of the sling or a bipod would cause minimal shift in the point of impact. The stock would be the Clifton with its disappearing bipod. When stowed, all that is visible is its feet, which look like a black fore-end tip. Because it must fit into the fore-end, the bipod is necessarily too short for any but the prone position, and it is more delicate than some, but its unobtrusiveness more than makes up for that. A bipod, incidentally, comes in handy when one must recheck the zero in field or camp, far from any shooting bench.

The stoutly built Clifton stock is not a feather. My FN Mauser weighs 9¼ pounds in working trim, enough to give lightweight enthusiasts the horrors. I will take a little extra heft any day to ensure solid reliability and improved ease of holding. Besides, it has been my observation that the fellow who cannot get up the mountain with a 9-pound rifle will not make it with a 7-pound one, either.

While it is unlikely that I'll ever afford to build this perfected "professional's rifle," my original one, with the improved scope and bullets, will do almost as well. In accordance with the KISS principle (Keep It Simple, Stupid), it has everything I really need, and nothing more. Especially, it is rugged enough to be reliable under almost any conditions I might encounter. Granted a heavy stopping rifle for the huge, short-tempered stuff, I would be content to hunt any other big game anywhere in the world with it. It is as close to being the perfect all-round, general-purpose big-game rifle as I can imagine.

Another Boost for the .35 Whelen

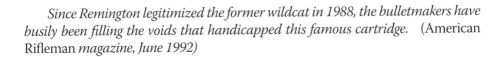

⊕ **Chapter 34**

Since Remington legitimized the former wildcat in 1988, the bulletmakers have busily been filling the voids that handicapped this famous cartridge. (American Rifleman *magazine, June 1992)*

When Remington legitimized the .35 Whelen as a factory cartridge in 1988, many of us were of the opinion that the .338-06 would have been a superior choice for a nonmagnum "medium" because better bullets were available for it.

At that time almost the only readily obtainable .35-caliber bullets suited to heavy game were the fine Speer 250-grain spitzer, 250- to 300-grain copper-tubing-jacketed bullets from Barnes Bullets, and a 250-grain roundnose softpoint (RNSP) from Hornady. All the other mass-produced offerings available were designed for use on deer-size game in the .35 Remington and .358 Winchester.

It is true that extraordinary, very expensive, and virtually handmade super-premium .35-caliber bullets were just starting to become available from small firms like Swift and Trophy Bonded Bullets. But .338-06 owners could load up with the superb 250-grain or 210-grain Nosler Partition bullets obtainable in any gun store and be sure that they would have ample penetration for the largest game one might need to slam them into on this continent.

The picture has lately changed considerably, to the Whelen's advantage. First, Sierra designed a streamlined 225-grain spitzer boattail that should be prime longer-range medicine in both the .358 Winchester and the .35 Whelen. Next, Nosler introduced a 225-grain Partition bullet, and Barnes its innovative X-Bullet in 200- and 225-grain weights in .358-inch size.

The Barnes X-Bullet is unusual in that it contains no lead. Instead, it is made of a homogenous copper alloy and is given a sophisticated cavity that ensures its expansion even at quite low-impact velocities. Typically an X-Bullet opens up like some exotic flower to show four long, narrow, sharp-edged petals. The expansion stops at the bottom of the cavity, leaving the rear two-thirds of the shank intact to drive the bullet on for good penetration. In softer tissue, the slashing petals remain intact, but against heavy resistance (or at high impact velocities), they tend to break off, thereby reducing the bullet's frontal area (and in effect increasing its sectional density), while possibly working as secondary projectiles to spread damage over a wider area.

Now, both Nosler and Barnes have added 250-grain projectiles to their premium lines, and Speer has recently introduced a 250-grain Grand Slam that ought also to work splendidly on the largest game.

The Swift Bullet Company's partition-type A-frame bullets with bonded front cores are offered in 225- and 250-grain weights, while Trophy Bonded Bullets' Solid Shank bullets, which have only a small, bonded lead core in the forward half, come in weights of either 240 or 270 grains.

The A-Square Company has 275-grain, .358-inch bullets in both its very stout "Dead Tough" and the softer "Lion Load" designs. Remington factory ammo is provided with a 200-grain Pointed Soft Point Core-Lokt bullet at a listed 2,675 FPS (24-inch barrel) and with two 250-grain bullets, a roundnose softpoint (by Hornady) and a pointed softpoint (the Speer, I believe), both at a nominal 2,400 FPS. Presently, this seems to be the only "ready-made" .35 Whelen ammunition available.

Up-to-date handloading data for the Whelen is to be found in the Nosler *Manual No. 3*, in the third edition of the *Sierra Manual*, in the latest (4th edition) *Hornady Handbook*, and in the 1992 Hercules *Reloaders' Guide*. The Nosler and Sierra books give data only for 225-grain and lighter bullets, while the last two list 250-grain bullets as well.

Data from the first three manuals suggest a maximum velocity of 2,650 FPS with 200-grain bullets, 2,500 to 2,550 FPS with the 225-grain bullet, and 2,400 FPS with the 250-grain Hornady bullets. But the Hercules manual claims 2,550 FPS for the 250-grain Hornady RNSP in a 24-inch barrel, with a maximum charge of 59.5 grains of Reloader 15 powder at a chamber pressure of 48,400 copper units of pressure (CUP).

For the 200-grain Hornady Spire Point, Hercules shows a charge of 60.0 grains of Reloader 15 as developing 2,675 FPS at only 44,800 CUP.

Remington informs me that the maximum average working chamber pressure for the .35 Whelen has been set at 52,000 CUP, which is the same as for the .308 Winchester and 2,000 CUP higher than the maximum for the .30-06. Normally, factory loads are, and handloads should be, kept decidedly below the maximum pressure to ensure safe and trouble-free functioning, even in badly fouled bores or at abnormally high ambient temperatures.

My own Whelen, built by Clyde Moore on a Mauser 98 military action, has a 22-inch Douglas barrel with a rifling twist of 1 turn in 12 inches, whereas Remington uses a 1:16 twist. (I chose the fast twist so as to be able to stabilize the long 300-grain Barnes bullets should I want to use them, but in fact a 1:14 twist will do that perfectly adequately and is probably the optimum twist rate for a .35 Whelen.)

This rifle has the standard-length magazine for the 8x57mm military round, which limits overall cartridge length to 3.295 inches for reliable feeding, although the chamber throat would permit most bullets to be seated out much farther.

With the pointed 250-grain Speer and Nosler Partition bullets (rather than the RN Hornady, for which I see no advantage) seated to fit the magazine, I ran into indications of higher pressures than I care for before reaching Hercules's maximum charge of 59.5 grains of RL15.

Using Remington .35 Whelen cases (not reformed '06s) and Remington 9½ standard large rifle primers, I settled on 58.0 grains of RL15, which recorded 2,550 FPS with the Nosler bullet at 15 feet on the Oehler M35P chronograph.

The 250-grain Speer and Nosler bullets come just about to the base of the case neck when seated to a cartridge overall length (OAL) of 3.295 inches, but because it contains no lead and is less dense, the 250-grain Barnes X-Bullet is longer and intrudes into the powder chamber. With it, 57.5 grains of RL15 gave 2,540 FPS.

When I seated the Nosler and the Barnes bullets out to a 3.38-inch cartridge OAL, which will work through a .30-06-length magazine, I was able to work up, gingerly, to Hercules's 59.5-grain RL15 load, achieving close on 2,600 FPS. But, again, I think pressures were too high for a working load, and I will not use over 58 grains in my rifle with those bullets. (The RN Hornady bullet that Hercules employed in its testing is shorter than any of the other 250-grain bullets, and it has a taper that gives it quite a short bearing surface.)

With the few copper-tubing 275-grain Barnes bullets I had on hand, a velocity of 2,400 FPS seemed to be practical, while 2,640 FPS with 225 grains and up to 2,675 FPS with 200-grain bullets were achieved with pressures that appeared to be nicely below maximum.

It might be of interest to some readers to note that the well-respected .350 Rigby Magnum (African professional John Taylor declared it one of the best of the "mediums") earned its African reputation with a 225-grain bullet at a nominal 2,625 FPS.

I compared the penetration and expansion of the Barnes X and Nosler Partition bullets, and a few other .35 Whelen loads, in wet newspaper against some .30-06 loads and the .375 H&H with 300-grain Nosler Partition bullets. In general, the Barnes X-Bullets gave the deepest penetration for their weight. I attribute this performance partly to the fact that their expanded petals tended to break off, leaving the bullets with a comparatively small frontal area and therefore a good remaining sectional density.

Penetration does not depend solely on sectional density—striking velocity, energy, and momentum, of course, undoubtedly count for something—but it is certainly a major factor. However, what matters is not necessarily the sectional density the bullet started out with but rather that which it retained during its penetration.

To illustrate the point, I calculated the remaining sectional densities of some of the expanded bullets recovered from the wet paper. The 275-grain Barnes copper-tubing bullet retained 94 percent of its original weight but expanded to an average diameter of .79 inch, showing the greatest frontal area of any of the bullets in the test.

Its remaining sectional density was thus about .059, compared to .067 for the 200-grain Nosler Partition in the .30-06 and .105 for the 250-grain X-Bullet in the .35 Whelen, both of which out-penetrated it, though with their lesser frontal areas they likely would create narrower wound channels in big-game animals.

In addition, I was curious about whether the X-Bullets would expand at lower velocities, so I tried them and the .35-caliber Nosler Partitions in the wet newsprint I use to test bullets at impact velocities of just below 2,000 FPS. They all expanded fully, which suggests that they ought to do so at ranges out to 300 yards or more, at least on mule deer and some larger game animals.

The .35 Whelen is sometimes disparaged by hunters and gun-magazine writers as being a short- to medium-range cartridge. I suppose this all depends on just how one seeks to define "long range," but the Whelen's trajectory with handloads is comparable to those of both the .30-06 and .375 H&H, and it is adequate for 300-yard shots if the man handling the rifle is capable of making them.

My rifle is now fitted with a Pacific Research Laboratories black synthetic stock. Designed by a custom stockmaker, it has handsome, classical lines and generous molded-in checkering patterns. Despite its light weight, it is robustly built with "ropes" of glass fiber reinforcing the critical areas and acting as pillars to support the action. It handles very comfortably, and altogether I like it better than almost any other synthetic stock I have tried.

The rifle is currently wearing a Burris Signature 1.5–6X scope sitting in Weaver mounts. It already has accompanied me on a number of hunts, including one very wet Alaskan trip, and has never given me even the slightest hint of trouble.

I think its power range is well suited to rifles of this type. When set at 1.5X it is nigh perfect for encounters of the close kind with bears or lesser game. While 3X or 4X is right for most hunting, the ability to go up to 6X has saved the day for me on occasion in poor light, or by enabling me to pick out the right patch of the beast to shoot at in thick cover.

When mounting the scope, I took care to ensure that the mount bases were exactly in line and exerting no bending strain on the scope's tube (epoxy under the rear base was necessary to achieve that). The Bushnell variable scope has stayed put and shows no shift whatsoever in point of impact (POI) as the power is changed.

Over the years I have killed more deer than any other game with the Whelen, and I have got good results on them with all bullet weights ranging from the 200-grain factory load to the 250-grain Nosler Partition, which does indeed expand even on our little central Texas whitetails.

The Whelen is a good deer cartridge! The lighter bullets are no doubt the sensible choice for this work. Unfortunately, with one exception, they do not shoot to the same point of impact (POI) as the 250-grain large-game bullets for which I prefer to keep my rifle sighted.

That exception is the 200-grain Remington factory PSPCL load, which prints to exactly the same POI at 100 yards. It is therefore my deer round of choice.

Actually, though, I am just as likely to use the 250-grain bullets on everything. It's just simpler.

An Alaskan friend has taken several brown bears and a number of moose and elk with the 250-grain Speer in his .35 Whelen. He says it works perfectly for him, and that no animal he has shot with it has ever gone more than 50 yards. I have used the 250-grain Nosler on a large, wounded, going-away brown bear at a range of perhaps 150 yards. The bullet broke the femur at the bear's hip joint, smashed part of the pelvis, and traveled forward into the big animal's abdomen.

With the same load I took a crack at a nilgai in south Texas. This goofy-looking beast from India has silly little spike horns, but a big one can weigh 600 pounds on the hoof, and the meat is excellent. The young bull I clobbered went about 350 pounds field-dressed.

It ran across the track sixty paces ahead of us. I swung with the cross hairs just in front of its chest and dumped it on its nose. The big Nosler had landed high on the shoulder. It went through the near-side shoulder blade, smashed the spine, broke the other blade, and ended up bulging the hide on the far side.

For the biggest bears, and especially for close-range stopping work, a heavier bullet like the 270-grain Trophy Bonded would be my preference. But in fact the 250-grain Barnes X-Bullet with its extraordinary penetration would likely be very near as good, and it or the 250-grain Nosler Partition are my choices for an all-round, use-it-on-everything load in the .35 Whelen.

The .35 Whelen was conceived seventy years ago to offer performance superior to the .30-06 on the larger game. In that it probably succeeded (albeit by a very small margin), and with the latest bullets and powders its potential is much enhanced. Now the cartridge is arguably the best of our nonmagnum mediums; it works well on anything without kicking up a great fuss, and reliability is its middle name.

The Tracker
by
Berit Aagaard

⊕ **Chapter 35**

In his book *African Hunter*, Baron Bror von Blixen-Finecke, who was one of the great professional hunters in Africa in the 1920s and 1930s, grasps the essence of the tracker when he writes: "In the exercise of his art—for an art it is—the tracker's qualities are tested to the uttermost. His patience must know no bounds, his physical endurance must almost exceed a marathon runner's, and his powers of observation must be keener than Sherlock Holmes's. These qualities enable him to say in the morning where the lion killed his prey last night, where the elephant lay down to rest during the darkest hours, where and between which animals nocturnal love duets to the death were fought out, when the wild beasts went to the watering hole, and where they are situated."

The first time my late husband Finn Aagaard mentioned Kinuno, who was to become his skilled tracker, expert skinner, reliable advisor, hunting partner, trusted employee, and loyal friend, was in a brief note in his journal from March 1964 after a private buffalo hunt. It simply states: "The tracker was a Mbere called Kinuno Mbogo. He did a fine job." Little did it herald the close working relationship and codependency that would develop between these two young men, both born in Kenya, but with such different backgrounds and heritage.

I remember Finn telling me how Kinuno initially worked on the farm he and his parents owned, cutting the tough sisal leaves that would ultimately be turned into fiber for twine and rope. One day during a conversation with Finn, Kinuno expressed an interest in hunting, and, shortly after, he started accompanying Finn in the bush. This was the start of a partnership that continued and flourished until legal hunting was banned in Kenya in 1977. Incidentally, Kinuno's last name is Mbogo, which means buffalo—quite fitting for a man who would spend many months out of every year hunting that impressive and challenging beast.

A professional hunter is about as helpless without his tracker as a ship's captain is minus his crew. Even though the hunter may find and follow game alone, and the captain could theoretically sail his ship solo, both these leaders depend heavily on their working partners in order to carry out their duties at the high level expected of them. Finn's relationship with his tracker Kinuno was no exception; the two hunted cordially together for years. On many occasions Finn would send Kinuno and the client off by themselves after some nondangerous game they had spotted; Kinuno always performed well, and always with a big grin on his face. The respect and admiration between the two men was mutual.

One such occasion had a somewhat unexpected outcome. Finn had sent Kinuno ahead with Charlie, a client, over a rise after a good warthog when a shot rang out. *"Simba!"* Kinuno exclaimed excitedly as Finn caught up with him and the client at the top of the hill. Finn had heard the shot, so he expected to see a worthy warthog trophy at their feet. What he saw was Kinuno shouting and pointing emphatically across to the next ridge about 250 yards away. After some searching, Finn did indeed spot the lion through tall, lion-colored grass. Kinuno insisted that the client's bullet had hit the lion, so Finn took a crack at him with his .375. They heard the thump of a hit, and then the lion jumped, growled, and took off!

When Kinuno and Charlie had crested the hill following the pig, there, to their great surprise, was a lion. Charlie desperately wanted a lion, but a week's baiting and blind building had been fruitless. It was the last day of the hunt, so this was too great an opportunity to miss. Kinuno felt somewhat responsible for the lack of Charlie's success with lions, so when they saw the big cat, Kinuno quickly told Charlie to *"Piga!"* (Shoot!) In his excitement and eagerness to please, Kinuno never thought of judging the distance . . . his brain was at that moment totally focused on the desire to get the client his lion.

The three men ran quickly toward where they had last seen the lion, but there was no sign of him. Finn sent for the hunting car where his .458 was, and they drove up the ridge as far as they could, looking carefully under and through bushes for the wounded lion. Finding nothing, Finn and Kinuno left the client in the Land Rover and started the unpleasant task of inching their way forward in hopes of finding the wounded and angry lion before he found them.

It was difficult to pick up the faint tracks and occasional drops of blood because the ridge was rocky lava covered with dry scrub bush and sansevieria, a vicious, spiky plant just tall enough for a lion to crouch under or behind. Slowly, cautiously the two men crept on, at any moment expecting to come face to face with a furious lion. Suddenly there were low, threatening growls ahead. They peered intently, looking into shadows and climbing up on a rock to see better. Nothing. They threw stones in the direction of the growls, still nothing. Advancing carefully to where they had heard the lion, they saw nothing. The lion had disappeared.

Finn and Kinuno must have looked at each other then and communicated silently as they so often did with hand motions; each one knowing the other's mind precisely after so many years as hunting partners. They advanced another fifty yards of painstaking tracking; all their senses were super alert. Suddenly there were more growls. This time Finn got a quick glimpse of the lion as he took off. Finn flung a shot after him, hitting a lava rock. Later Finn would discover that a piece of bullet or lava had found the top of the lion's back.

The two advanced up the ridge, and as they moved forward they heard growls emanating from a particularly dense bush. Finn got up on a rock from where he had a good view of both sides of this clump of vegetation. He instructed Kinuno to put a .375 bullet into the bush, which Kinuno did. The lion shot out to the right in a long low leap, emitting guttural growls as he went. The .458 swung like a shotgun, spoke, and caused the lion to jerk as he disappeared in the thicket. Finn took after him running, hoping to get another shot. As Finn rounded the bush, he practically stumbled over one very dead lion!

The close and intimate work relationship between a professional hunter and his tracker is legendary; the two have different strengths, play different roles in the hunt, and all are equally important. Finn always reckoned that Kinuno was the better hunter of the two; his tracking skills were phenomenal, and he had an uncanny way of "smelling out" where game had moved. A sense of total trust developed between the two men; they were often faced with sticky situations like the little lion incident where cooperation was essential; their silently mouthed communication and use of subtle gestures spoke volumes. If a hunter was hired by another outfitter, it was presumed and accepted that his tracker came along as well; the two were considered an inseparable unit.

Early in their relationship Finn decided it would be sensible to teach Kinuno to shoot since he would often be carrying the second gun while hunting. After a certain amount of target practice from various practical positions and instructions on shot placement, the two went out after game. Kinuno's usual big smile reached beyond his ears as they returned with a *kongoni* (Coke hartebeest), and Finn was as proud of him as if he had been one of his own sons. We would sometimes arrange informal shooting matches amongst the staff, and Kinuno generally did well.

More than once did his limited experience of shooting come in handy. Robert Stark from Orange, Texas, shot an oryx in the wide open semidesert of northern Kenya. There was no cover; the oryx was becoming restless while the hunters were still a good ways off, and Robert's shot did not drop it at once. Several guns fired, but it was Kinuno's shooting that did the trick. Using Finn's .375 at a distance of four hundred yards, he hit the ground in front of the animal. That's when it got interesting. The bullet ricocheted into the oryx's neck, went through the spine, and dropped him in his tracks!

Of all the shots Kinuno contributed over the years, the most spectacular one was undoubtedly on a wounded lion. Camp was on the edge of the Great Rift Valley, where a small river dropped over the edge of the escarpment surrounded by rocky, brushy hills and plenty of cover for lions. There was a lot of game, but also a lot of Masai cattle. The first day in camp a group of Masai came and informed the hunters that four lions lived in this area and that they had recently killed a cow.

This was exciting news, and Richard, our client from Texas, immediately began imagining his lion trophy displayed proudly in his den. For several days the hunters looked for signs of the lions, but saw nothing. Presently a report came in that lions had made an unsuccessful attempt on some more cattle. After a lot of searching, Kinuno found fresh tracks. The local Masai insisted the tracks were found in the lions' home range; furthermore, they said the lions would leave the area only for short periods to hunt, but would always return.

Finn and Kinuno discussed the strategy of how to hunt these lions and decided the best thing would be to set up a "fly camp" in the area. With no road, not even a track, to drive on, some serious "bundu-bashing" (bush whacking) would be the order of the day to get there. They knew getting into the area could prove difficult or impossible without getting lost in the predawn dark. So they came back to the "area of operations" with a tent, blankets, and other bare essentials. Next they proceeded to shoot a zebra for bait and dragged its guts all over the area leading to a suitable bait tree. The tree was in a little valley by a water hole with plenty of rocks and thick brush, which would help the lions feel safe when they approached the bait. They built a blind, and then the men set up their little camp on a ridge about a mile away, not forgetting to mark the path back to the blind with toilet paper.

The view from behind the camp was spectacular, with the whole of the Rift Valley spread out in front of them. There, they could see gleaming soda lakes rimmed by pink flamingoes, dramatic extinct volcanoes punctuating the deep blue sky, and in the distance the Ngong Hills defining the far edge of the escarpment. Buffaloes grazed their way out of the bush, three klipspringers played on some rocks below, and beyond them were herds of impalas and zebras. The three men spoke in hushed voices by the evening campfire, wondering what the next day's lion hunt would bring. Everything around them was peaceful. There were few of the usual night sounds—they heard no lions at all and no hyenas serenaded them.

The three hunters were not very hopeful as they crept down to the blind in the dim light the next morning. Quietly they moved inside the blind, and Finn and Kinuno pulled out the grass they had stuffed into the peepholes. It was then Kinuno mouthed he could see the bait swinging. Then Finn saw something light-colored lying underneath the bait. As the light improved, they made out a lion on the bait, and eventually they saw all four lions, just as the Masai had told them. They were all males, two young ones and two larger ones. None of them had impressive manes, but both the older ones had presentable ruffs.

The men observed them for a while, listening as the cats tore off flesh and crunched bones. In low whispers they discussed the merits of each cat as they moved about the bait. Richard took about three seconds to decide he wanted the largest one, but he had to wait awhile before the lion presented a good side shot on the bait. Just as he was about to squeeze the trigger, the lion dropped into the long grass below and flopped down, out of sight.

Presently, one of the others came over and nudged him, so he got up again, and they stood side by side rubbing noses as lions do when greeting each other. At that point, one body was shielding the other, so they again held their fire, for they could not risk getting two lions with one shot. Eventually the bigger one moved forward a little, and Finn motioned to Richard to take him, but

293

just as Richard fired, the lion turned some more, and the bullet angled a bit too far forward. The lion fell, but immediately got up again, growling. Kinuno then belted him with the .375 and very luckily hit his spine at the hips, thus immobilizing him, so Richard was able to finish him off.

Finn was undoubtedly relieved that the lion did not make it any farther, for the bush was wickedly thick and inhospitable—deadly terrain with a wounded lion in proximity. The Masai were very happy as they flocked to camp, and to show their gratitude, they put on a show for the three men by leaping in the air, singing their praises, shaking their hands, and thanking them for dispatching the cattle killer. Finn made certain the Masai knew that it was really Kinuno who had saved the day, which of course pleased him to no end.

A telling entry about the wounded lion and the thick, lion-colored brush sums up their close relationship and demonstrates Finn's well-known flair for understatement: "One tries to avoid having to dig hurt, dangerous game out of the bush, but when one is actually doing it, one realizes there is an awful fascination about it; for a while one really lives. Kinuno and I certainly had our share of living that day!" No bravado, but I can well imagine the thrill Kinuno experienced, and how pleased Finn must have been by his hunting partner's participation. The two depended on each other; the mutual trust and bond between them was strengthened by every close call.

Kinuno had frequent opportunities to practice the refined art of tracking, even though it was not necessary in this particular case. Years later while following wounded deer, we remembered and wished we could master his uncanny skills to see a pebble out of place or a bent blade of grass. It seemed to me he could find tracks on bare rock. He detected blood where no blood was to be found, and he had an understanding of animal behavior that enabled him to search for signs in directions that remained mysterious to most mortals. During the years they hunted together, Finn and Kinuno learned from and fed off each other's skills and experience, resulting in a mutual trust and lasting friendship.

Richard and Kinuno had another adventure together when they were hunting for lesser kudu in the parched country outside Tsavo Park. Composed of dry, gray, thin scrub, the area was at one time famous for elephants, rhinos, and lesser kudus. One morning after glassing from the top of a hill, Finn and Kinuno spotted a small herd of lesser kudu that contained at least three good bulls. Finn was feeling a bit under the weather, so he sent Kinuno with Richard after the kudu while he sat on the roof of the Land Rover and directed them using hand signals.

Suddenly kudus exploded from the bushes in front of the two hunters, white tails flying. In a flash they were gone—before Richard was able to get off a shot. That was the last Finn saw of the two men for the next two hours. Finally he heard a shot from way down the valley, followed by the reassuring thump of a bullet strike. When Finn reached them, he saw a lesser kudu lying on the ground. And what a kudu! The horns seemed to go on and on—it was the biggest kudu ever taken by any of our clients in Kenya. Finn was not one to whip out the measuring tape at the drop of a hat, but for once he measured, and measured again: It was 29 inches by the Rowland Ward measuring system (not around the curl), easily qualifying for the record book.

Kinuno had been hot on the tracks the whole time, for he knew that this one was a trophy. He told Richard that he was determined to follow him all day if necessary. The big kudu had gone in a large circle, shedding the other kudus en route. When the hunters did catch up with him, they were quite close to where the chase had started. All they could see when the shot rang out was a square foot of striped hide; even so, Richard made a perfect behind-the-shoulder shot. Finn always reckoned that if Richard came back, he would not feel he needed a PH with him as long as he had Kinuno to back him up!

The closest Kinuno ever got to being thumped was once by a very angry buffalo, and on that day disaster was only a few inches away. When faced with a buffalo herd, our client Ed had gotten a bit excited; consequently, he not only shot poorly, but he also aimed at the wrong animal in the herd. As Ed fired, Finn managed to put a .458 bullet into its midsection before the buffalo disappeared into the thick forest.

Suspicious noises from within made the men very alert and cautious; they did not go straight in but circled carefully for about fifty yards to the right before they ventured into the thicket. Advancing step by step and examining anything that would indicate where the beast was hiding, Kinuno got a little ahead while he was looking for tracks. Suddenly, there was a tremendous snort and sounds of crashing bushes, and Kinuno came tearing out past Finn and Ed, hotly pursued by an extremely irate and hurting buffalo.

Kinuno was in line with the buffalo and the bull was gaining on him, but nobody could shoot until he was level with them. There was some extremely fast and cool shooting from both Finn and Ed at a range of about ten feet, both hitting the buff well in the shoulder and rolling him over only a foot behind Kinuno. That was a race too close for comfort; Kinuno's usual grin when photographed with a client and his buffalo was conspicuously missing from the picture.

Thirty years later there are still clients who remember the tracker that so faithfully followed their PH; they recall his remarkable skills in finding game, his cheerfulness, dedication, and his ready smile. To us who employed him, he became almost like family because his loyalty and dependability went a lot further than what would be considered a professional obligation.

Some might have classified him as a savage, for he picked thorns out of his feet with a machete, ate raw tips of buffalo tongues because they gave him courage, and savored drinking the stomach content of eland because it was believed to be the best thirst quencher. We who were fortunate enough to know him "privately" knew a different, softer Kinuno.

Here was a man who worried so much during Finn's father's illness that he donated blood when asked, something that was very foreign to most Africans. He brought me special honey when I was pregnant to strengthen the baby and give me more milk; he had his wife weave me an intricate basket after I had given him some hand-me-downs. One memory particularly stands out. Kinuno had been on safari for several months and had not seen his own family, but he knew that his Bwana had had a new baby boy, and he wanted to pay his respects. Instead of going straight home, he took the only bus of the day, got off at the small town near where we lived, and walked for several hours to get to the house to see us. When I close my eyes, I can still see him gently holding baby Harald, only days old, with his enormously powerful paws and looking down into the little face with such obvious pride and love.

This to me described the essence of the man, a tough crust with a heart softer than most. Years later when Harald visited Kenya, he met Kinuno. Harald told me how the then old man had grabbed his hands and exclaimed with obvious delight: "He looks just like his father did when we started hunting together!" Memories flooded back and filled the old man's eyes, for he felt as strongly as ever that Finn and Finn's family were an intrinsic part of his own family, a relationship that neither time nor distance could ever change. To the Aagaard family, Kinuno will always be "The Tracker."

The Tracker Revisited
by
Berit Aagaard

 **Chapter 36**

T he road was terrifying and the traffic indescribable as we fought our way through downtown Nairobi to the Machakos Bus Station. Hordes of loud, diesel-spewing buses, rattling trucks in various states of disrepair piled high with odd-shaped bundles, and endless masses of people hurrying about added to the chaos. Handcarts weaving their way at a snail's pace held up traffic, and shouts and curses in many tribal tongues outmatched the din of barking dogs and squawking chickens. Unbelievable filth and pollution attacked us from all sides. What were two mature white women doing in this sea of African humanity?

I was back in Kenya, the land of my young adulthood, where I had married and raised my three children. I had returned for the purpose of showing my new husband, Bill, a land I had come to love so that he, too, could appreciate and share some of the beauty and wonders that I had lived and experienced. Simonne and I had driven to the bus station to meet Kinuno, my late husband's Finn Aagaard's tracker and longtime hunting partner. We were looking for one certain young man in this melee who was bringing his old father, Kinuno, to see me.

We discovered the young man standing on a corner, and somehow Simonne managed to squeeze her car into an empty space outside a nearby ramshackle building. As we got out and waited while the young man brought his father to us, I felt very blonde and very white—not threatened, mind you, only conspicuously out of place. It was not open hostility I sensed, rather annoyance; body language told us we really had no business there.

As Kinuno walked slowly toward me, I remembered all the hours I had followed this strong and loyal tracker out in the bush while hunting with Finn and how safe I had felt in his presence. He had taught me the art of caping a trophy and had shared with me choice morsels of game; he had brought me raw honey to enhance my breast milk when my babies were born. I recalled his joy seeing our children come along, one after the other, and how he held them so gently as infants in his work-hardened, paw-size hands.

Multiple clients had made special requests that he accompany them on safari; his reputation as a first-class, dependable magician of the hunt was widespread. Finn had more than once stated that although he was the boss, Kinuno was the better hunter. Finn's diaries are full of reference to his old friend Kinuno. He describes Kinuno as "My gunbearer/tracker/skinner/ and hunting companion of many years." This statement merely touches on the trusting relationship between Finn and Kinuno. Only by having watched the two interact during the hunt and been involved in some of their hairy situations, can one have an inkling of the importance of their mutual dependence.

Kinuno's eyes were exceptional, and his hearing was far better than Finn's. One morning as they were tracking buffalo in thick forest Finn writes: "We started to poke carefully around the edge of a glade when suddenly Kinuno put up the cross-sticks. Bob, (the client) aimed and shot almost before I had seen the bull. As the wounded buffalo reached dense bush, it abruptly turned and came thundering down the slope toward us. We all opened up; the air was about ⅔ lead. Everyone had a marvelous shoot-'em-up; we figured we had 12 shots in him. Even Kinuno got in two shots with my .375 which absolutely made his day."

When Finn had two clients with him and time was running out to get all the trophies they wanted, he would send Kinuno with one of the clients after nondangerous game. A picture in the diary shows a happy client and a good lesser kudu; the caption reads: "The kudu John and Kinuno hunted on their own for two days whilst Ron and I sat (unsuccessfully) in a leopard blind."

Early on Finn taught Kinuno to shoot. While hunting dangerous game he often carried Finn's .375 and more than a few times he pounded additional lead into wounded animals, either slowing them down or stopping them all together. After one safari Finn noted in his ledger: "Kinuno hit Ron's buffalo; he hit Ron's elephant; and he hit Ron's rhino. . . ."

Memories like these flashed through my mind as I spotted the old man emerge through the mass of humanity; his face was the same, only older; a wide smile spreading as he saw me. His big hands grasped mine, and I realized they too had changed; they were no longer like the rough sandpaper I remembered; now they were merely old. Greeting me, he immediately asked about the children, the all-important question in an African country where there is no one else to take care of a man in his advanced age. My Swahili had become very rusty, but I assured him that they were all well, and that I had pictures.

The spectators around us must have grasped that something special was happening between the two of us; this was no ordinary meeting. They must have seen the emotion on the old man's face, and how he clutched my hands in warm greeting. I felt strongly a wave of goodwill coming from the crowd gathered around us as I helped Kinuno, slowly and painfully, into the car because of his arthritic knees. Here was an elderly, distinguished *mzee* (a revered title for an elder), one of their own, smiling and being helped by a stranger. There was an obvious, unconditionally accepted relationship between us; the frowns around us turned into smiles and friendly faces. This was the Africa I remembered, uncomplicated, happy people, quick to smile with none of the modern chips on any shoulders. It was so reassuring to see that it still existed.

We had tea on Simonne's front veranda. Leading the old man by the hand through the house, I sensed his hesitation, realizing this was not a common occurrence. Forty years earlier it had not been the custom for the African staff to be invited into a white man's home; neither did the expatriates expect to visit their employees' homes. There was a strong loyalty and trust on both sides, but there was also an unspoken understanding of certain invisible boundaries respected and accepted by all. Even in camp there was a mutually honored distance. Just as the staff would serve dinner in the mess tent, but would never dream of joining us for the meal, I would never enter the kitchen area without calling *"Hodi"* and waiting for the customary welcoming reply *"Karibu."*

Bill had been anxious to meet the old man; he had heard so many stories about him and understood how important he had been in my early life. Bill greeted him warmly and I introduced him as my "new bwana." The old man nodded his approval and beamed. Our hostess handed Kinuno his cup first, as a greeting to show him that he was in fact the guest of honor. He grinned, and then he again asked about the children. The young son acted as an interpreter, switching between English, Swahili, and Kikamba, their own language.

He studied the pictures over and over, asking questions, laughing. He remembered these faces as toddlers, now grown with children of their own; it must have struck him that time had indeed passed and we had all grown older. Then I handed him a picture taken of him and Finn when we had visited in 1990, the two longtime friends and hunting partners sitting side by side. This time they were not pursuing buffalo or lion, merely birds, but the pleasure of being together again showed in their faces, and Kinuno was delighted at the memory.

Finally I presented him with a denim vest that had been Finn's and told him that my boys had wanted him, Kinuno, to have it. He put it on with reverence, a shy smile crossed his face, and he sat stroking the vest for a long time without saying a word. It fit him well and he wore it the rest of the day. Through his son, I tried to tell my old friend what a special person he had been to Finn, to my family, and to me. He had been a significant part of our lives in that Finn could and did depend on him during every hunt, and we at home felt safe knowing the two were a team. We would always remember him for that, and whenever we thought of him, it was with respect and gratitude. The old *mzee* remained silent through all this, but his eyes were smiling, and he kept looking intently at me. I hope he understood what I so very much wanted him to know.

We took pictures; I had to share this moment with my kids. I put my hand lightly on his shoulder, and then something very special and intensely emotional happened. Out of respect Kinuno had never before touched me, except when shaking hands or guiding my hand while teaching me to cape an animal in the field. Now he shyly, ever so gently touched my hair. It was such a demonstration of love and nostalgia, of trust and acceptance; it brought tears to my eyes. Not only had he meant a lot to us; we must have been important to him as well.

I promised the old man I would send greetings to the children; he kept repeating over and over that he wanted them to get his greetings. Through the son I tried to explain e-mail, and that I could send them a greeting that they would get "today." Later in the day, after he had lain down for a while, I visited him in his quarters, as did Bill, and the first thing out of his mouth was about the greeting to the children. He smiled and was happy when I told him that messages with his greetings had been sent to all three.

(The following is from Bill, Berit's husband: After Kinuno's nap I went to his quarters for a brief personal visit. Kinuno was lying on his cot as I approached; he turned with a big smile on his face and his hands reached out to mine. It was a long contact; I have never felt so welcomed. It's hard to explain the emotional quality of the moment. Face to face with Finn's most trusted African friend, I saw before me a man of courage, skill, and, oh yes, dignity. His son came in and through him I told Kinuno how pleased I was to meet him and how proud I was of his role in Finn and Berit's lives. He smiled warmly as we shook farewell.)

The following morning we returned to the chaos of the bus station. Again people were impatient and irritated over seeing our vehicle parked in an awkward spot until they saw us help the old man gently out of the car, and Kinuno took my hands in his. We stood there looking at each other, tears welling up. The same wonderful experience happened as the day before, the mass of faces suddenly smiled, and a benevolent atmosphere encircled us. I wanted to hug the old man, but knew this would embarrass him and ruin the goodness between us. Instead I squeezed his hands tightly and thanked him for coming to see me. Barely audible with a quivering old voice he answered: *"Ti onana siku ngine."* (We will see each other another day.) Then he leaned heavily on his son's arm and melted slowly into the crowd toward the bus.

Simonne and I picked our way through the milling throng, dodging handcarts and lorries not saying a word to each other for a long time. Both of us were keenly aware of the beautiful thing that had happened between people of different cultures who had history together and respect for each other. Time and distances had evaporated; only friendship and priceless memories remained, overshadowing the hustle and bustle around us.